Black Film as a Signifying Practice

Cinema, Narration
and the
African American Aesthetic Tradition

Gladstone L. Yearwood

Africa World Press, Inc.

P.O. Box 1892

Trenton, NJ 08607

P.O. Box 48

Asmara, ERITREA

Africa World Press, Inc.

P.O. Box 1892
Trenton, NJ 08607

P.O. Box 48
Asmara, ERITREA

Copyright © 2000 Gladstone L. Yearwood

First Printing 2000

Cover and Book Design: Jonathan Gullery

This book is set in Janson Text and Futura.

Library of Congress Cataloging-in-Publication Data

Yearwood, Gladstone, Lloyd.
    Black film as a signifying practice ; cinema, narration & the African-American aesthetic tradition / by Gladstone L. Yearwood.
       p. cm.
    Includes bibliographical references and index.
    ISBN 0-86543-714-9. -- ISBN 0-86543-715-7 (pbk.)
    1. Afro-Americans in motion pictures. 2. Afro-Americans in the motion picture industry. I. Title.
PN1995.9.N4Y43   1998
791.43'089'96073--dc21   98-41078
                                                CIP

For Harriett

CONTENTS

Preface

Tradition is not a luxury that we can ignore. This is part of the reason Thomas Cripps has repeatedly called for the black film movement to instill a sense of the past and acknowledge its own traditions as part of its self-consciousness. Cripps' pioneering histories of blacks in film were inspirational to me in mapping out the territory of an emerging field of study. I believe that it is important for new developments in black film studies to recognize the work of all those who have contributed to the growth of this increasingly rich and provocative cinema. I view my work as building on the foundation prepared by earlier black film critics. I have found this somewhat frustrating in teaching black film during the past two decades in the United States, Nigeria, the Caribbean and Canada. Many black film critics often overlook the existence of a critical tradition and some even neglect to mention important historical work. As a result, a fuller account of black film studies only began to significantly emerge in recent years with the publication of several important studies and books.

Black Film as a Signifying Practice provides an introduction to black film studies, an overview of black cinema and black film historiography and a commentary on the significant ideas that have shaped the black film movement. I am particularly concerned with issues of aesthetics and theory especially as these relate to the development of the black independent film movement, the relationship of the black cultural tradition to black cinema and the influence of the history of black intellectual ideas on black film studies. The exploration of the aims, purpose and functioning of black filmmaking stands as the central motive of this study of black film as a signifying practice. This book presents an account of black cinema by examining a range of fundamental issues that can give a new reader a firm foundation for understanding black films. It can also equip film students with new conceptual tools for viewing black films.

I am particularly fascinated with issues in aesthetics, theory and criticism in black film. This interest began years ago when I first studied photography in Brooklyn with Ray Francis, Lou Draper, Herb Randall, James Mannas and Fred McCrae. These photographers introduced me to the importance of images and image production. As teachers, they insisted on technical excellence. They also emphasized a visual aesthetic that was rooted in sources coming from the black community. They gave their students a direct connection with an aesthetic that was informed by the black cultural tradition and pioneering photographers such Roy de Carava. Their artistic sensibility reflected a commitment to the black community that was buttressed by their professional experiences as photographers during the Civil Rights movement and their desire to teach their art in community settings. But most of all, they taught us 'how to see.' They believed that a community had to produce images of itself and its history. These photographers found a place for aesthetic expression as part of our everyday lives. When I worked as a journalist with Reggie Workman and the Collective Black Artists (an organization of musicians that was based in New York City), I learned about the power of black expression, the resilience of the black cultural tradition and the importance of searching for new forms in black art. My good friend Robert Peppers, associate professor of art at Ohio University, helped me to better understand how the black expressive tradition is articulated in the visual arts. I am also grateful to Bill Miller, professor of Telecommunications at Ohio University in Athens, for his insights on aesthetics and criticism.

My foray into film theory, semiotics and narration is indebted deeply to Peter Lehman, currently professor of film at the University of Arizona, who encouraged me to apply new developments in film studies to black cinema. Vattel T. Rose, chair of the African American Studies Department at Ohio University where I taught for several years, was very supportive and shared many ideas that clarified issues arising in the black literary tradition. My early work in black film was aided immensely by Pearl Bowser and St. Clair Bourne, who provided information on films and general advice on understanding black cinema. These ideas were further developed when I conducted a seminar on black independent cinema in the Honors Program at North Carolina Central University, Durham, NC. Rick Powell was generous in his support, especially in providing the opportunity to further develop this work by teaching a seminar on African American Aesthetics in the Art History Department at Duke University. These friends and mentors offered encouragement, discussed new and controversial ideas or made it possible for me to advance my work in black film theory. In sum, they each played a key role in facilitating my ability to pull together various pieces that would work to solve the puzzle, which resulted in this book. All this was used as a springboard for building bridges and making interdisciplinary connections between different modes of the black expressive tradition. Although I am thankful for all the support I have been given, let me express caution by pointing out that I am fully responsible for the ideas and interpretations expressed in this book. I must also thank Beverly Miller, who teaches in the English Department at Fayetteville State University, for reading the manuscript and Kassahun Checole, publisher at Africa World Press for his generosity in making this book a reality.

Gladstone L. Yearwood
Orlando, Florida

Chapter One

Perspectives on Black Film Theory and Criticism

■ ■ ■ ■ ■ ■ ■ ■ ■

INTRODUCTION *WHAT IS A GOOD BLACK FILM??*

Black Film as a Signifying Practice is an investigation of the philosophical ideas that have shaped the theory and practice of African American cinema. Its aim is to enrich our knowledge of the black experience through the study of African American film. Its purpose is to deepen our understanding of African American aesthetic theory, especially as it is articulated in the cinema. It focuses on questions of value in black cinema: how filmmakers use the aesthetic values of the black cultural tradition and what expressive elements distinguish a work as a good black film? The study is also concerned with the ideas and concepts that filmmakers and critics use to talk about good black film. It is based on the assumption that narration plays a foundational role in filmmaking. Hence, the study of black film as a signifying practice is principally devoted to exploring the uses of narration in African American cinema.

narration in what sense?

Part one presents an overview of black film and an introduction to black film culture. It surveys the emergence of the black independent film movement as a 20th century development in the evolution of the black aesthetic tradition. Then it examines the major theoretical approaches and issues that have arisen in the black film movement through analysis of the concepts, terminology and debates that have shaped it. Part two presents an intensive examination of black film narration. The focus on narration offers the opportunity to scrutinize the internal features of the film as text. This allows us to observe the play of the film's narrative strategies and it's signifying practices. Examining

the narrative texture of black film involves paying close attention to how elements of film form, structure, and film language
are shaped and mediated by the African American experience.

AFROCENTRIC VALUES IN THE CINEMA

Despite the material progress most Americans enjoy, the full
promise of American society still eludes significant numbers of
the African American population. Whether it has to do with aver-
age life expectancy, job opportunities, income levels or health,
blacks generally fall short when these kinds of measures are
applied. As we move into the 21st century, political and economic
inequality remains a difficult problem as the social and economic institutions that have been so important historically to black
survival have been eroding. A moral drift and waywardness is evident in many parts of the black community, reflecting the nihilism
that Cornel West (1993) describes as pervasive in contemporary
African American affairs. Consequently, the need to find meaning in our lives and create knowledge useful for black life to flour-
ish rank high among the priorities of any black intellectual activity.
Black film—as a mode of inquiry—examines fundamental issues
related to the existence of blacks; and black film theory—as a key
epistemological activity—articulates models for exploring alternative ways of seeing and understanding the black experience.
Theory is important not only as a form of scholarship in itself,
but for its central role in contributing to the larger understanding of film and the African American expressive tradition.

Although African American existence is defined in relation
to a dominant white world, in studying black culture it is useful
methodologically to proceed from a point of view located within the black experience as opposed to an over-determined use of
the dominant society's point of view. The methodological shift
from a view of black film as defined by the dominant society provides conceptual tools that are better suited to accounting for
the expressive strategies and cultural mechanisms that have sus-
tained the black art experience. The critical approach that
informs this work foregrounds a cultural framework that "has its
own autonomous systems of values, behavior, attitudes, sentiments, and beliefs" (Lardner, 1972, p. 80), which positions the
black experience as an integral mechanism blacks use to negotiate their day-to-day activities. This signifying matrix has an
Afrocentric function, in which black film is properly understood
as a cultural expression that reflects the survival impulse of

African-Americans. It also serves to identify and clarify research
priorities useful in black film theory and criticism. Most importantly, it recognizes that the criteria for evaluating black film are
shaped in a fundamental way by the black experience because
culture functions as a point of power. —> *enter Michel
Afrocentric practice compels black film theorists to consider certain basic issues. What is black cinema? How do we know
a black film? How does a black film work? These are the kinds
of questions generated from an Afrocentric view of black film
culture. Using critical strategies based on traditional film studies hinders the ability of black film theory and criticism to address
the dynamic nature of black cultural products and the multiple
intersections of signification fundamental to the black expressive tradition. Traditional Western aesthetics is unable to adequately address Rap and Hip-hop influenced forms such as music
videos or films such as *Girl-6*, directed by Spike Lee and written by Suzan-Lori Parks, which develop intricate systems of signification that invoke significant intertextual elements of the
black tradition.

The black female group En Vogue's *Whatever* (1997) music
video highlights the way African American art complicates the
analyses of traditional forms of criticism. Undoubtedly, the audio
recording of *Whatever* is a work that can be located within the
African American cultural tradition. However, the only way for
critics to establish how En Vogue's music video works as a logical expression of the black cultural tradition is through recourse
to Afrocentric aesthetic criteria. Do we reject the video's science
fiction mise-en-scene as alien to the black cultural tradition or
can the tradition be extended to encompass the music video's signifying imagery? The tendency to declare the *Whatever* music
video as an African American work of art because it features black
performers diverts attention from the rich productivity of the
music video as text.

Theresa Randle plays the title role in *Girl-6*, which is the
story of an unemployed actress who uses her acting ability to
enliven a stint as a phone sex operator. The film, which received
lukewarm reviews because of its unusual narration, uses a variety of narrative techniques informed by the African American
tradition to explore cinematic expression. Lee's use of narration
in this film is related to the work of African American musicians
such as Charles Mingus or Archie Shepp whose art draws on a
wide variety of source material and expressive techniques. The

narration in *Girl-6* uses elements of orality and improvisation. It incorporates monologues, direct modes of address, jump cuts, flashbacks and hallucinations against an aggressive soundtrack by Prince. Director of Photography Malik Hassan Sayeed relies on bright colors to create Lee's unfettered cinematic ambience, which is developed through unusual camera placement, compositions and editing sequences. The film's narration includes historical references to figures such as 20th century cultural icon Dorothy Dandridge, Pam Grier's *Foxy Brown* (1974) and *The Jeffersons*—a television sitcom which ran from 1975 to 1985. One also finds intertextual references featuring cameos by contemporary popular cultural figures such as Halle Berry, Naomi Campbell, Madonna, and Quentin Tarantino. *Girl-6* is a most unusual African American film. Rather than conveying its ethnic character by relying principally on traditional definitions of subject matter, Lee creatively explores narration and intertextuality from the perspective of the African American experience.

Whereas, for the most part, critics studying black film narration have principally used literary models for analysis of storytelling, narration in contemporary black culture draws on aesthetic sources that often exist outside the established canons of art legitimized by the dominant society. Narration is an organizational and interpretative paradigm for human activity, which involves language, performance and culture in the African diasporic tradition. We can strengthen black film theory by specifying on which the artwork develops and extends elements of the black expressive tradition. Not doing so robs us of the opportunity to witness how change functions in the black cultural tradition. Furthermore, it denies the very essence of the African American cultural tradition, whose fabric is constructed from hybrid or Creole experiences.

A dynamic quality, a concern with process and the embrace of change are integral features of the black cultural tradition. We must question the conservative tendency to limit black filmmaking to an expressive language based on the Hollywood classical film narrative and its preoccupation with realism. Why should this be a privileged and defining criterion of black cinematic expression? By endorsing the dynamic characteristic of the black cultural tradition, we can better explain, for example, how African American cinema relates to American cinema and how a film such as *Girl-6* creatively straddles the line between Hollywood and the African American expressive tradition.

THE IDEA OF BLACK EXPRESSIVE CULTURE

It is important to examine black cinema as a phenomenon in its own right, having its own cultural traditions and expressive norms, that is, within its own cultural perspective. We cannot understand the culture and traditions of African diasporic peoples by using the dominant white culture as its principal frame of reference. Similarly, it is equally problematic to adequately appreciate black film by using the standards and aesthetic principles of the Hollywood cinema. This forces us to pay attention to the formative characteristics of film and its status as a product of the black cultural tradition, instead of other relevant, but less important criteria. Toni Cade Bambara emphasizes the importance of contesting film language because "it is key to the issue of cultural-political autonomy in the development of a national cinema" (1993, p. 127).

The term black cinema describes a specific body of films produced in the African diaspora which shares a common problematic. If blackness is articulated as a symbolic construct of the Western Unconscious (especially given the historical encounter of Europe with Africa), then shared diasporic experiences of blackness can be demonstrated to span geographic and cultural boundaries. In this sense, the work of black filmmakers throughout the diaspora is of reciprocal significance to each other. Yet, caution is warranted because it is foolhardy to collapse unique African diasporic experiences in order to find a transcendental black culture. However, to a very important degree, the development of black cultural expression in various parts of the New World shares a common problematic. "For many people . . . blackness is less a color than a metaphor for a political circumstance prescribed by struggles against economic exploitation and cultural domination: a state of consciousness that peoples of various pigmentations have experienced, empathized with, and responded to" (Powell, 1997, p. 10). A primary assumption is that black culture is syncretic in nature and reflects hybridized forms that are unique to the Americas. This process of creolization, which is evident in African American classical music (Jazz), represents the forging of a new ontology and epistemology. It is the product of cultural practices that have developed from the experience of slavery, the struggle for freedom from oppression and the recognition that interdependence is the key to our survival.

For centuries, blacks in the Caribbean and the United States have shared many cultural forms. Folk-tales share motifs (for example, animal figures) and techniques of narration. Elements of African traditional religions emerged in parts of the American South and in the islands of the Caribbean. African-based folk music such as calypso and the blues are related in their modes of expression. Forms such as the slave narrative share expressive characteristics in the New World. Blacks in the Caribbean and in the United States have also had significant reciprocal influences on each other's culture and politics. Coastal communities in North Carolina, South Carolina and Georgia to this day still retain cultural continuities with the Caribbean. Shared cultural expression can also be found in the architecture of the Shotgun house, which is rooted in African history, emerged in the Caribbean and then flourished in the southern United States. During the War of American Independence, blacks from the Caribbean journeyed North to fight against the colonial rulers. The development of African American fraternal organizations owes a tremendous debt to Prince Hall, a Caribbean immigrant. Twentieth century African American politics and culture also reflect the influence of figures such as Marcus Garvey, who led the largest grass-roots mass organization of blacks in American history; Malcolm-X and Louis Farrakhan, who trace part of their ancestry to the Caribbean; writers such as Claude McKay who helped shape the aesthetics of the Harlem Renaissance and Paule Marshall; Susan Taylor, editor of *Essence* magazine; and General Colin Powell, who has had a powerful influence on contemporary American political life. This list by no means exhausts the long history of mutual cultural exchange between African diasporic culture in the United States and Caribbean. Since his death, Bob Marley has become an inspiration and icon of cultural resistance in the African American community. Young African Americans have acknowledged the richness of African diasporic culture through their incorporation of Caribbean rhythms and musical forms in Hip Hop and Rap music. Styles of oratory and a peculiar polyvalent narrative, central to contemporary Rap music, was developed in Jamaica during the mid-1960s by musicians who added a counter narrative to popular melodies. All this points to a common problematic in contemporary black culture that can enrich and strengthen black cinema.

Afrocentric art critics suggest that African American artists are now part of a movement of pan-African artists representing people of African descent from around the world who now live *[handwritten top margin: The African diaspora (and culture) is expanding]*

in the United States. In the 20th century, communications technology and immigration patterns have created a powerful manifestation of the African diaspora in the United States, which is redefining what it means to be African American. Black artists from many countries have become a part of the contemporary African American mix. The films of Haile Gerima (Ethiopia) and Euzhan Palcy (Martinique) are widely regarded in African American film circles. African American visual arts reflect a veritable smorgasbord of African artistic and cultural influences, which Howard University artist and professor Jeff Donaldson describes as TransAfrican art. Theorists and practitioners who are not black also endorse the spirit of pan-Africanism to advance TransAfrican aesthetic ideas.

> They are intrigued by issues of color . . . they are inspired by the African legacy, and they are committed to the art of the outsider. The source of their interest is the excitement created by the recent arrival of blacks from South America, the Caribbean, Africa, and Asia, who bring their various hues and cultural allegiances with them. The bond of these people of color seems to be Africa, not only because many share this legacy, but because African Americans have paved a path for universal cultural redemption through their telling of the African story. (Morrison, 1995, p. 38)

[handwritten right margin: but this is also fairly broad and sweeping.]

Using the framework of an Afrocentric model moves away from a preoccupation with black film as defined by the majority culture and focuses more on how the expressive strategies and cultural mechanisms that have been critical to black survival influence black filmmaking. In essence, the criteria for evaluating black film are shaped in a fundamental sense by the black experience. In this view, black film is a cultural expression that reflects the survival impulse of African American culture, which has had to struggle against the marginalization that results from institutionalized racism and its popular cultural expression in the Classical Hollywood cinema. When we examine black film from a perspective informed by Afrocentrism, we can dismiss attempts to establish Hollywood film as the yardstick against which all others are measured. Because most film scholarship has not delved into the cultural world of the black experience, black film has predominantly been viewed through the lens of the domi-

[handwritten bottom margin: of that tradition again, are people not able to?]

[handwritten right margin: which is good for everyone.]

nant white American experience and its cultural limitations. The
Afrocentric impulse endows black film theory and criticism with
a powerful agency in its view of black film as a legitimate cultural expression emanating from the black experience. It is not
that Hollywood is irrelevant to black filmmaking; but rather
Afrocentric film theory suggests that the black experience functions as a more fundamental layer of signification in understanding black film. Of course, it is folly to attempt to define
African American film as completely separate from the history
of American cinema because contemporary criticism has suc-
cessfully demonstrated the polysemic and often contradictory
nature of any cultural phenomenon. Using the black experience
as the context for theory and criticism compels us to pay attention to the specific textual circumstances of a film, while being
reminded that as a cultural artifact black film cannot be adequately understood when it is removed from the black cultural
experience.

From its very beginnings, traditional cinema as an institution has operated from a model of production, signification, distribution and exhibition within which less powerful social and
ethnic groups have been positioned subordinately. The
Hollywood classical narrative demarcated an ideological area in
which valiant heroism was reserved for the white male; beauty,
dependence and containment characterized the woman; while a
definite inferiority and comic emasculation were attributed to
other ethnic groups. This regime underscores a foundational
premise of black film theory that black people need to produce
images of themselves and heroes of their own making, or signifying mechanisms that speak to the black community's social
needs and articulate its cultural traditions. Any community needs
to be a major producer of the popular signification—the images
and media—that occupies and promotes its social agenda. As a
collective social mechanism, consumption without production
only opens a group of people to economic and ideological
exploitation.

While cinematic technologies and languages are products of
dominant social and political ideologies, at the same time the
cinema—as a social institution—aids in their continued reproduction. Black film critics have always questioned the dominant
epistemological premises in American film history, which have
articulated assumptions that defined blacks neither as active
agents in film production, nor as creators of filmic signification.

The paradigms of traditional film emanate from a white patriarchal point of view in which blacks are represented principally as objects and rarely as subjects. In the Classical Hollywood cinema, blacks are deprived of the power to create. In contrast, black independent filmmakers have always attempted to explore an alternative terrain, which has resulted from their interest in forging different representations of race. Their work has inquired into how the black experience can be adequately expressed using cinematic means. A black aesthetic and critical tradition, which questioned the subordination of the black experience in film, has existed since the early days of cinema. *The Birth of a Race* (1918) is one of the earliest film examples of the search for an alternative tradition. Thomas Cripps comments that, " . . . A surviving sequence in the film . . . , along with a one-line music cue, suggests an African American centrality that would have been uncommon in American movies either before or since *The Birth of a Race*" (Cripps, 1996, p. 51). A vigorous campaign condemned the negative paradigm of racial representation in D.W. Griffith's *Birth of a Nation* (1915). The attention to cultural restitution in the work of black film pioneers such as Oscar Micheaux provide graphic evidence of the search for an alternative Afrocentric historical consciousness in the cinema.

Despite the acknowledgement of the deleterious consequences of racism in the film industry, most black film scholarship still tacitly accepted the epistemological and aesthetic assumptions of the dominant cinema. Until recently, black film critics did not fundamentally question the established knowledge of film, the way critics talk about film, or how the film experience and the definition of a good film differ across cultures. Traditional black film scholarship acquiesced to the conventions and received values of the Classical Hollywood cinema. Consequently, there was little concern with altering the structural relations that govern American society and the film industry. Furthermore, official histories of American film developed a paradigm of exclusion in relation to black filmmaking, so that black film was invisible to most white American film scholarship and traditional black film scholarship was motivated by premises of inclusion. Black film scholarship sought to guarantee greater access for blacks and a larger share of the film industry pie without calling for the requisite transformation of the social and political values of the dominant society. A progressive black film scholarship moves beyond social paradigms that foster a victor-victim, powerful-subordinate mentality to develop alternative modes of knowledge and social organization.

Instead of viewing black film as a poor imitation of Hollywood, an Afrocentric stance locates black film within a long history of cultural expression, refusing to see black film as a deviant cultural product. While a deficit model of African American cultural expression theorizes black film as a wannabe high cultural product, in contrast, Afrocentrism offers a basic conception of black cinema as a legitimate cultural expression of the black experience. Inscribing a notion of blackness and black people in the context of deviance is directly related to the marginalization of blacks as a group and their ability to impact on these definitions. Blacks have not had the power to destroy these negative labels, which "could have only come from the ability to provide the definitions of one's past, present and future. Since blacks have always, until recently, been defined by the majority group, that group's characterization was the one that was predominant" (Lardner, 1972, p. 75).

Certainly, the black cultural tradition offers a dynamic conceptual and expressive framework for black film studies; however, most black film criticism has ignored the significant achievements of African American expressive forms and its complementary systems of aesthetic thought. When we view black film within the problematic of 20th century African American arts and black film criticism as part of the intellectual tradition of African American aesthetic thought, we find a provocative dialogue between the arts and a rich cultural reservoir that informs black film. A vigorous discussion of aesthetics and issues in the philosophy of African American art has been ongoing in the black community. The debate has dealt with critical issues that include: the cultural sources of black creativity; the role of folk expression in black art; the function and purpose of black art; whether black art should be representational or non-representational; how race is socially constructed in artistic production; the relationship of art to the black community; the aesthetic criteria for good black art; and the role of the critic as detached observer or active participant. Most of all, the African American intellectual tradition provides a history of intertextual conditions that are directly useful for the study of black film signification.

THE CHALLENGE OF BLACK INDEPENDENT FILMMAKING

A major problem facing the black independent film movement is that the voice and the vision—that is, its signification and the symbol—producing framework that have produced African American music, for example—are not as astutely present in African American films. This may be the result of the relative infancy of the cinema as compared to the deep traditions of music and oratory in the black cultural experience, which extends thousands of years. The art of literature is founded on the written word. It encompasses the techniques for using words to express complex thoughts and stylistic elements for combining phrases. In contrast, film is the art of cinematography, the art of the camera. It is, in essence, a way of seeing—a way of framing and producing aural and visual images. The challenge for black filmmakers is to explore the sophisticated expressiveness that is characteristic of the African American tradition and use the raw material of film to do what African American musicians have done with their art. The task is to let film speak from the formal structures of the black cultural tradition and to appropriate the tools of the cinema as an expressive form within the black experience.

As a social institution, the cinema has been a popular vehicle for the production and reproduction of an exploitative system of racial representations. The challenge facing the black independent film movement is how to move beyond the prevalent regime of popular images and dominant film languages to excavate its own terrain and establish its own aesthetic values. Because traditional Hollywood cinema is constructed on a series of relationships that position blacks in a subordinate relationship to political and social power, black independent cinema necessarily moves beyond dominant paradigms to explore alternative film forms and narratives that undertake the requisite transformation of popular filmic signification. A black independent cinema gives priority to producing its own expressive paradigms, which redefine the nature of entertainment as a social institution and narrative as a means of encoding the world based on its own cultural requirements. Narration is a form of social history that plays a central role in the promulgation and reproduction of dominant ideologies. Narrative has a mythic function that facilitates the institutionalization of a group's lifestyle and choices. The black filmmaker's primary task is "to create, by definition, reality for the members of his or her community, to allow them to perceive their universe in a distinctively new way. This new way is built on tradition, only now reformed to be valued anew. This is the black poet's mythopoetic role: to predict our future through his or her sensitivity to our past coupled with an acute, almost intuitive awareness of the present" (Gates, 1987, p. 177).

At its best, film is an art form capable of delving into the depths of a culture, and art is capable of playing a powerful role in black community restoration. It can help us find meaning in our lives. As film has become a powerful agent of socialization and a communication medium par excellence in contemporary society, its narratives play a critical role in the production and transmission of social meaning. Additionally, society invests the medium of film with a powerful sense of authority, believability and legitimacy. An important premise of the black film movement is the recognition that film can play a role in the formation of social perceptions and in the articulation of a culture's worldview and experience.

EVALUATION AND AESTHETIC JUDGMENTS IN BLACK FILM

The need to justify evaluative judgments in film criticism has long been a sore spot for film studies. In their book *Authorship and Narrative in the Cinema*, William Luhr and Peter Lehman argue that, "Film criticism crawls with unreliable witnesses, people quite often intelligent ones, who give responses to works based on assumptions they seldom specify" (1977, p. 14). Likewise, black film critics must plead guilty to this charge. Speaking specifically of the African American expressive tradition, Henry Louis Gates, Jr., finds that "Black critics have enjoyed such freedom in their discipline that we find ourselves with no discipline at all" (1987, p. 41). Cripps—the pioneering historian of African American cinema—lends his voice, commenting that "Black film has not been blessed with a critical tradition, merely celebrants or traducers; worshippers or infidels" (1978, p. 143). Undeniably, black film studies will reap tremendous benefits from giving careful consideration to theoretical and methodological issues and through grounding aesthetic judgments on sound conceptual criteria, so that a richer understanding of black film results without any need to limit the filmmaker's creativity.

To address the methodological issues facing black film theory and criticism, two important tasks need attention. The first requires a fuller documentation of how black filmmakers use the tools, techniques and raw materials of the cinema; the second involves analysis of how the black cultural tradition informs filmmaking. Recent advances in textual criticism, narratology and semiotics have given us more advanced tools for film studies. This has enriched black film criticism because content-based criticism and the historical preoccupation with images of blacks betray an over-reliance on subject matter, which is inadequate for addressing the broad range of contemporary black film. While subject matter has a role to play in black film criticism, a broader and more encompassing critical focus is needed, which can speak to these kinds of issues, which are often overlooked. What the black filmmaker does with the film's subject matter should be one of our prime theoretical concerns. Given the structuring, shaping or molding influences that form exerts on content, it is important to ascertain how the specific structuring constraints of a film's formal elements redefine subject matter. The fact that most black film criticism is silent on the subject of how films are made and how film form as a cultural product functions to generate ideologies and values that reproduce the system of dominant social relations signals a major weakness.

Methodology remains a significant problem in black film criticism because most critical studies do not articulate the methods they use for film analysis and drawing conclusions. Despite the fact that theoretical and conceptual issues such as what is black film and how to understand a black film have been hotly debated for years, adequate attention has not been given to methodology in black film studies. Greater focus on methodology would clarify concepts and develop appropriate procedures for studying black films. Methodology is a central undertaking in film theory and criticism because it provides critical tools or a set of procedural rules for engaging the text. These rules contain assumptions about the nature of the object of study and elucidate the procedures and processes critics use to study film.

The relevance of a critical methodology is based on the assumption that film can be better understood by using a conceptual model or framework specifically designed to analyse film that emerges from the black experience. Ultimately methodology is not a miracle elixir that will resolve all critical problems; however adherence to a focused set of procedures and rules for studying these films can yield untold advantages and deepen our knowledge of black film. In addition, students of black cinema need to have access to critical methods that can be replicated and extended to the study of new films, so that they can examine the procedures critics use to make conclusions, better evaluate films and make more informed judgments on how particular films work. Although a respect for difference is an important element in the black cultural experience, we still can point out that black film criticism is too often unsystematic, antimethodical and riddled with excessive subjectivity. We must demand that critics make judgments that are based on sound methodological criteria and that they separate their opinion of a filmmaker from the actual textual conditions identified in the film. Black film criticism cries out loudly for greater conceptual and methodological development.

During the past 30 years, important advances in black film studies have been made. Several good works on black film are available. However, we are still at a loss to identify a body of critical work that spells out its methods in a way that we can creatively apply them to the study of specific films. The attention to methodology in black film criticism highlights the importance of focusing on the films themselves and identifying modes of analysis that can be productively applied to a wide range of films dealing with the black experience.

The development of reliable strategies for the critical viewing and close reading of films will produce untold benefits for black film studies. The project of a close reading necessarily focuses on the film itself, how a film is made and how its component parts function together. In contrast, it is far easier to proceed using global approaches to film criticism that make political and ideological statements about the relevance of film to the black community without taking the time to properly engage the film itself. A close viewing means that we pay attention, first of all, to the film and the internal conditions that govern it as a text. This requires study of the film's narrative strategies and its signifying practices, which then necessitates an assessment of how the African American experience mediates elements of film form, structure and film language. How the African American tradition renders these factors as malleable, as capable of being shaped to express the black experience, are of direct interest in this critical strategy. To speak authoritatively about African American film, it is necessary to engage the film on its own terms before

[handwritten marginalia:] it's difficult to do this from outside Hollywood conceptions of film functions

seeking out its intertextual and contextual relationships. Conceptually, we look at the film as an entity in its own right, and then ascertain how it functions as a work within the African American tradition. Equally important, we investigate how its structure and forms are derived from the black cultural experience. Presently, the most important factor has to do with the way filmmakers use the cinema as a unique vehicle of the African American experience to fashion narratives that may unfold using a unified story-line or may favor other narrative techniques. This critical strategy emphasizes the textual production of the film and provides a method for assessing how the film relates to its intertextual and contextual sources.

Developments in contemporary critical studies inform us of the polysemic nature of texts. In addition, we have learned that their construction draws on a variety of historical and cultural sources. Undoubtedly, black film reflects a certain heterogeneity that reflects the postmodernist sensibility of the African American quilt in which plural and often competing tendencies are part and parcel of the fabric of the text. For example, black film falls into the problematic of American cinema and the range of cinematic sensibilities abroad in particular regions and in the larger culture. Yet, it betrays an intimate reflexive sense of self, a sense of the black experience that is not represented historically in American mainstream cinema and which the dominant cinema is at a loss to adequately represent. We urgently need more advanced tools for viewers and students to better understand the diversity of American film in order to create more access to the work of black filmmakers. It is also critical to establish the fact that black film is best understood as the product of a specific historical and cultural tradition as opposed to a view of black cinema that conceives of it within the framework of a white cultural point of view. Hence, it is necessary to fight against collapsing film into a dominant paradigm of a master narrative and avoid the tendency to define what cinema is and then conveniently find films to meet our ends. Although art has universal implications, it is, first and foremost, a specific symbolic act that occurs within a particular cultural and historical context. To view this relationship the other way around leads us to misread important aspects of the artwork. When we universalize artworks, we rob them of their specificity and their social, cultural and historical relations. Artistic production is characterized best as a symphony involving visions and viewers. So as not to deval-

ue black film, we must develop appropriate hermeneutic models that allow film as art to be seen as part of the problematic of
the black experience, in which we relate film to the cultural roots
of that expressive tradition. Although the nature of film does not
lend itself to the direct affective relationship that exists between
artist and audience in African American musical forms, nonetheless, it would be an error not to explore how such elements of
the tradition impact on black film. It is impossible to analyze
black cultural expression without reference to its socio-historical context, its sense of community, modes of address, aesthetic
stances and values the tradition foregrounds. The exploration of
how a black film text relates to other texts within the African
American tradition, from the vantagepoint of their signifying
practices, signals a critical advance for the study of black independent film. A vibrant black film theory and criticism will benefit enormously from this necessary excavation and
foundation-building activity.

THE RICHNESS OF BLACK CINEMA

There are many strong opinions on what constitutes a good black
film and which films represent good black cinema. In film classes, students are often eager to establish a neat definition, which
specifies a set of rules for classifying and excluding particular
works in the black film canon. This reminds me of the story of
a student who travels far and wide across the earth to find the
meaning of life. After an arduous journey, the student finally
reaches a village deep in a Central African forest. In a small clearing in the forest, he finds an old griot who gestures wistfully with
his open hands and whispers that the secret of the meaning of
life is a deep well. For a moment, the student is speechless, thinking of the many perils and treacherous experiences of the journey. Disappointed and in disbelief, the youth leaves mumbling
the words of the sage. The lesson we learn from the old griot
echoes a point of view articulated by the filmmaker Melvin Van
Peebles, who believes that black film should be as rich and varied as the black experience. Van Peebles argues that the public
should not expect black filmmakers to all make the same kind of
films, speak from the same voice with the same point of view and
use the same stylistic devices. "You don't ask Pushkin why he
doesn't sound like Dostoevski or Tolstoy," Van Peebles says.
Black film is capable of articulating the rich plurality of the black
experience so that we, in the African diaspora and the world, will

in its varied forms

come to a deeper understanding about the soul of black culture.

Taking the griot's advice, *Black Film as a Signifying Practice* is not a search for the true black film or the essential characteristics of a black cinema. Of course, some films more accurately reflect black cultural expression, while others can be more productively understood in other related or overlapping contexts. These issues will be addressed, but the desire to find the true black film is not among my objectives. Simply put, the focus on definitions is a requisite part of theory formation in black film studies. Definitional issues function in this work as part of the process of excavation and investigation, and not a final outcome that will determine, once and for all, the true nature of black cinema. We are better poised to make meaningful statements about specific signifying practices by clarifying what we mean when the term black cinema is used to describe a body of films. Signifying practices can be defined as the special way filmmakers use expressive forms and systems of signification to reflect the cultural priorities and historical exigencies of the black experience. From the perspective of a signifying practice, we can see how the symbol-producing mechanisms that inform black filmmaking function within the black cultural tradition and how black film narratives use the formal structures of the black experience to organize story material. A people's world and their world-view are codified in their stories; and the basic elements of a culture are reworked and repeated in its narratives. By specifying how the black experience selects, arranges and uses story material, we can observe how black film functions as a signifying practice and better understand how the African American expressive tradition utilizes its own vernacular space and time for storytelling. Because narrative is a fundamental mechanism through which humans signify, one of the major goals of this work is to explore how narration works in the African American expressive tradition and in black independent cinema. To better understand this relationship, it is critical to inquire into the intertextual linkages between black film criticism and historical developments in African American philosophical thought, which provide a substantive and accumulative aesthetic and critical context for black film studies.

Part One

Theory and Historiography

Chapter Two

The Emergence of the Black Independent Film Movement

ALTERNATIVE NARRATIVE

Historiography occupies a prominent position in black film theory and criticism because blacks have fought relentlessly to construct an alternative narrative that provides a context and historical framework for understanding the black experience. Black film historiography questions the dominant epistemological and aesthetic assumptions in American film history. It differs from traditional film historiography in that it seeks to reveal knowledge of the cinema that has been neglected and often rendered unknowable. We can produce this new knowledge by bringing to the foreground an interpretative framework that draws on the rich depth and diversity of the black experience. Black film historiography provides thick descriptions that introduce more complex ways of documenting and compiling the historical record, which in turn inform the functioning of analytical and critical systems, the application of methodologies and procedures and the study of arguments used in black film criticism.

MODERNISM IN 20TH CENTURY BLACK CULTURAL THOUGHT

In the early years of the 20th century, African Americans embarked on a journey of realization and self-discovery as a new black awareness took root in black communities. Several events and personalities played a role in this developing black consciousness. The Pan-African Congress of 1900, which was held in London, made an important contribution to bolstering the value of an African identity and elevating Pan-African awareness among blacks. The idea of Pan-Africanism had broadened to include not only political but cultural concerns as well. W. E. B. DuBois' Pan-African history helped cement a diasporic consciousness. Organizations such as the NAACP, which was founded in 1910, confirmed the need for collective struggle for political and economic justice. Marcus Garvey's Universal Negro Improvement Association (UNIA) also contributed to the creation of this powerful new black awareness. Garvey's UNIA attracted large numbers of followers with its appeal for economic independence and black cultural pride. This period was marked by an emerging recognition of the value of an African consciousness, which incorporated the idea of African redemption, African diasporic relationships and the need for Pan-African unity. It gave new impetus to the study and discussion of the long history of African achievement and the persistent power of the African spirit as a creative source. African creativity and its aesthetic forms had influenced the development of modern art in the 20th century and innovative artists such as the Cubists borrowed elements from African traditional cultures, reworking them into challenging artistic expression that would reshape the history of European aesthetics.

The Great Migration had brought large numbers of blacks from the South and the Caribbean to urban centers in the North. The development of black cosmopolitan culture and the internationalization of African diasporic consciousness helped fuel a powerful notion of black cultural signification. A rich set of black symbols and iconography was created to represent the modern black experience. The momentum behind the emerging black consciousness was crystalized in the vision and voices of the Harlem Renaissance. Philosophers such as W. E. B. DuBois and Alain Locke encouraged African Americans to embrace and build upon the folk sources of the African American tradition. Locke's aesthetic would draw heavily on the ancestral connection of blacks to Africa. Along with the redefinition of self and community, the black self-help movement—which had been organized during the Reconstruction era to counter the effects of racial segregation—had begun to bear fruit. It had functioned to create wealth in black communities, giving birth to a black middle and professional class, black colleges and universities, businesses, mutual societies and social organizations.

Blacks rallied to the racial pride and self-help appeal of the UNIA, which became an active broad-based grassroots organization with branches in North and South America, Africa and the Caribbean. The UNIA moved masses of blacks "to an appreciation for literature and the arts on a scale not often equalled in other communities" (Martin, 1983, p. 2). This was all part of the growth of artistic, cultural and political expression of blacks in the 1920s. "As the 'New Negro' defined the self through creative expressions, the 'New Negro' also examined and interrogated with increasing vigor those creative representations, particularly in race magazines such as *Opportunity, Crisis, and Messenger*. With the change in leadership in the early years of the 20th century from the accommodationist policy of Booker T. Washington to the radical protests of W. E. B. DuBois, African Americans became racially conscious and self-assertive, affirmed their humanity, and demanded respect" (Mitchell, 1994, p. 3). Artists and intellectuals explored the soul of the black community from artistic, cultural, social and political perspectives. An emerging aesthetic principle defined the black artist as "an interpreter, a voice that makes intelligible the deepest, most meaningful aspirations of the people, a channel through which their resentments, hopes, fears, ambitions, and all the other unconscious drives that condition behavior are expressed and become explicit" (Lewis, 1978, p. 4). The movement of writers, actors, musicians and artists of the Harlem Renaissance helped shape an artistic and cultural agenda that included the work of black filmmakers. "The 1920s and 1930s . . . were quite special since they marked the emergence of the African American artist who could say something significant, in so many different ways, about life in this country. The African American participant in the Harlem Renaissance inherited a legacy of expression from those of an earlier period and in using it transformed it into a powerful, relevant statement that would greatly influence succeeding generations" (Franklin and Moss, 1994, p. 380.)

The black cultural renaissance of the 1920s and 1930s saw the development of two divergent expressive strategies of African American aesthetic thought. The African American modernists rejected the social realist absorption with subject matter (that is, the preoccupation with portraying particular uplifting images of black life) to focus attention more on formal issues in art. When we look at African American modernist art, our attention focuses on how cultural traditions influence the artist's sensibilities, expressive techniques and how the artifacts are produced. We are interested in their symbolism rather than their approximation of reality. African American modernism focuses on the way black expression incorporates certain forms and survival techniques germane to the black experience. Because African American life evolved in a hostile social and political environment, many ideas and opinions although deeply felt by blacks often are not expressed openly or directly. African American modernist forms are structured to question American social reality through details rather than a focus on obvious content. When considered as a whole, the work suggests messages far more profound than its parts could ever transmit.

Marked by an ongoing search for new cultural models, it rejects the philosophy and values of the conservative black middle class leadership, deliberately avoiding the stoicism of African American social realist ideas. Incorporating elements from black rural and working class urban experiences, the African American modernists exemplify an artistic tradition that looks inward, celebrates historical roots, and refuses to engage in self-denial for the sake of assimilation. It was simultaneously defiant and humanistic. Claude McKay's poem, "If We Must Die," from 1919 summarizes these ideas:

> If We Must Die, let it not be like hogs
> Hunted and penned in an inglorious spot,
> While round us bark the mad and hungry dogs,
> Making their mock at our accursed lot.
> If we must die, O let us nobly die . . .

We also witness this pride in Langston Hughes' (1926) statement that black art did not exist to please white audiences and that black artists would "express our individual dark-skinned selves without fear or shame." Drawing on the blues as a healing source, these new black voices embraced muted folk themes of revolt.

By the mid-20th century, two black worlds had emerged. One was made up of the upwardly striving middle class favored by the social realists, and the other was inhabited by the masses of working-class blacks that had left the rural South hoping for a brighter future in the North with hopes of entering the American mainstream. However, their dreams of a new day went unfulfilled. "Too often their dreams were deferred. These disappointments led to disillusionment. Outward rejection led to introspection as a means of survival, to seeking affirmation of self in one's own heritage, and to a search for personal significance through the celebration of Afro-American folk traditions and institutions. Out of this retreat into self came a revival and renewal of some of the forms of cultural and personal folk expression that had long been repressed. This spirit of discovery of self, combined with the demands of city living, spawned a whole new tradition in black (art) . . ." (Yearwood, 1987, p. 145). African American modernists turned inward to reflect on black life. They focused on the daily pain and joy of being black. They celebrated their blackness and reached out to consummate their cultural kinship. In particular, they explored a perspective on cultural expression that was unique to the black experience in America. There was no sense of cultural shame, no sense of an ethnic inferiority. There was also no need to accept assimilation at the expense of their cultural and ethnic identity.

African American modernists aim for a universalist appeal that uses the black experience as a vantage point from which the artist creates. Their artistic sources are rooted in African American folk culture, and these are combined with the melodies and lyrics of urban working class life. Although blacks are the primary audience for this work, others are not excluded. A major objective of the modernists is the exploration of the human condition using the black experience as their focal point. African American modernism stresses the centrality of aesthetic sensibility in art. Yet, the artist's racial identity serves as a reservoir from which the artwork flows. In a sense, there is a self-consciousness in black art. Art is a primary cognitive activity capable of producing knowledge of social relations. In this view, black art is conceived as a product of a particular socio-cultural formation. Because serious vexing problems continue to plague black life, African American modernists see art as an opportunity to forge new knowledge of society, which in turn can be useful in our understanding and resolution of social problems.

Early black filmmakers shared the problematic of cultural restitution and the recuperation of the comic black image that had been popularized as a demeaning, low-comic blackface minstrel caricature with the commercialization of popular culture. The blackface syndrome of low-comic minstrel images defined blacks as lacking intelligence and humanity. However, a range of signification developed within the black community that defined black life not in terms of a dehumanized caricature but from a point of view that endowed it with a fundamental morality and humanity. This alternative signification marks a site of black resistance similar to what bell hooks describes in the metaphor of Homeplace, which is the space "where all that truly mattered in life took place—the warmth and comfort of shelter, the feeding of our bodies, the nurturing of our souls. There we learned dignity, integrity of being; there we learned to have faith" (1990, p. 42). It is a space in which social roles were redefined and racial and gender positions articulated outside the purview of the dominant society. This cultural mechanism allowed blacks to maintain a sense of dignity, and did not relegate black women to minor roles of subservience. "Historically, African American people believed that the construction of a homeplace, however fragile and tenuous (the slave hut, the wooden shack), had a radical political dimension. Despite the brutal reality of racial apartheid, of domination, one's homeplace was the one site where one could freely confront the issue of humanization, where one could resist. . ., where we could restore to ourselves the dignity denied us on the outside in the public world" (hooks, 1990, p. 42).

The black community created a congenial environment within which the black independent film movement and an alternative filmic signification emerged. "It was more important for blacks to maintain a separate existence socially and culturally than it was for them to do so economically. Whites in the South and, to a considerable extent, in the North kept a discreet distance from the everyday lives of blacks, and as the problems of migration and existence in a complex industrial society multiplied their difficulties, blacks had to work out their own formulas for survival" (Franklin and Moss, 1994, p. 285). This private psychic space was articulated not only in the extended black family, but also in the church, mutual benefit societies, business associations and educational institutions. The extended family and community institutions provided an infrastructure and impetus for the development of black art and culture. This mechanism which allows for development and interaction within a nurturing environment functions simultaneously as a private and communal space. It can be found in the islands of the Caribbean, historically black colleges and universities and historical black towns such as Eatonville, Florida. It accounts for the richness of Zora Neale Hurston's work, which was centrally organized around this powerful sense of self and community that provided a secure nurturing image of the black person as an autonomous entity despite the existence of oppressive social and political conditions. Blacks understood the power of naming and imaging as well as the importance of telling their own stories and documenting their experiences. This is the background against which the Lincoln Motion Picture Co. and the Oscar Micheaux Book and Film Co. came into being. These companies enjoyed a modicum of success because of the existence of infrastructural supports for black cultural products in black communities across the country.

CIVIL RIGHTS POLITICS AND THE CRITIQUE OF POPULAR IMAGES OF BLACKS

In 1940, the NAACP urged President Franklin D. Roosevelt to integrate blacks into all aspects of service in the armed forces without discrimination or segregation and to encourage the same in American industry. Integration became the major objective of the Civil Rights movement, and its elevation as a political philosophy signalled an important moment in American history. The political philosophy that marked the integration era (1947 to 1965) had a direct impact on images of blacks in film. In the black community, the integration controversy was far-reaching, reflecting "a range of historical arguments within the black freedom struggle, including debates around questions of the cultivation of a black aesthetic, community control, black economic and political development, black nationalism, and assimilation amongst others" (Simpson, 1990, p. 25). By the 1940s, the influence of the NAACP-led protest movement helped reduce the most flagrant low-comic images of blacks on screen. Yet, blacks remained marginalized on the fringes of the film industry, and there still was little meaningful reformulation of the limited filmic signification that had become commonplace in Hollywood.

Civil Rights ideology represents an African American social realism that speaks to a politically conservative and socially accommodating black middle class, which is involved in a perennial Sisyphian struggle for legitimacy with the dominant society. Social realism describes the philosophical direction of a dominant view in African American aesthetics at the beginning of the 20th century. Among its values, we find "a strong belief in the redemptive powers of Christianity; the moral right of the democratic ideal; DuBois' hope of a talented tenth; Booker T. Washington's doctrine of social accommodation; and even

Marcus Garvey's cultural and political rejection of Eurocentric values" (Yearwood, 1987, p. 139). Although some of these positions contradict each other on occasion, on the issue of representation and the use of artistic languages, they all share a similar problematic. As a form of black cultural expression, social realists advocate the representation of positive dimensions of black culture. African American social realism is interested in evoking the emotional vitality of the black experience, which is considered to be so powerful that there is little need for the artist to be overly concerned with art as an expressive language. It is concerned with racial uplift and is filled with optimism for the social and political aspirations of the black community. The absence of themes dealing with the black underclass is a prominent feature of African American social realism. Social realists countered the popular mode of blackface minstrel imagery with an alternative, more respectable image of blacks. As such, they favored black middle class values. "Inasmuch as the Afro-American character had become the butt of the national joke in 19th century America, Afro-American social realist art of the early 20th century defined black life proudly, in terms of a Christian stoicism with dignity and success. It depicted certain ideal views of black life through characters and situations that would serve as models for black aspirations, despite the social circumstance of racial discrimination. Art was to function as a vehicle for building racial consciousness, consolidating a sense of community, and solidifying a sense of identity . . ." (Yearwood, 1987, p. 143).

Political justice and social equality were two core elements of African American social realist philosophy. In contrast to the modernists, the social realists were willing to subordinate their Afrocentricity to the desire for integration into the dominant society. In their concern with creating a corrective that was powerful enough to subvert the negation of the black film presence, adequate attention was not given to developing the cultural specificity of the black film experience. Schomburg curator Lawrence D. Reddick wrote that a principal objective was to have black life admitted to the full range of human characterization, to eliminate the 'race linking' of vice and villainies, and to have black actors on screen treated like everybody else. Reddick classified films as being anti-black when the presentations were limited to stereotyped conceptions of the black in the American mind and pro-black when the presentation proceeds beyond these stereotypes to roles of heroism, courage and dignity. Black film critics repeatedly made the point that racial segregation "created barriers of ignorance that perpetuated the creation of racial stereotypes" (Cripps, 1977, p. 145). Peter Noble's *The Negro In Films* (1948), examined the history of stereotypes in cinema and V. J. Jerome's *The Negro in Hollywood Films* (1950) used a Marxist critique to analyse the racial barriers that supported the propagation of stereotypes. Critic and film educator Albert Johnson was also concerned with the rehabilitation of the filmic signification of blacks. Calling for honest depiction of blacks on the screen, Johnson wrote that. "Such films as *Home of the Brave, Pinky, Lost Boundaries* and *No Way Out* were particularly memorable because they attempted to portray the (black man) in a predominantly white environment; and as a figure of dramatic importance, the (black man) has long been overlooked or carefully avoided on the screen . . ." (1959, p. 38).

Other voices in the black community questioned the adequacy of integrationist philosophy as a paradigm for black liberation. Harold Cruse (1967) maintained that because the Civil Rights movement was too concerned with legitimizing its "social aims with American standards," it could not provide effective leadership to the black movement. For Cruse, it was ironic that black Civil Rights ideologists would subordinate themselves to the same cultural values of the dominant society that marginalized and exploited blacks. In this view, racial integration was a trap because it required that blacks shed their culture and, in turn, accept the full set of values of the dominant society even though racial inequality persisted.

Cripps argues that the institutionalization of American cinema in Hollywood engendered a political alienation and isolation from progressive social forces. As a result, the film industry developed in an idyllic western setting geographically divorced from the burgeoning metropoles so vital to America's ethos in the 20th century. American film identified with upper-middle class aspirations, separate from the working class and non-white underclass. It constructed a world of lavish spectacle and dreamlike fantasies. Its emphasis on consumption tended to minimize attempts to create a visionary approach to filmmaking. Gradually, the aura of Hollywood, escalating costs of popular filmmaking and the power of studio bosses steered film production to create a product that was easily digestible—what Roland Barthes describes as a 'readerly' text—for mass market consumption. The pervasive consumerism and the white middle class cultural values of the Hollywood model had a deleterious impact on the development of African American film. Early efforts toward the building of a black cinema were hampered by the absence of a clear conceptual schema for articulating a viable black aesthetic and the over-reliance on the Hollywood paradigm, whose motivating premises tended to be more reactive than proactive. While paying scant attention to the specificity of black film, most critics believed that the work of black filmmakers was inferior to commercial Hollywood film. Black film critics tacitly accepted Hollywood's definitions of film, the nature of the institution of cinema in a multicultural society, and the relationship of film knowledge to the socio-economic status of marginalized groups. They accepted the alleged superiority of the cultural values of the Hollywood cinema as the measure of all filmmaking, and the pressing ideological questions of the dominant cinema as an institution remained muted. Despite the fact that early black film critics broke ground that was repressed by the dominant society, they did not question the signifying processes that reproduce popular stereotyped signification.

Reddick and his generation (of critics) left little room for the growth of a black independent film industry because their objectives sought greater inclusion of blacks in the film industry at the expense of developing an alternative black film culture. Despite the progressive advances made by social realist critics, black culture still faced the danger of being submerged for the sake of integration. Ultimately, the burden rested with blacks who would have to make the major sacrifice and prove themselves worthy of being treated as human beings. From the beginnings of the 20th century until the post-Second World War period, the preoccupation with the cultural restitution of the image of blacks would serve as the dominant problematic of black film criticism. Even today, many black film critics tend to overlook the elements of resistance in the work of filmmakers such as Micheaux, who seek to recuperate the position of blacks from the margins of the film industry and present alternative paradigms of black film narration. The refusal by early critics to reformulate the conventions of the Hollywood classical narrative created severe problems for black cinema. The tacit acceptance of the Classical Hollywood cinema as the defining criterion for black film is premised on an aesthetic principle based on a narrative whose model is alien to and repressive of the requisites of a viable black cinema. To accept the traditional Hollywood film narrative as the driving paradigm of a black cinema aesthetic is to implicitly legitimize the accompanying restrictive baggage of the Hollywood paradigm. In doing this, there is a silent endorsement of the predominant models of filmic signification and their alleged 'natural' ways of seeing. Inevitably, a black cinema seeks the demythification of dominant ideologies especially as they proscribe the ontological, epistemological and aesthetic bases of the film experience. In spite of this tendency, early black film provided a fuller range of imagery that extended beyond the limited stereotypes prevalent in the dominant cinema. The body of films produced by the pioneer black filmmakers contributed to a redefinition of the larger perception of black life and culture and the imagery they produced played a complementary role in reflecting an alternative signification of the black experience.

BLACK FILM CRITICISM
AND THE POLITICS OF INTEGRATION

Civil-Rights inspired black film criticism reached its apex in Cripps' engaging social historical work, *Slow Fade to Black* and Donald Bogle's *Toms, Coons, Mammies, Mulattoes and Bucks*. The forging of a new black cinema and the attendant writing of black film history would have been a more difficult undertaking without the supportive atmosphere created by these pioneering works. The study of images of blacks implicitly introduced the reflection hypothesis to black film criticism. The reflection hypothesis was a paradigm drawn from Marxist criticism, which averred that film images tend to reflect the socio-economic structure and values of the dominant society. As a result, the reflection hypothesis gave critics the tools to link the film image to larger questions of the social position, legal status and political disenfranchisement of blacks. Despite its limitations, image studies established an explicit relationship between society's superstructure and the film industry in so far as superstructural relations impact on the organization of the film industry and its portrayal of film images.

More recent black film scholarship disagrees with the aims of this kind of criticism, which views the Hollywood model as the solution to problems of the black film movement. This newer scholarship questions the legitimacy of the Civil Rights paradigm of black film studies. For example, J. Ronald Green queries whether "Hollywood can handle—in the interest of any group seeking assimilation—differences of identity as significant as the color line, economic status exploitation, partriarchal sexism, or sexual taboo" (Green, 1993, pp. 30-31). With the passing of the social activism of the 1960s, the retreat of white liberal support- ers into the materialism of the Reagan years, integration as a social doctrine increasingly went into crisis and the Civil Rights movement was under attack. After all, legal desegregation had been accomplished, blacks had the right to vote, there was a rise in the black middle class and apparently blacks had ascended to the highest political and educational institutions. But despite the gains made by the Civil Rights movement, a permanent black underclass persisted.

AN OUTLINE OF BLACK FILM HISTORY

The Black independent film movement dates to the beginning of the second decade of the 20th century when the medium of film and the fledgling film industry were both in a formative peri- od of development. A short called *The Railroad Porter* (1910) by Bill Foster is cited as the first black film produced in the United States (Sampson, 1977, p. 30). Two brothers—George and Noble Johnson—set up the first known black film company—the Lincoln Motion Picture Co. in Los Angeles and started a branch in Omaha, Nebraska. Lincoln's films included *The Realization of a Negro's Ambition* (1916), *The Law of Nature* (1917), *A Man's Duty* (1919), *The Trooper of Troop K* (1920), and *By Right of Birth* (1921). Adrienne Lanier-Seward argues that the first films produced by the Johnsons "did as much to herald the advent of the 'New Negro' as the writings of James Weldon Johnson, Claude McKay, Langston Hughes, and Nella Larsen of the Harlem Renaissance" (1987, p. 196). Cripps also observes the importance of Lincoln's contribution to the black aesthetic expression. "The Johnsons carried the notion of a black aesthetic to its limits as a social force. Unlike the efforts of Emmett Scott and the NAACP, the efforts of the Lincoln Company sprang from black roots in Los Angeles, and their idea spoke to blacks rather than to whites" (Cripps, 1977, p. 76). Lincoln's films were distributed using an exhibition circuit made up of black communities in towns and cities scattered across the country. By the 1920s, about 700 movie houses existed in diverse black communities. These auditoriums comprised the main exhibition facilities for black film during this period. "They were not the picture palaces of downtown, but in these theaters black audiences were not restricted to balcony seating arrangements. They were also free to enjoy the work of black filmmakers" (Murray, 1973, p. 7). Films were also viewed in community arenas such as churches, school halls, tent screenings and on special days in white theaters. The system designed to stop blacks from taking part in the new white dominated ritual of movie-going helped create the market for films featuring blacks and aided black filmmaking (Diakite, 1980, p. 43).

The Micheaux Book and Film Company took over where Lincoln left off when it produced its first film *The Homesteader* (1918) and another *Within Our Gates* (1920) soon after. Another early pioneering black film outfit was The Norman Film Manufacturing Company, whose films include *The Crimson Skull* (1921) and *The Bull Doggers* (1923). However, it was Micheaux, who would make the most impact on the development of the black film movement. He was a homesteader on the Dakota prairie, and was a novelist who turned to filmmaking after an unsuccessful deal with the Lincoln Motion Picture Company. He was bold in his treatment of controversial subjects and themes. His films tackled social problems that included the clash of rural and urban values, the issue of color caste among blacks, corruption in the black church as well as black-white social relations. Micheaux's films reveal how blacks chose to represent themselves as opposed to how the dominant society represented them. They often dealt with issues that were relevant to the black community but generally neglected by the mainstream cinema. Importantly, his work represented blacks in family settings. His films acknowledged the black Southern experience—a fact that has been substantially repressed in subsequent black filmmaking.

Micheaux based his films on controversial themes. For example, *Body and Soul* (1924) which demonstrated the filmmaker's style and approach to narrative represents a courageous film for a director to make in the 1920s. It is the story of a sadistic, corrupt minister—played by Paul Robeson—who rapes, tortures and blackmails a young woman (Isabella). The minister, Reverend Jenkins is depicted as a con man who served time in prison. The young woman's mother, Sister Martha Jane has a strong position in the narrative as the character who calls the preacher to account. She is in control of her actions and does not need a male to do so in her behalf. When she accuses the preacher, he is mobbed and beaten by the church congregation. *Body and Soul* stops short of demonizing the villain. The narration builds toward redemption and forgiveness. As it concludes,

Martha Jane tries to protect the preacher. Micheaux uses flashbacks to drive his narration, which is a device to hold the audience's suspense. The framing narrative is presented as a dream,
which contains two flashbacks. The daughter Isabella's running
away from home is revealed in flashback; so is her confession to
her mother about the rape and theft of money.

The relationship between Isabella and her mother is not the
typical depiction of black domestic life during the period in
which the film is made. The fact that there is no male father figure in the family is not presented as a liability or deficiency.
Isabella is not a delinquent. Although there are angry moments
between the mother and daughter, there are visible examples of
caring between the two. Micheaux calls attention to women in
his films through his choice of attractive, light-skinned actress-
es to play various roles. Yet, the narration does not develop an
excessive voyeurism and its attendant sexism. However, there is
relentless criticism of the macho black male. The setting of *Body
and Soul* is not presented as an idyllic black segregated world.
Unlike a dominant depiction in many black genre films,
Micheaux presents a relationship with the white community.
Black independent filmmakers made a significant contribution
to maintaining the psychic space that helped preserve the black
community. In *Body and Soul*, the narrative has a happy ending.
The conflict is resolved and is revealed to have been an elaborate dream. The preacher drops to his knees and begs forgiveness telling the congregation that church members pampered
him.

Micheaux's cinematic style focused on developing a black
visual iconography. His sets include black pin-up girls on the
walls of the saloon. Renderings of Booker T. Washington and
religious scenes featuring Jesus decorate the home. The film
favors the use of a stationary camera and iris transitions. Contrary
to the Hollywood style, Micheaux uses loose framing and a conservative approach to composition. Generally, his sequences are
lengthy. The narration begins with a loose plot and conceals a
lot of plot information, which is exposed later. There is little tendency to develop a dominant image. The camera does not lead
as is common in the Hollywood style. As a matter of fact, action
always seems to be center stage and is played out for the camera. There is an infrequent use of close-ups, so that the sequence
containing close-ups of hands stands out.

Micheaux had released his fourth feature film by the ending

of 1920. *The Symbol of the Unconquered, A Stirring Tale of Love and Adventure in the Great Northwest*, like *The Homesteader*, emphasized wide, open settings. "The frontier, for Micheaux, is the mythic space of moral drama and the site of opportunities seemingly free of the restrictive and discriminatory laws and social arrangements of the rural South and the urban metropolis" (Bowser and Spence, 1996, p. 61). Despite lean financial times, Micheaux—the first black director to make a sound movie, *The Exile* (1931)—worked consistently, averaging one film a year until 1940. He made his last film in 1948.

In the 1920s, The Colored Players Film Corporation, a company with white financial ownership and creative control used all-black casts to produce a series of films that included the well-received *Scar of Shame* (1926) and *Ten Nights in a Barroom* (1926). The Colored Players created stylish films and focused on topical issues relating to the black community. Of all the white-controlled companies making black films at this time, the films of the Colored Players require careful attention and raise significant questions relevant to the discussion of a black cinema aesthetic. However, other white-controlled outfits like the Ebony Motion Picture Company of Chicago began to turn out exploitation films (or race movies as they were called), featuring black subject matter aimed at black audiences. As the 1920s rolled on, "The filmmakers were undaunted by any topic; the whole black world was their stage, and their regional roots gave a varied flavor to the black experience they recorded on film" (Cripps, 1978, p. 24). By the 1930s, white companies increasingly began to view the black community as a lucrative market for films. "Many newer films of the 30s were commercial projects aimed at black neighborhood theaters: westerns, detective stories, and romances written, produced, and directed by whites in black locales with black actors. These films were cheaply made, but the circumstances were different. Their producers were financially able to do better, yet they turned out B-plot pictures with titles like *Bronze Buckaroo, Dirty Gertie From Harlem*, and *Murder on Lennox Avenue*" (Murray, 1973, p. 12). Approximately 150 companies produced hundreds of films that ranged from imitation black Hollywood images to images that showed diversity and depth in the black community (Bourne, 1994, p. 20).

Spencer Williams' 1941 film *The Blood of Jesus* exemplifies the cultural significance of early black independent filmmakers. It utilizes African American religious iconography and practice as structural and stylistic devices. African American spiritual music functions as an integral formal element of the narration. William's cinematic style attempts to bring black folk expression to film. The narrative revolves around Martha Jackson, who accepts Christ and submits to baptism. She encourages Ralph, her worldly husband to join her in coming to Christ. However, soon after her baptism he accidentally shoots Martha. An angel comes to her deathbed and brings her back to life. As a consequence, Martha undergoes a journey to test her faith. Williams' narration invokes the fantastic device of an "out-of-body" experience to depict Martha's faith. Her journey is structured around a vivid exploration of black religious themes and black folk imagery of good and evil. In this civilizational struggle between the power of God and the devil, the strength of Martha's faith keeps the devil from claiming her soul. Adrienne Lanier-Seward finds that *The Blood of Jesus* is an important black film because of its use of African American religious ritual. Her criticism is refreshing because it emanates from a concern with how Williams' film is constructed using formal parameters located in black folk culture, especially the way it sources its narration in the orality and communicative style of the sermon in the black tradition. Lanier-Seward writes that "*The Blood of Jesus* is the best example of early black filmmaking that employed structures and themes from Afro-American folk drama and religious expression to simultaneously entertain black audiences and acknowledge the culture's expressive style" (1987, p. 198).

The black film movement can be considered in four phases: 1919-1949; 1950s to the late 1960s; the 1970s; and 1980s to the current time. The first phase of black filmmaking (1919 to 1949) had several objectives that included promoting the contribution of blacks in film and proving to the world that blacks were capable of making films. Early black filmmakers recognized the emergence of a black audience at a time when black life was rendered invisible by the dominant society. Segregation had given root to black communities in different parts of the country and a black entrepreneurial class had sprung up to service the needs of blacks because the apartheid system placed restrictions on interracial contact. Inherent in these films was the notion that American society could be enriched by black culture. During the first phase, the practice of black filmmaking existed on the margins of Hollywood and black filmmakers did not attract the levels of finance necessary to mount adequate competition with

Hollywood filmmakers. They also were unable to command the subsidiary resources of well-equipped facilities and highly trained technicians to make Hollywood-type films. Because the white-financed companies existed on the margins of the black community, their products did not have the urgency and did not reflect the core values of the black experience. "In the absence of movies that spoke directly to black concerns, a kind of black underground grew outside the major studios. Although largely white-owned, it nonetheless attempted to reach the black audience that was untouched by Hollywood. Strapped by poor distribution channels, paltry budgets, amateurish actors, technical failings, and untrained crews, these production companies were somehow able to release films for black audiences throughout the silent era. Their films reached beyond mere representation of Negroes on the screen to depict Afro-Americans as a presence in American life" (Cripps, 1978, p. 24).

By the late 1930s, "independent filmmakers reawakened interest in black genre film by simply recreating Hollywood genres, i.e., gangster movies infused with black cops, crooks, judges, and jailers. Where the first generation of black filmmakers had examined black social issues, the new crop, including many whites, focused on tried and proven Hollywood genre formulas recast in black form, with an admixture of racial awareness" (Cripps, 1978, p. 38). The almost total capitulation of black film themes and characters to the Hollywood formulas helped bring about the demise of the first phase of black filmmaking. Murray explains that there were several reasons for the decline of the black film circuits in the late 1940s because theaters—mostly owned by whites—tended to be marginal enterprises and economic downturns in the 40s and 50s hurt business (1973, p. 14). The fact that black audiences were becoming accustomed to the narrative formulas and entertainment values of the Hollywood studios also helped to push black independent film to the background.

A formulation of black cinema that calls into question the cultural imperialism of the dominant cinema tends to shift concerns away from superficial change to the underlying structure of social signification itself. This was the hope of early black filmmakers. In retrospect, despite the immediate emotional satisfaction and equilibrating therapeutic value of black heroes (gangsters, detectives and cowboys), there was little transformation in the structure of representation of blacks. As a result, tra-

ditional ideologies in the cinema were, to some extent, reaffirmed
and a radical black cinema aesthetic was denied. A new problematic emerged in black cinema following the Second World
War. It was related to developments in the Civil Rights movement, the historical process of decolonization in Africa and the
Caribbean, a search for new expressive forms and new political
contingencies, and most of all it was the result of the struggle to
forge a new social order.

In the 1930s and 1940s, Paul Robeson loomed large as a
powerful black cultural icon. However, there was confusion of
Robeson's real-life politics with his film characterizations which,
for the most part, were checked by the constraints of the film
industry and never assumed the political importance he hoped
they would. His Hollywood roles, for example, in *Showboat*
(1936) and *Tales of Manhattan* (1942), contain Robeson's explo-
siveness and couch it in the thunder of his voice. His European
films revolve around a black hero (often an expatriate from the
New World), a neocolonialist figure who invariably functions as
the leader of the Africans. For example, Bosambo of *Sanders of
the River* (1935), Umbopas of *King Solomon's Mines* (1937), *Zinga*
of Song of Freedom (1936) and the title role of *Jericho* (1937) offer
no significant reformulation of the black hero. As in the
American independent production of Eugene O'Neill's *Emperor
Jones* (1933), Robeson's heroes represent the dominant ideologies and political relations of the status quo. At base, they represent a black heroic tradition, which treats blacks in Africa and
the Caribbean as exotic, unsophisticated savages whose leaders
derive their raison d'etre from the assumed superiority of
Western cultures. Robeson has a strong and definite presence in
these films. Yet, there is a certain reactionary sentiment in which
the representation of the black hero merely shifts traditional paradigms of power from a structure of race and class in society to
an intraracial framework in which class positions are fused with
the supremacy of Western values. There is a contradiction inherent in the ideology of a black hero who does not challenge the
dominant system of power and who seeks to establish a subsidiary
system of power within the dominant one. This kind of hero who
poses little conflict, but rather complements the economic and
political status quo, is undoubtedly one of equivocation.
However, it is important to separate the figure of Robeson—the
black cultural activist from—the film roles he played. Robeson's
personal political stance explicitly opposed the ideology pre-

sented within the narration of his films. Robeson's life and films bring to light a very important observation regarding signification in the cinema: meaning arises not so much in what precedes the film, for example, the actor's personal politics, but more so through the concrete circumstances or the process of production governing the film image. What we seek to know is how the political activist Robeson performed traditional roles such as Joe of *Showboat*. The bothersome factor here is how the "real-life" black hero is sabotaged and rendered powerless in film. Robeson's case emphasizes the importance of conceiving cultural products or films as resulting from specific, ongoing struggles, namely economic, political, ideological and signifying practices.

After the Second World War, Hollywood had begun to redefine the black male image in film. Canada Lee's Joe in *Lifeboat* (1944), James Edwards's Peter Moss in *Home of the Brave* (1949), Juano Hernandez's Lucas Beauchamp in *Intruder in the Dust* (1949) paved the way for the silent, dignified screen persona of actor Sidney Poitier in the 1950s and 1960s. Poitier meant a lot to blacks and whites alike, albeit different things. "In this integrationist age Poitier was the model integrationist hero. In his films, he was educated and intelligent. He spoke proper English, dressed conservatively, and had the best of table manners. For the mass white audience, Sidney Poitier was a black man who met their standards. His characters were tame; never did they act impulsively, nor were they threats to the system" (Bogle, 1994, pp. 175-176). For blacks, Poitier's screen persona was one of intelligence, quick wit and control of his circumstances.

The genre of neorealism provided the vehicle for a series of interesting films about the black experience in the early 1960s. John Cassavettes' *Shadows* (1961), Shirley Clarke's *The Cool World* (1963), Sam Weston and Larry Peerce's *One Potato, Two Potato* (1964) and Michael Roemer's *Nothing But a Man* (1965) took sincere steps to move away from traditional delineations. Using black and white photography, films such as *Nothing But a Man* and Charles Burnett's *Killer of Sheep* (1977) attempt to restrict the pleasures of the traditional cinema by emphasizing the less illusionist and less glamorous aspects of film. These two films use different points of view to explore the meaning of black manhood in American society. Duff, the protagonist in *Nothing But a Man*, "wrestles between the poles of black male freedom and domesticity; he is driven to the verge of vengeful violence, puling back in time to keep his integrity; he descends into the

wretched black city, only barely escaping its baleful forces that
destroyed his own father" (Cripps, 1978, pp. 118-119). Duff is a
working class protagonist who is a strong, defiant figure. In *Killer
of Sheep*, the narration develops a notion of black manhood as
fighting against the law of the jungle (American society). One of
its characters opines, "That's the law of the jungle." Another
states that "You can't live according to the white man's rules."
However, Stan—the film's protagonist—prefers not to live
according to the law of the jungle. Despite the travails and harsh
circumstances of this existence, he lives a noble life. When one
of his friends associates Stan's existence with poverty, he angrily responds telling him "We ain't poor," thereby making an
important distinction between poverty of spirit and the lack of
material things.

aesthetic
structure

The soundtracks of *Nothing But a Man* and *Killer of Sheep*
function in the black expressive tradition as more than background accompaniment and actually work to provide structure
for the narration. *Nothing But a Man* features a Motown soundtrack with cutting-edge Rhythm and Blues recording stars from
the early 1960s such as Martha and the Vandellas, Stevie Wonder,
The Miracles, Mary Wells, Holland and Dozier and the
Marvelettes. *Killer of Sheep* juxtaposes Paul Robeson's powerful
rendition of *What is America to Me?* with visual sequences of a
child's toy—a spinning top. Burnett crafts one of the most
poignant scenes in black film history in the dance sequence featuring Dinah Washington's *This Bitter Earth* playing while Stan,
the protagonist, and his wife are locked in a moving embrace.
Killer of Sheep is marked by a blues aesthetic, which emphasizes
repetition and thematic development of visual imagery and the
resilience of black survival amidst hard times.

Move away from
black middle
class.

These African American neo-realist films are about ordinary
people living very ordinary lives. Their protagonists are drawn
from the working class. While their existence is defined by the
white society, the character of their lives implies a steady resistance to and a tension with the established order. The world of
Charles Burnett's *Killer of Sheep* is a frightening amalgam of sheep
on their way to the slaughterhouse, blacks struggling against difficult jobs and unemployment, and the small joys that have contributed to black survival. Burnett's film uses a cyclical metaphor
in its narration. However, in an improvisational maneuver the
cycle of sheep going to the slaughter is reversed. When we first
see the sheep, we see cuts of meat and the narration ends with

the sheep going to slaughter. *Killer of Sheep* is an excellent example of poetic narration in black cinema. Its central image of the
slaughterhouse speaks directly to the dehumanization of the
black man. The film makes a probing poetic statement about
black survival, black manhood, work, the black family and the
relation of blacks to the majority society. The film's lyrical quality builds on an intricate interplay of visual and sound images.
The narration informs the viewer that the filmmaker is deliber-
ate in setting up his compositions and framing, although the camera does not call undue attention to itself. One finds a reflexive
quality that offers a succinct commentary on filmmaking and the
contemporary black experience itself. In addition, the placement
of the individual in the frame draws attention to the relationship
of the black individual to the larger society. *Killer of Sheep* makes
no attempt to develop a temporally driven narration. In contrast,
it uses spatial narration, often lingering and exploring variations
in its sequential structure paying attention to what may appear
to be insignificant detail and concretizing the existence of off-
screen space.

The African American genre of neo-realist film certainly
pushes the idea of a black hero to the limits of realist film languages. There is very little idealization and sexual exploitation
of the female body. In *Killer of Sheep*, the females are varied, representing a variety of body types and temperaments. The intense
identification that is developed between the audience and the
protagonist in a film like *The Learning Tree* (1968) is visibly
absent. These neo-realist films are poignant, touching and provide an important social critique of exploitation and oppression.
However, their black heroes are dignified, somewhat rebellious
and present an implicit challenge to the power of the dominant
society. Yet, these heroes are trapped men who are ever subject
to the phallic control of the white society, which is a basic characteristic of the genre.

As the Civil Rights movement made gains during the 1950s
and early 60s and increasing attention was given to bringing
blacks into the mainstream film industry, the black independent
film movement underwent a hiatus. However, the development
of infrastructural supports for black film was taking place. Black
writers, directors and other filmmakers were being trained in a
variety of circumstances. Some studied in the black theater movement. Others honed their craft in television and Hollywood.
Documentarian William Greaves, for example, spent several

years in Canada where he worked with the National Film Board.

Black documentary filmmakers also made important contributions to the reformulation of black film signification. During the Second World War, Carlton Moss wrote *The Negro Soldier* (1943) for the U.S. Armed Forces, which presented images of blacks in contrast to the prevalent depictions of that time. But the black film documentary did not reach critical heights until the late 1960s and early 1970s when a group of black documentarians led by William Greaves produced the *Black Journal* series on National Educational Television. "The mission of *Black Journal* was to show black spectators the world as seen by black observers, an overdue innovation in motion picture media. Black documentarians like (William) Greaves, (St. Clair) Bourne and many others began working to recode the non-fictional representation of black experience" (Taylor, 1988). *Black Journal* took a strong stand " . . . in its insistence that (black) people in our films speak for themselves as much as possible and, if narration was used that the narrator assume a tone of advocacy" (Bourne, 1988, p. 12). In catalogue notes that accompanied the Whitney Museum's New American Filmmaker's Series presentation of Bourne's work, Taylor (1988) states that his films—especially *The South: Black Student Movements* (1969), *The Nation of Common Sense* (1970), and *Let the Church Say Amen!* (1973)—have moved beyond a mere functional recording of events to engender a sense of empowerment through the film image. "The key to his construction of black subjectivity is not merely performance, but the expressivity of his subjects as cultural archetypes."

By the late 1960s, Hollywood had begun to take a new look at blacks. The impact of Sidney Poitier's screen presence and his box-office success in films such as *To Sir With Love* (1967) and *Guess Who's Coming to Dinner* (1967) demonstrated the existence of an untapped movie-going market among blacks. Gordon Parks' *The Learning Tree* is a transitional work in African American film history, creating a bridge between black filmmakers of an earlier period, their successors in the 1970s and the shifting characterization of the black male in the 1960s. *The Learning Tree* summarizes significant stylistic and structural elements of the work of early black filmmakers. As a transitional film, it presents signifying paradigms from early black cinema and also incorporates later developments in black film.

The Learning Tree represents black family values in terms of a certain universal humanism. It differs thematically from the point of view that a black humanism was undesirable, which was developed in the spate of 70s films that followed. In contrast, a dominant thematic approach depicted blacks as engaged in struggle against an oppressive system and importantly showed them winning symbolic battles in film narratives. Protagonist Newton Winger, who is symbolic of innocence, freshness, youth and promise, signifies the liberal humanist black hero. His antagonist rival, Marcus Savage represents the 'vicious, criminal, uncivilized and angry black voices' who want to strike out at the white society, Marcus is imprisoned and later killed by a white law enforcement agent. In a true Christian faithfulness, Newton decides to turn in Marcus' father for an unsolved crime. Later, he defeats a revengeful Marcus in a miniprize fight. The hero of *The Learning Tree* is an equivocating figure who is unable to act out his own freedom, reflecting the liberal, Christian tradition of Western society. The film employs mythic themes of change: good versus bad and lawfulness versus outlawry. Parks' heroes implicate these poles of existence in such a fierce manner that they are powerless to act. This film remains within the problematic of traditional cinema in its aesthetics and narrative structure. Its black heroes are trapped within a debilitating tension that functions ultimately to reaffirm the status quo of blacks in society and the structure of representation, which remains substantially unchanged.

Critics usually distinguish between black films and 'blaxploitation' films in the 1970s. Blaxploitation films compromised black cultural signification because they were contemporary white productions in blackface. These films were produced by whites (and some blacks), featured black casts and were set in black communities. Economic exploitation of the black audience was the principal reason for their existence. After the success of *Sweetback* (1971), *Shaft* (1971) and *Superfly* (1972), the industry moguls snapped to attention and began to turn out exploitation films with startling regularity. "Sometimes it even looked as if the same movies were being remade time and again" (Bogle, 1994, p. 240). The rush to capitalize on the popularity of black film often resulted in the marginal rewriting of plots and the overuse of stock characters.

Insofar as films of the 1970s continued to support the ideological system prevalent in the dominant society, it was not unusual to find that women of all races were rendered in traditional terms. The black woman is represented as passive and sex-

Paris
Gins

ual. Invariably, she plays the role of the homemaker—dependent and ready to please the hero. Eventually, the phallic woman became another representation of the black woman in 1970s films. This 'new' black woman seems to break out of her careful containment. In films such as *Coffy* (1973), *Cleopatra Jones* (1973), *Foxy Brown* (1974), and *Friday Foster* (1975), we find a black female heroine who appears to have captured the power from a male-dominated world and is out to reek revenge. Yet, her representation in traditional gender terms equivocates any change in the narrative representation of the black woman.

 Instead of reformulating the traditional signification of the woman in popular entertainment, the phallic black woman reaffirmed and celebrated the sexual objectification of women. The 'black woman as heroine' series of films falls far short of presenting a new problematic of the woman in cinema, for there is a certain regime of traditional male pleasure in these film. Hence, the sexy, guntoting heroine in these narratives is but a variation of the traditional treatment of women in society. The representation of the white woman is reverse. She is a siren, an alluring sexual creature whose narrative function is generally irrelevant except to build the machismo of the hero.

 Without a reformulation of the traditional narrative, films such as *Shaft*, Michael Schultz's *Cooley High* (1975) and Ivan Dixon's *The Spook Who Sat by the Door* (1973) will represent the limits of black film possible in traditional models. Although these films delve deeply and richly into the question of the black hero in film, their over-reliance on the traditional narrative tills unproductive soil. The problem with these films is that, to some extent, their protagonists are similar in important respects to traditional Hollywood heroes. This establishes the efficacy of social realism as a poignant form, but it also clearly points out the severe problems of conservative ideology and filmic signification that characterize this genre. Despite the radical political tones of *Spook's* content, the nature of its revolt is still contained within traditional outlines. In that these films are not just simple Hollywood films with blacks, they continued the movement toward developing the potential of a black cinema. However, they place themselves within the problematic of traditional cinema in as much as they posit a central focus upon narrative content and refuse the radical possibilities of fusing film form and content into a new cinematic experience.

Bill Gunn's *Ganja and Hess* (1973), which developed an

unusual cinematic ambience and innovative narrative about the contemporary existence of an ancient African vampire, countered the blackface mode of exploitation cinema in its representation of complex black characterizations and the exploration of African source material. However, the increased activity during the third phase of black cinema in the 1970s did not significantly question the nature of filmic narration and the code of the Hollywood hero. Films such as *Shaft, Superfly, or Cooley High* attempt to subvert, or at least question, the dominant tradition in the cinema, but they are effectively harnessed by it in their usage of the Hollywood model as the basis for the development of black heroes. Despite the fact that these films present examples of the possibility of a black hero, they are unable to get rid of the historical baggage and ideological circumstances arising from the mythology of the Hollywood hero.

The hero of Gordon Parks, Sr.'s *Shaft* is a haughty black detective who straddles rebellion and acceptance of the dominant society. The protagonist in Gordon Parks Jr.'s *Superfly* wants out of a life of crime under the control of crooked white cops. Both Superfly and Shaft are virile masculine figures within traditional sex-role delineations. Their world is one in which blacks can challenge the political and legal authority, but not in a way to reformulate the basic system of power relations. It appears that blacks in these films merely wish to replace the white power structure with one controlled by blacks. In these films, the woman continues to be represented in the mode of sex object. Interestingly, there is the figure of the white woman who must succumb to the sexual power of the black hero. The film adaptation of Sam Greenlee's novel *The Spook Who Sat By The Door* has an unusual anti-CIA theme for a film produced in Hollywood. It is the story of a black hero who defects from a United States government intelligence agency and trains a team of subversives in urban guerrilla warfare during the turbulent 1960s. These films were made by black directors, but produced within the Hollywood system. Inasmuch as they rely on the narrative conventions and film language of the Classical Hollywood cinema, they are restricted in their attempt to articulate a full-blown black hero. However, they make significant advances that contributed to the continuation of a black aesthetic tradition in the cinema. For example, in *Shaft* and *Superfly*, the use of music functions not so much as a secondary support for the visuals, but on occasion serves as a primary driving force in the flow of the narrative. The black hero as the outsider, who is often an out-law existing on society's boundaries is also developed in the plot of these narratives. These films exemplify a tremendous tension between the ideological requirements of the classical system of film narration and the evolving outlines of a black independent cinema. In 1977, the filmmaker Larry Clark directed *Passing Through*, about a black musician's struggle against exploitation in the music industry. Clark's hero suffers the humiliation and oppression of America's blacks, but he strikes back refusing the castrated existence so clearly inscribed upon traditional black heroes. *Passing Through* creates a narrative structure derived from African American music. Clark's hero is uncompromising and his experimental uses of film languages mark a significant advance for black independent cinema.

An Afrocentric-based filmmaking practice effectively ques-tions the cultural imperialism of Hollywood cinema and shifts concerns from minor superficial changes to the underlying struc-ture of the narration itself. In the history of black cinema, we find incremental change in the depiction of black images. The black independent filmmakers were instrumental in building and continuing a black cinematic tradition that would not signifi-cantly emerge until the late 1960s and early 70s. In retrospect, one must surmise that despite the immediate emotional satis-faction and equilibrating therapeutic value of their black heroes—black gangsters, detectives and cowboys—the need still existed for a more thorough transformation of the structure of representation of blacks.

AFROCENTRIC FOUNDATIONS OF BLACK FILM CULTURE

The notion of black art and the establishment of criteria for understanding it were both firmly established by the 1960s when the black nationalist movement undertook a major thrust to rede-fine and reclaim black history, culture and identity. In their wide-ly read book, *Black Power: The Politics of Liberation in America*, Stokely Carmichael and Charles V. Hamilton describe the Black Power movement as a "struggle for the right to create our own terms through which to define ourselves and our relationship to the society" (1967, p. 35). While many critics decry black nation-alist aesthetics of the 1960s, Houston Baker argues that the Black Arts Movement made an important contribution to the estab-lishment of an African American critical tradition. He finds that,

"The faith that postulated that 'Blackness' as a distinctive category of existence is seen as the generative source of a new art, politics, and criticism nullifying the interpretive authority of a white, critical orthodoxy" (1981, p. 297).

The roots of the Black Arts Movement can be found in the longstanding tradition of African American protest, which sought to change the system of social and political relations in society, especially as these impacted on blacks. Protest in African American cultural expression can be traced to the encounter of enslaved Africans with the plantation system and their narratives of freedom. In the 20th century, the oppressive social conditions and structural inequality that most blacks continue to face have functioned to fuel black protest movements. Following the migration of blacks from the South to the North and from rural America to urban centers in the early 20th century, activism increased as blacks began to sharpen their sense of ethnic identity, deepen their knowledge of their cultural heritage, and articulate a more aggressive political vision.

The philosophy of black cultural nationalism has been a seminal historical influence on African American social protest thought. Black cultural nationalists argue that solutions to the socio-political problems of blacks must involve a spiritual linkage with the African heritage and the recognition of the psychic ties that link African diasporic cultures through an emphasis on pan-African unity. Art is conceived as being inherently political; its political function is the liberation of blacks; and the artist is viewed as an active participant in the struggle for racial dignity, cultural resonance, political empowerment and economic autonomy. The aesthetic function of African American protest art is to visually embody the political message of the black consciousness movement. Inspiring black unity and dignity, articulating the black community's needs and embodying the experiences and potential of blacks through art are some of its major concerns (Fine, 1973, p. 195).

In African American social protest art, there is no separation of aesthetic expression from social and political issues. Good black art is believed to reflect and support black liberation, and any art that does not contribute to the liberation struggle is considered invalid. Social protest art is associated with political activism and agitation. It functions as a symbol of political ideology and a weapon for social change. Maulena Karenga succinctly summarizes the aesthetic position of social protest art,

stating that the black liberation struggle does not need pictures
of oranges in a bowl or trees standing innocently in the midst of
a wasteland. "If we must paint oranges and trees, let our guer-
rillas eat those oranges for strength and use these trees for cover
. . . All material is mute until the artist gives it a message, and
that message must be a message of revolution" (1971, p. 34).

'Black Aesthetic' criticism is a related development of the
tradition of social protest art. It is a term used by Hoyt Fuller in
response to the exclusion of black artists by the white establishment. Fuller "was exasperated by the irreverent treatment of
black artists by some white establishment critics on the assumption that their work was not to be taken entirely seriously"
(Fowler, 1981, p. x). 'Black Aesthetic' proponents wanted to
break loose from the academic confines of 'fine art' to forge closer links with the black community and create forms that speak
directly to black concerns for liberation. They foregrounded the
political and economic relations that reproduced racial exploitation, which has been a central issue in African American artistic
expression. They advocated the establishment of separate black
institutions as an antidote to the pervasive oppression of the
white society. Today, these ideas range from the ideology of black
street culture to what has been described as 'gangsta' history.

The rhetoric of Black Power, its iconography, modes of communication and sources of authority differed significantly from
that of the Civil Rights movement. "Whereas the rhetoric of the
Civil Rights Movement was Southern and familiar to the rural
as well as to an urban audience, that of the Black Power movement was decidedly Northern, strictly urban and often derived
its logic and authority from the ethics of the streets where many
of its early adherents struggled for survival" (Sanders, 1986).
While African American social realism gained momentum from
the rise of the black middle class during the late 19th and early
20th centuries, black protest aesthetics flourished with the urban
explosion of the late 1960s and 1970s during the cultural consciousness, nationalist and racial awareness movements of the
period.

Protest art pays little attention to traditional artistic values,
which are favored by the academy and which might detract from
the force of the message of revolution and the need for change.
Addison Gayle describes it as a "corrective—a means of helping
black people out of the polluted mainstream of Americanism"
(1971, p. xxiii). Karenga argues that "All art must reflect and sup-

[handwritten margin note: NOT European - American aesthetics]

[handwritten margin notes: Afrocentric film + aesthetic]

port the black revolution, and any art that does not discuss and contribute to the revolution is invalid" (1971, p. 33). In this aesthetic, the black experience functions as the unequivocal locus from which to evaluate black art. This explains why Larry Neal invoked the framework of Ethics as necessary to the question of aesthetics. Neal asked whose values should serve as the basis for a black aesthetic and whose vision of the world should be more critical to African American art—an Afrocentric vision or that of the dominant white society ? He also questioned the nature of truth, asking "whose truth shall we express, that of the oppressed or the oppressors?" (Neal, 1972, p. 259). Drawing on the aesthetic theory emanating from African traditional culture which views artistic expression as part and parcel of everyday life, the African American protest tradition views film as a tool in the struggle for black liberation, self-determination and political empowerment. Afrocentric critics find it impossible to divorce art from political activity. Political practice is viewed as an integral feature of the black artistic impulse.

The activist aesthetics of the 1960s and 1970s influenced a new generation of blacks who were attending film school and studying film in university programs. A new Afrocentric aesthetic stance was emerging. It was poised to produce a more sensitive and responsive climate for black film. The rise of black studies as an academic subject and the attention to the black experience in theory formation provided critical approaches that were capable of discerning and providing a radically different context for viewing and studying black film. The appearance of black film festivals complemented the new cultural environment. In 1969, Pearl Bowser organized the First Black Independent Film Festival in New York. "Films that had not been seen in more than 40 years were located and put on exhibition. *Scar of Shame* (1927), *Body and Soul* (1924) and *God's Step Children* (1938) were among the discoveries to reopen an area of American film history that scholars had ignored or just passed over" (Bowser, 1981, p. 1). In 1976, the Los Angeles County Museum of Art presented a retrospective of black film, which included St. Clair Bourne's *Let the Church Say Amen* (1973), *Black Shadows on the Silver Screen*, and *The Emperor Jones* (1933). When the Black Filmmakers Foundation convened the first conference of African American filmmakers in 1979, several new voices—St. Clair Bourne, Ayoka Chenzira, Julie Dash, Reggie Hudlin, Alile Sharon Larkin, and Spike Lee—attended, and they would help alter the course of

[handwritten margin note: film making]

[handwritten margin note: LACMA]

the black independent film movement. The African Film Society in San Francisco, Oliver Franklin and Toni Cade Bambara in Philadelphia, Chamba Educational Film Services in New York City, and the Black Film Institute, Washington, D.C. characterized the grassroots organizational activity that began to spring up around the country.

Although resistance to exclusion and marginalization remained high on the agenda of black filmmakers, in the late 1960s the black film movement turned its attention to other issues. This new direction, which was Afrocentric in orientation, involved the articulation of a genuinely black independent film culture and the shaping of an expressive film language that draws on and addresses the black experience in very specific ways. New critical approaches to black film also emerged, which coincided with the coming of age of black film and the production of a significant body of highly acclaimed films. This criticism incorporated developments in linguistics, psychoanalysis, structuralism, Marxism and black cultural studies to produce an increasingly sophisticated theoretical framework. Mbye B. Cham and Claire Andrade-Watkins define this movement as one of redefinition, involving " . . . a studied awareness of self, rooted in individual and collective memory, visions and aspirations, as well as of the other, now decoded and recoded anew." Furthermore, this critical strategy generates a multi-faceted artistic, cultural, social and political method which functions as "a reading of the imaginative, the cultural and the socio-political experience and challenges of individuals and societies linked by a common heritage and a history of struggle against similar, and in many cases, the same forces of oppression and domination" (1988, p. 9). Cham explains that this project "is a strategy to rediscover and appropriate the diversity of the black experience in order to construct a new, more authentic sense of identity" (1992, p. 4). Jim Pines stresses the need for new black cinema to break away from the old-style problematic of race relations and multiculturalism. He suggests that black filmmakers develop a broader, more critical strategy, which would stress a completely different set of political and cultural concerns, such as the retrieval and re-presentation of black people's own histories through archival excavation. It would also involve the use of film language to construct a filmic signification that conveys a more complex sense of contemporary black experiences from a black perspective (1988, pp. 26- 27).

Since the 1970s, black film criticism has increasingly been

seen as a distinct discipline characterized by the publication of histories, criticism and bibliographies. Several studies such as James Murray's *To Find an Image* (1973), Lindsay Patterson's *Black Film and Filmmakers* (1975) and Thomas Cripps' *Black Film as Genre* (1978) used the method of sociological criticism. Patterson captures the broad social appeal many black film critics shared. He writes, "Make no mistake about it, movies have a psychological and sociological impact on societies that is frightening. They set tones in morality and dress (one only has to walk through the urban centers of America to see how pervasive this influence is) for millions of people throughout the world" (1975, p. ix). Murray was also concerned about film's social impact. "The chances are great that visual media will play an increasingly important role in direct education as well. Since the media exert such influence, and because they have historically excluded blacks to the detriment of the black image, blacks, if they are to rectify this omission, should use the media to create their own versions of society" (1973, p. xiv). These writings reflected a politically committed criticism and put an explicit focus on questions of race to film studies.

In the 1980s, the black independent film movement moved ahead on several fronts that included organizations to promote black film, film screenings, festivals and the emergence of scholarship committed to a black independent film culture. Pearl Bowser played a major role in these events as a film archivist, researcher and curator. She organized a major exhibition in Paris of African American cinema—*A Retrospective of Independent Black American Cinema, 1920-1980*—which opened in 1980, a pivotal year for the black film movement. Ten filmmakers and specialists in black history took part in debates with the audience. They explored issues in black film theory—such as the question of defining black film, the use of music in film, and how the influence of jazz and an African heritage shaped the look and sound of black films (Bowser, 1981, p. 1). A new agenda for black film and black film criticism was now firmly established, bringing about a shift in the integrationist appeal for inclusion in Hollywood. Black filmmakers were free to pursue work in Hollywood, while developing their own independent projects.

Madubuko Diakite's *Film, Culture and the Black Filmmaker* (1980) was published at an important moment in the establishment of the black independent film movement. Diakite examines cinema as a cultural product and explores the relationship between black film and the sociocultural environment of the community that produces it. In particular, he focuses on how black filmmakers reflect their perceptions of the world through the medium of film. Diakite's analysis moved black film criticism away from the earlier preoccupation with a black Hollywood to address the failure of critics to "venture into the wider study of expressive meanings" (1980, p. 126). His framing of a phenomenology of black film expression stands as a seminal contribution to black film historiography. He describes it as "a method of analysis that looks 'Zu den Sachen' (to the thing itself) as it functions within a sociocultural community with which it shares values and meanings" (1980, p. 161). In contrast to a popular vein of criticism that found little aesthetic value in black independent cinema, Afrocentric theorists succeeded in focusing attention on the cultural functioning of black art and black film. "If the values reflected in black-made films are seen as mere reflections of a white culture, then the realities of black life, hopes, and aspirations are unjustly being overlooked, an occurrence which white Hollywood has refused to deal with, but one that black filmmakers dealt with in spite of handicaps whenever possible" (Diakite, 1980, p. 51).

Instead of viewing the black experience as a liability or a deficiency, a more advantageous assessment conceives of it as a creative force. J. Ronald Green (1993) argues that although the dual consciousness of African American life has inherent difficulties and is not a condition to be envied, nonetheless it "is a knowledge worth having." Instead of viewing the black experience from a deficit model, the positive reliance on the black cultural tradition as the source for the development of black independent film made an important contribution in identifying a primary focus on the black experience. Bowser's archival work in the 1970s has been very valuable in this regard. She raised questions about the relative obscurity of black film history especially in the post-First World War period of a black art and cultural renaissance. Bowser was persistent in probing why the cultural renaissance of the black writer, actor, musician and artist during the 1920s and 1930s was well documented, while the role of the black filmmakers of the same period remained unheralded. Describing the existence of a fledgling black film industry between 1915 and 1939 as "a bit of lost history," Bowser played a pivotal role in helping to clarify and establish the importance of early black filmmakers. For thousands of movie-goers in the 1920s and 30s,

with benefits for all

these films "must have offered a glimpse into a fantasy world that reflected their own hidden dreams of heroes and villains . . . Blacks saw themselves for the first time on film, cast in dramatic roles created by other blacks . . ." (Bourne, 1973, p. 33).

In the early 1970s, *Black Creation* (published by the Institute of Afro-American Affairs at New York University) issued a series of articles that helped set the tone for a new historiography of black film. Describing film as a tool for liberation, Roscoe C. Brown, Jr., (1973) sketched out the context within which black film was developing. He described the 1960s and 1970s as "years of black awakening from years of accommodation—a reawakening of black pride and concern for our heritage, an awakening to the need for massive political and social action to change the conditions affecting black people in the nation and the world." In highlighting the demands for liberation, he saw a major role for black arts in helping to raise the social and political awareness of the black community. What is most interesting about the *Black Creation* series was a view of film not only as art, but also as business. "It took a 'revolutionary' film that . . . dared white patrons to walk into the theater, to crystalize the image of a substantial black audience. In 1971, Melvin Van Peebles's *Sweet Sweetback's Badasssss Song* became the first major black-produced feature film since the 1930-era of men like Oscar Micheaux to draw audiences that were consistently in excess of 80 percent black. And within weeks, a stampede in the ailing industry which had lost hundreds of millions of dollars, was on" (Murray, 1973, p. 26).

Black film historiography and criticism benefited from the momentum to develop Black Studies courses and departments in American universities. The first black film curricula focused on image studies and presented comparative analyses of diasporic black film. The academic study of black film would grow substantially, and by the 1990s, a wider range of universities began to include black film studies in their class schedules. The 1980 symposium on Black Cinema Aesthetics at Ohio University crystalized the impact of the new generation of black filmmakers and scholars. The conference focused on the cultural and artistic specificity of black independent film and it explored the use of black expressive traditions and historical forms in filmmaking. This black film scholarship conceptualized the issue of black cinema in broad terms as a phenomenon in and of itself. The aims, goals, and purposes of a black cinema were acknowledged to be different from those of Hollywood, especially in the representation of blacks. Black independent cinema was defined as challenging the institution of traditional cinema and the social understandings on which it was based, and the best black cinema explored cinematic models and content outside the conventions of the Classical Hollywood cinema. The black experience was conceived as a rich cultural matrix upon which to build an alternative black cinema. "Because of the subordinate position of blacks in relation to the system of power in society and the particular history of oppression visited upon blacks in New World societies, many believe that the black experience offers a vantagepoint from which special insights on society and the human condition could be gleaned. Related to this is the view that black film (much like black literature) is capable of functioning as a vehicle for expressing the unique aesthetic sensibilities that emanate from the black experience" (Yearwood, 1982, p. 10).

The Ohio conference was a unique historical gathering of filmmakers, historians, critics and educators. Conference participants discussed a broad range of issues in the aesthetics and philosophy of African American film. Part of the significance of the Ohio conference was the cumulative impact of bringing together leading voices in the black film movement and the range of concerns that were addressed. Bowser presented a historical overview of the representation of black women in the cinema. She urged caution in rehabilitating the black male image at the expense of the female. Her isolation of gender issues within black cultural expression signaled a critical moment for black film scholarship. Bowser explained that the black response to the negative imagery by the white industry was to create its own counter images, which often did not go far enough in its representation of women. "Early independent companies such as The Lincoln Motion Picture Company established in 1915, Reol Pictures and others, focused on the black woman as though she were germane to the white woman; she was helpless, in need of protection, and frail. She was the symbol of status for the hero; and the fact that she often looked white, spoke to the acceptance of white standards of beauty among the black 'achievers' of the period" (Bowser, 1982, p. 46). Despite a wider range of imagery and attention to social issues affecting blacks in early black film, Bowser observes that the struggle against male bias was still not considered as important as racism or colonialism. In summary, she finds, "The black woman in race movies (as they were once called) was rarely a winner, often unlucky in love, frequently losing the man, her status, or both. Black filmmakers of race movies glorified athletic heroes, cowboys, soldiers and men on their way up; but rarely, if ever, did the woman move beyond the romantic love interest or maternal figure" (1982, p. 50).

Seeking to ground the emerging black film culture within a strong historical framework, Cripps argued that the new black cinema movement had much to gain by including "a sense of the past in its own self-consciousness." He lamented the fact that in the 1970s surge of interest in black film, there was a general tendency to function as though there was no black film history. Cripps suggested that this forgetfulness might have led to the disastrous end of the epoch. He appealed for a black historiography of film that was truly historical and highlighted the need for an incisive critical canon. He stated that the black independent film movement could not afford the luxury of ignoring its past. "The next class of black filmmakers, having never known or having forgotten this history, seems doomed to repeat a variation on it, unless history is included in the concerns of black filmmakers" (1982, p. 21). Haile Gerima shared Cripps' sense of history. He noted that black filmmakers must always assume that "There must have been somebody before me; otherwise I would not exist" (1982, p. 111). He stressed the importance of a strong sense of history in black film because the filmmaker finds his or her freedom in that history. He posed the question: "How long can Afro-American artists be travelogue artists, taking white America into the underworld . . . into the worst negative conceptions of black America, which happen to titillate and fascinate white America?" (1982, p. 112). History provides a context and a meaning for black film, and struggle plays a central role in the course of this history. Gerima argued that cinema is an integral player in the development of social perceptions through the way it functions to present certain points of views as social norm and others as social problems or as being illegitimate. Gerima identified a sense of equivocation in the achievements of early black film. Although early black filmmakers agreed that self-expression was necessary for blacks, their "rebellion was still levied within white American ethnic expression. And in doing so, they damaged the whole historical movement of a powerful and significant transformation of our people's lives" (1982, p. 109). In Gerima's view, cinematic language should be poetic, but its poeticism must be rooted in the writing of a different social history.

Two divergent trends in black film historiography were identified at the Ohio conference. While both call for the development of alternative imagery in black film, they differ as to the
means of achieving it. Gerima's criticism of Sweetback for its
repetition of images of blacks associated historically with negative stereotypes represents one approach. This point of view is
based on the notion that because popular stereotypes seem to be
endowed with a potent and overpowering range of negative
meanings, a new black cinema must overvalue 'positive' images
and depict blacks with a greater sense of pride and dignity. The
second is illustrated by the position held by Van Peebles, which
focuses more on the construction of social meanings and proceeds by attacking the perceptual bases of what we know as reality and how we understand it. Inherently, Van Peebles is not
concerned with presenting stereotypes of blacks in his films. But,
he is interested in using popular stereotypes as a means of social
satire (*Watermelon Man*) and as a point of initiating a struggle
against them (*Sweetback*). Part of the significance of the 1980
Ohio Conference was the application of new methods of criticism to black independent film. "Van Peebles' approach to the
presentation of images in film is allied to certain modernist critiques of the image as sign. In and of itself, the image does not
constitute a problem; but the problem is how the image becomes
stereotyped. Thus Van Peebles emphasizes the historical conditions within which particular images arise as stereotypes. He confronts the stereotype and refuses any repression of it. Whereas
there is criticism of *Sweetback* in terms of the image, the filmmaker seems to place more importance on process, that is, how
the image is constructed in the first place and how it can be
deconstructed in political terms" (Yearwood, 1982, p. 15).

The difference between the theoretical positions held by
Gerima and Van Peebles could be further explained through a
comparison of their films. The evidence of a history of oppression surrounds the heroine of Gerima's *Bush Mama*. Yet, she is a
noble character who has managed to retain an essential humanity amidst the devastation of welfare and ghetto life. In
Sweetback, Van Peebles' hero cannot display the remnants of a
humanity that survives poverty and social oppression because
these are viewed as a fiction of bourgeois society and as a lie
which the oppressed are subtly encouraged to believe as a means
of denying the harsh brutalities of a history of slavery and cultural dislocation. In this historical materialist view, blacks can-

not have an innocent humanity, an inner peace until the material conditions of their existence are altered. All Van Peebles is
willing to concede is the necessity of struggle. Van Peebles'
Sweetback is submerged in what Bowser calls the graphic pain
of reality. Without recognition of the deep scars of this painful-
ness as well as the transformation of social consciousness and
social reality, the humanity that Gerima's characters experience
and cherish is not possible for those of Van Peebles.

Vattel T. Rose raised a critical issue for black film culture
when he suggested that black literature provides a rich cultural
treasure available as source material for black films. Although
forms of black expression are bound by historical traditions and
practical limitations, nonetheless historically they "have freely
taken from one another forms, techniques, and ideas as they seem
appropriate" (Rose, 1982, p. 27). He observed that many of the
problems faced by a fledgling black cinema in search of an aesthetic foundation had already been experienced by Afro-
American literature, which could help chart productive
directions for the newer art form. Rose mentioned the fecundi-
ty of the African American folk tradition, which could be
reworked and incorporated into more contemporary forms of
expression. Warning against a black cinema aesthetic that satis-
fies itself simply with easy protest against the system and mere
opposition to Hollywood cinema, Rose urged that at its deepest
levels black film "must explore the full dimensions of the Afro-
American experience in all its complexity, contradictions, vitality, triumphs" (1982, p. 38).

Bourne noted that political action was an essential ingredi-
ent in the development of a black film culture. "As filmmakers,
we had to be concerned with . . . broad-based social, economic,
political, and legal matters. Because of that we deliberately tried
to function as artists and not technicians. We tried to interpret
and define the issue that affected our lives. Technicians record;
as artists we knew we had certain fundamental power and respon-
sibilities to those—our community—who had trusted us enough
to stand with us and support us" (1982, p. 99). Bourne expressed
concern about the tendency of new black filmmakers to de-
emphasize a view of black film as a voice of the black experience,
while placing an emphasis on technical questions, what he
described as the priorities of the filmmaking circle. This could
lead black filmmakers to lose touch with the black community.
But he cited a new group of black filmmakers (that included

Gerima, Charles Burnett and James Fanaka) whose agenda
stresses the continuation of "the tradition of developing and
expressing African-based cultural models on film. This ranged
from content to the structure of their films. They did not devalue the political message, that is, the oppression of our people and
how a resistance movement developed. They mastered the narrative form; and this meant much more to the people . . ." (1982,
p. 10). The overall impact of the often heated symposium of filmmakers and scholars at the Ohio conference was twofold. First,
it helped to systematize the concept of black independent film
culture by foregrounding a view of black film as art that was committed to the development of the black community, and it served
to emphasize the significance of an expressive tradition emanating from African American history and related to black expression in the arts. The project of black film was outlined as seeking
to establish a viable independent black cinema and using film as
a means of transforming popular entertainment and prevalent
representations of blacks.

NEW DIRECTIONS IN BLACK FILM

The conscience of black cinema in the 1970s came from a group
of filmmakers that Toni Cade Bambara describes as black insur-
gents whose artistic consciousness was influenced by the activism
of the sixties. The articulation of a film form that reflected the
historical and cultural experiences of blacks, which could resist
absorption by Hollywood, was a fundamental critical concern of
these filmmakers. They emphasized accountability to the community over taking their place in a film industry that denigrates
and contributes to the oppression of blacks. They stressed the
importance of the black community and its development as the
arena for their film work as opposed to the over-determination
of aesthetic issues and the preoccupation with narrow technical
concerns. They expressed a desire to reconstruct cultural memory by refinding black literature and bodies of knowledge germane to the black community and objected to the slavish
imitation of white models and the classic texts of a Eurocentric
academic world. The UCLA group also believed it was important to establish linkages with international film culture (Cade
Bambara, 1993, p. 119). "The revolutionary breakthrough of the
UCLA school was to draw on Micheaux's work, yet shift its social
subject matter from a middle-class to a working-class milieu in
which black labor struggled against white capital" (Masilela,

1993, p. 109). The UCLA group included Charles Burnett, Ben Caldwell, Larry Clark, Julie Dash, Haile Gerima, Pamela Jones and Billy Woodberry. Drawing on the work of Clyde Taylor, Bourne comments that "what is remarkable about this movement was the portrayal for nearly the first time, of black women with a legitimately positive existence for themselves. Although varied in approach, the films of Julie Dash, Alile Sharon Larkin, Pamela Jones and Barbara McCullough began exploring the interior complexity of the black woman persona" (1994, p. 22).

The Los Angeles school of black filmmakers played an important role in helping to establish a viable black independent film culture. "The intellectual and cultural co-ordinates of this black independent film movement are inseparable from the political and social struggles and convulsions of the 1960s. For these African and African American filmmakers, imagination was inescapably wedded to political and cultural commitment. The Civil Rights movement, the Women's movement, the anti-war movement, and activities in America in support of national liberation struggles in Africa, Asia, and Latin America informed the political consciousness of the members of the group" (Masilela, 1993, p. 108). These developments laid the groundwork for subsequent gains in black filmmaking. *Black Journal*, which began to air on public television in 1968 was a direct response to the murder of Dr. Martin Luther King. The idea was an overdue response to the Kerner Commission report on U. S. race relations, which called for the media to expand and intensify coverage of the black community and to the growing mood for self-determination in the black community. *Black Journal* captured national attention, and its producers saw the need for trained filmmakers. The *Black Journal* Film Workshop helped to fill this void. It also created a pool of filmmakers who worked not only on *Black Journal*, but on other productions as well (Bourne, 1988, p. 12). James Snead links the gains of the Civil Rights movement to the increasing educational and professional opportunities gained by a new generation of black filmmakers. Many of these filmmakers belonged to the black middle class, but unlike many of their precursors in the 1920s and 1930s, they insisted on an Afrocentric orientation engaging problems that addressed the diverse experience of all segments of the black community. They became the politically engaged beneficiaries of a stylistic and technical revolution in the world of film. "Skeptical about the ability of the mainstream American film industry to put its house in order, this new generation of black independent filmmakers decided to exploit film's full aesthetic and political potential. They set about recoding black skin on screen and in the public realm by revising the contexts and concepts with which it had long been associated" (Snead, 1994, pp. 115-116).

Instead of viewing low budgets as liabilities, politically conscious black independent filmmakers of the 1970s developed a cinematic ambience shorn of the illusory glitter of traditional cinema. The politics of film occupied a prominent place on their agenda. "These films are not what one may term advocacy films, or simple propagandistic work. There is a centrality of the artistic expression of ideas through the medium of film. Without a doubt, these filmmakers deal with explicit political themes. These films contain a political commitment to the liberation struggles of black and other oppressed peoples. However, these filmmakers are not interested in ghettoizing black cinema. As filmmakers, they hold a fundamental commitment to advancing the rights of black people; but they never hesitate to speak to larger audiences" (Yearwood, 1982, pp.11-12).

The first phase of black independent cinema to some extent reflected the ideological priorities of traditional American cinema. However, elements of resistance can be identified in the work of filmmakers such as Oscar Micheaux, who did not fully succumb to Hollywood. Significantly, Foster, Micheaux and the Johnson brothers championed an Afrocentric perspective through their use of narrative forms and subject matter germane to the black experience. The aesthetic value of the early black independent film movement goes beyond a simple concern with black subject matter and the iconic representation of black life. Micheaux's filmic signification of the black experience differs widely from the Hollywood models of African American reality. In contrast to the Classical Hollywood cinema of the period in which representations of blacks almost always retained a romantic nostalgia for the life of a servant or a slave, the characters in Micheaux's films were often members of the black middle-class. His "portrayals of black people . . . project a reality that Hollywood preferred to overlook. His portrayals of features of the reality of black life in defiance of Hollywood's overwhelming influence was radical and perhaps militant; it also was very much a part of the theoretically active thoughts and writings of the freedom movement of the period" (Diakite, 1980, p. 129).

An unenlightened historiography was not capable of evaluating the work of early black film pioneers from the point of view of a black expressive tradition. The Classical Hollywood cinema was placed on a pedestal as the epitome of film art, and the use of African American vernacular expression in film was greeted with negative criticism by both black and white critics. Diakite explains that "no thought at all was given to the fact that Micheaux was making a completely different type of film art" (Diakite, 1980, p. 65).

Inherent in these films was the notion that American society could be enriched by African American culture. The third phase of black independent cinema, which paralleled the period of the Civil Rights movement, consciously explored concerns outside the traditional perimeters of Hollywood. "This new wave of black creative activity, which arose from the ashes of riot-torn ghettoes, rejected art that appealed to white America's aesthetic morality" (Reid, 1993, p. 75). The phenomenon of the irreverent black film emerged full-blown in 1971 during the third phase of the black independent film movement, when "Melvin Van Peebles dropped a bomb. *Sweet Sweetback's Baadasss Song* was not polite. It raged. It screamed. It provoked, Its reverberations were felt throughout the country. In the black community it was both hailed and denounced for its sexual rawness, its macho hero, and its depiction of the community as downpressed and in need of rescue" (Cade Bambara, 1993, p. 118). To explain *Sweetback's* significance to the third phase of black independent filmmaking, Bourne describes Van Peebles as "the Charlie Parker of American cinema." He argues that *Sweetback* was instrumental in re-establishing African American films as a cultural force: "When Melvin Van Peebles started production on *Sweetback*, he had no idea that his pioneering efforts would produce not only another film but an attitude. That attitude, based on Van Peebles' desire to see images of African American life as he had perceived it, was reflective of and energized by the Civil Rights and Black Power movements. Melvin Van Peebles, in creating his own images that tapped into the black rage of the times, encouraged a generation of others to create their own visions of life on film as well" (1994, p. 21). Nelson George points out that *Sweetback* remains a vital memory for black filmmakers of what could be, and "its bastard child blaxploitation" stands as a bitter reminder of what they should avoid. No black filmmaker had produced a feature film without mainstream Hollywood involvement since Micheaux's early days, and Van Peebles' achievement wouldn't be duplicated with similar impact for another 15 years (1992, p. 5).

By the 1990s, the best black independent films displayed two major influences. One focused on film form and film language as exemplified in the work of Haile Gerima (*Sankofa*, 1994) and Julie Dash (*Daughters of the Dust*, 1991). The other paid more attention to subject matter. This work favored the traditional film narrative model as exemplified in the work of Spike Lee (*Do the Right Thing*, 1989 or *Malcolm-X*, 1992, John Singleton (*Boyz 'N the Hood*, 1991) or Leslie Harris (*Just Another Girl on the IRT*). On the one hand, we find interesting black independent filmmaking in Norman Loftus' *Small Time* and Wendell Harris' *Chameleon Street* (1989). We also find a series of nihilistic 'hood' genre films such as *Menace II Society* (1993), which stands on the fringes of the black tradition, but fully within the problematic of Hollywood. This phenomenon has led veteran filmmaker St. Clair Bourne to lament that the "current generation of working black filmmakers seems to move to a different ideological drummer, distinct from African American independent filmmakers. For starters, their films do not invoke the theme of 'resistance,' and in some instances actually avoid an upfront sense of politics, a traditional characteristic of independent black films. They eschew the same political sensibilities that enabled these filmmakers to be where they are" (1994, p. 22). Other critics also address Bourne's uneasiness with neo-blaxploitation and the elimination of political questions from some of these films. Ed Guerrero observes that while the blaxploitation wave featured movies made by whites for blacks, the 1990s wave finds black directors producing films for black audiences, but these filmmakers maintain a keen eye on the possibility of attracting a large white crossover audience.

> If black independent filmmakers tend directly to resist or oppose cultural and political domination through their avant garde languages, forms, socially urgent narratives, and insider depictions of the black world, then those directors who work within the 'mainstream' tend to be more concerned with learning and perfecting the conventions of dominant cinema language and addressing their projects to the colonized desires of the vast consumer audience

this emphasis seen as white privilege.

encompassing blacks, other non-white minorities, and ... crossover marketing to whites. (1993, p. 181).

Contemporary black filmmaking can boast of an increasingly sophisticated use of cinematic languages. However, some critics fear that the tendency to locate black independent filmmaking within the problematic of the Western aesthetic tradition, which privileges artistic technique at the expense of communicating with the black community, is counter-productive. Taylor warns that a meaningful black independent film movement is threatened "by the trap of the 'intellectual' or artistic posture that has been coded into it, which has become a means of shielding filmmakers from ideas, from new historical formations, perspectives and challenges" (1996, p. 439). He uses the term "intellectual filmmaking" to describe films produced by the film school generation of black filmmakers, which give higher priority to formal elements. Although this generation of filmmakers has had some success in having their work accepted in 'art and culture' circles, the question remains as to whether that limited success functions to conceal the filmmakers' failure to reach large segments of the black community and to explore issues of self-definition through the lens of the cinema (Taylor, 1995, p. 434).

Manthia Diawara equates the best contemporary black independent films with the European New Wave in that the filmmakers see their work in dual terms: as artistic expression and political struggle.

1970's. Film school generation.

> "Politically, they are dissatisfied with commercial cinema's lack of courage to address certain issues. They feel that they have to make their own films if they want to see those issues on the screen. Artistically, they want to explore new ways of telling stories; they want to experiment with the camera, the most powerful invention of modern times, and engage the infinite possibilities of storytelling." (1993, p. 6)

The significance of the contemporary black independent film movement is found in its dual exploration of the aesthetic and political potential of film.

As American society emerged from the era of segregation and the emerging Civil Rights Movement de-emphasized black vernacular expression and valued a politics of integration, a

which is perhaps all what all films should be.

'crossover' yardstick was used to evaluate black art. Black film, very much like black life, was defined as revolving around the concerns of the dominant society. The preoccupation with integrationist politics subordinated the black vernacular to forms of expression comfortable to the dominant culture. As a result, black film as artistic and cultural expression suffered because it was not valued as an entity in its own right. Black film signification is properly constructed on particular aesthetic strategies rooted in the black experience, which give vernacular structure and form to cinematic and narrative elements. Our special concern is with black cinema as a signifying practice, which is "the process through which the symbol is constructed and elaborated as language. It is the way in which we make our films, the sum of cinematic languages, aural and visual languages, languages of color, and languages of imagery" (Yearwood, 1982, p. 73). As a signifying process, we emphasize the expressive forms through which story information is processed.

THE SEARCH FOR NEW CULTURAL MODELS IN BLACK FILM

In his book, *Black Film as Genre*, Cripps observes that great traditions demand great syntheses, which rest on a body of systematic criticism (1977, p. 150). The challenge to black film culture is to delineate a critical project that functions in a similar manner to the Constructivists and Soviet montage theorists who developed an environment within which film masterpieces could be created. It would do for black independent film what Andre Bazin and the *Cahiers du Cinema* critics (Jean Luc Godard, Francois Truffaut *et al*) did for the French New Wave. A film movement usually is bolstered by the existence of an accompanying intellectual and critical tradition. Auteur theory offers a good example of a body of critical thought that creatively redefined its object. Before auteur criticism, most American film was often discussed as kitsch, in terms of popular culture and not as serious art; but auteur criticism posed new questions, and in the process, uncovered film gems in American cinema. The auteur theory of criticism framed the problematic of American cinema in a different way, and established a critical framework that allowed a creative re-reading of Hollywood films and the restitution of the films of John Ford and Howard Hawks. Film scholarship dealing with the black experience ought to pose questions that frame black cinema in new and exciting ways. A carefully elaborated theory of black cinema can provide a critical frame-work that finds aesthetic value in filmic elements other than the tight dictatorial structures of the Hollywood classical narrative film and elevates style not necessarily as an element of narrative but as a filmic element in and of itself.

The increasing sophistication and crowning achievement of contemporary black film criticism is reflected in Diawara's *Black American Cinema*(1993). The collection seeks to examine a film aesthetic that focuses on the black filmmaker, his or her representation of the black imaginary, and his or her place within broader communities; and second, issues of film spectatorship within the black film experience. Diawara emphasizes an approach to film from an Afrocentric perspective, which reveals continuities among black filmmakers from Micheaux to Burnett, Singleton and Dash. He finds that "the modes of existence of a black film culture are linked to black institutions, nationalist versus integrationist politics, black American literature and literary criticism, and issues of realism in representation" and that black film spectatorship includes "a history of film reception, generic expectations, patterns of spectatorial identification, and the possibility of political resistance" (1993, p. ix).

The paradigm shift in black independent cinema has now taken full root. Snead captures the ambience of the new black film culture, observing that since the 1960s these films have been developing "the feeling of intimate conversations between film-maker and audience." These films deal with issues relevant to the black community without feeling the need to create a theoretical white viewer as the film's principal audience. "The viewer achieves, in the best of these films an understanding of a complex black world from within, rather than caricature of it from without" (1994, p. 117). As the confidence of the black film movement grew, a cinematic sophistication and intellectual probing could be discerned. Snead explains it this way: "Instead of seeing blacks purely in terms of white norms and practices, these films show blacks securely positioned in their own environments, discussing and dealing with their own problems, ignoring or at best belittling the toys and games of the dominant white culture" (1994, p. 19).

Black film had now become more reflexive in its ability to cast a more critical eye on its aesthetics and its relationship to the black community. Questions about the type of film language appropriate for black film expression began to enter the debate.

and its need to distance itself from Hollywood.

For example, Gates found lessons for black American film in the
black British import, Isaac Julien's *Looking for Langston* (1993).
In his examination of the use of experimental languages in black
independent film, Gates speaks specifically about the avant garde
film style used by British film collectives. He finds that this cinema opens itself to being criticized as "elitist, Europeanized,
overly highbrow; as a black cultural product without a significant black audience, its very blackness becomes suspect." He suggests that the poetic career of Langston Hughes, which explored
modernist art languages, might be an appropriate model for black
art. Writers such as bell hooks added to the range of theoretical
and methodological issues in black film scholarship by introducing black feminist ideas to the study of black film. She identifies an "oppositional black gaze" that emerged with the
development of black independent cinema, which created conditions in which blacks could experience a sense of agency and
resistance (1993, p. 288).

    In the search for new cultural models to adequately address
the complexities of the contemporary black experience, Taylor
urges black film to make an epistemological break from the seduc-
tions of first-world ideology. "Postaesthetics"—as Taylor
describes this kind of activity—extends beyond the cultural par-
ticularism of ethno-aesthetics to interface with the revisions in
knowledge posed by feminism, class analysis and some of the dis-
sidents of postmodernism. (1988, pp. 80-2). The cultural model
Taylor presents seeks to free the text from its specious autonomy,
which separates cultural production from social and material production; thereby, it opens up black film to intercommunication
with other texts as well as to the significations of everyday experiences. Sylvia Wynter endorses Taylor's project stating that "Such
a model would . . . call for scholars first to free themselves from
their addiction to the 'opiate of aestheticism,' if it were to serve
the purpose of bringing to black cinema a perception of its cultural practices as a crucial site of the contest out of which the
human is being rewritten" (1992, p. 240).

    The significance of this insurgent paradigm is to break down
cognitive barriers so that our "cultural imaginary" is constituted in a new way. The deciphering practice germane to this aesthetic reveals its own rules of functioning rather than merely
replicating and perpetuating existing rules, thereby avoiding the
problems of what Wynter calls an ethnoaesthetic trap. "Rather
than seeking to 'rhetorically demystify' . . . a deciphering turn

seeks to decipher what the process of rhetorical mystification does. It seeks to identify not what texts and their signifying practices can be interpreted to mean but what they can be deciphered to do, and it also seeks to evaluate the 'illocutionary force' and procedures with which they do what they do" (Wynter, 1992, p. 267). This calls for a new frontier of knowledge that would serve as an intellectual underpinning for a black film culture, thereby generating a different and more productive set of critical questions.

Wynter argues that the cultural belief system that arose out of the humanistic revolution in Europe in the 15th century underlies the systemic social ills—such as poverty, joblessness, environmental degradation and racial stratification—in contemporary society, especially as they affect black life. The problem is not that the black underclasses are beyond help; rather the crisis that characterizes the dominant philosophy and world-view allows society to tolerate and accept the wretched conditions that affect large numbers of people. She contends that the nihilism threatening significant numbers of blacks is a product of the dominant system of knowledge that governs social perceptions. It, therefore, becomes necessary to change the conditions of knowledge as well as the rules that regulate modes of perception and the behaviors to which they lead, which further calls into question the methodology we use to construct our cultural paradigms, our historiography, and the models for making films. This involves the excavation of new ground, the forging of a new way of thinking that informs discursive practices and governs human behavior.

Wynter proposes a set of practices that reject the Cartesian and Darwinian notions of people having particular predispositions of human nature because in her view our world is knowable and therefore it is alterable. This deciphering practice is knowledge producing and contains the potential to be "as far-reaching as the first intellectual mutation of humanism, which made possible the realization of the natural sciences" (1992, p. 239). A new black film culture fosters discourses that not only are capable of countering existing stereotypes, but can proceed beyond prevalent analytic paradigms to create a critical space that aids in the production of new forms of knowledge. Fowler makes the point that "black criticism emerges as a tradition of demystification" because these kinds of concerns have been central to its historical development (1981, p. xiv). The dominant tendency in black film history has been to agitate for an inclusivity, which moves marginalized groups from the periphery to the center. This is a movement whose goal has been integration—to become one with the status quo. In contrast, a new deciphering turn seeks to transform the center so that it also encompasses the margins, not because blacks have a monopoly on truth, but rather that their experiences and the discursive practices they use to encode them can produce knowledge beneficial to the larger society, providing modes of problem-solving and analysis generally rendered insignificant.

TRANSFORM
THE
CENTER

Chapter Three

Theorizing Black Film

B lack film aesthetics is a key epistemological activity that is relevant not only as a form of scholarship in itself, but for its central role in articulating and exploring paradigms that offer a more incisive grasp of film in relation to the black expressive tradition. Theory formation in black film studies should reflect the socio-historical and political-economic conditions of the black experience. It should provide concepts, tools and strategies for initiating and maintaining a struggle against the way the black world is marginalized and shaped by forces beyond its control. Theory should also explore ways to "win over, defeat, or neutralize those forces arrayed against its emancipation, growth, or development" (Harding, 1987, p. 8). From the perspective that cinema is an area of cultural production, black film theory and criticism is premised on a notion of culture as the socially and historically situated process that involves social signification and the concomitant production of meanings. Our principal interest focuses on "modes of production and modes of signification" (Barret *et al*, 1979, p. 10). Production is intrinsic to understanding culture because cultural products and practices are defined in relationship to the material conditions of their existence and their functioning as representations that establish the conditions for producing meanings. Black film aesthetics interrogates the discourses generated in film as well as subsidiary discourses in society about films and filmmaking. It examines the methods and techniques critics use to study film and foregrounds issues involving audience reception of black film. Historically, black film aesthetics has focused on a few fundamental problems: first, there is an emphasis on reformulating the nature of film images; second, a preoccupation with the way filmic signification helps to establish or challenge social meanings; and third, a

focus on the relationship between the cinema as a social institution and the dominant system of power.

A CRITIQUE OF EUROPEAN AESTHETIC THEORY

The 19th century European concept of aesthetics claims that
certain arts (the fine arts) have special aesthetic qualities that
make them superior to other forms of artistic expression. These
other forms of art are often described pejoratively in terms of
utilitarianism in that they served functional purposes. This distinction was used to label African artistic expression as not worthy of serious attention. Popular art, as well, is said to be not as
morally valuable or intellectually stimulating as fine art. In the
20th century, a strident critique of the 19th century European
concept of aesthetic theory has developed. Critics point out that
the idea of the 'fine arts' (that is, a special form of art produced
by Europeans) amounts to a baseless racist ideology. Other critics have established that Western philosophical aesthetics is not
value free and innocent (as it has claimed); but that it is disin-
genuous in its assumption that it has no political agenda. We find
that Western art and its aesthetics are thoroughly riddled with
ideological values.

> Ideology does not question the foundation, the lim-
> its, or the root of representation; it scans the
> domain of representations in general; it determines
> the necessary sequences that appear there; it defines
> the links that provide its connections; it expresses
> the laws of composition and decomposition that
> may rule it. It situates all knowledge in the space of
> representations, and by scanning that space it for-
> mulates the knowledge of the laws that provide its
> organization. It is in a sense the knowledge of all
> knowledge. (Foucault, 1973, p. 241)

Black film theorists agree that traditional aesthetics is far from
being an innocent discourse. Invariably, their view of aesthetics
contradicts the European definition, which has been unmasked
as an ideological construct generated by powerful social and
political forces that use their power to repress and marginalize
competing views. The major criticisms of European aesthetic
theory disallow its claim to a value-free intellectual detachment
from political and ideological issues and to any universal validi-
ty. Furthermore, it is most deficient in its failure to acknowledge

that different cultures respond differently to the question of value in artistic expression and what is good art. The fact that individual cultures use culture-specific modes of aesthetic expression provides theoretical ammunition for the development of a black film aesthetic.

Hence, a reformulated aesthetic theory is relevant to black film studies. In its most fundamental understanding, it helps clarify our focus on the functioning of art and artistic expression within the black cultural tradition. We can define aesthetics as a broad concept that includes references to the arts, artistic creation, the philosophy of art (which describes a discourse about questions of beauty), the sublime and what people value as being good in art. In this view, we can examine the arguments black film theorists use to talk about black film and the strategies they articulate to clarify ideas and theories about it. Aesthetics as the philosophy of African American art reflects the arguments, the critical and reflective activity that writers, critics, scholars and ordinary people put forward to explain art. In this sense, African American aesthetics alludes to the historical existence of a philosophical tradition in the African American community (Fowler, 1981, p. v).

The notion of aesthetic sensibility is relevant to black art. It has to do with forms of knowledge and modes of perception and expression that are intuitive and sensory-based, as opposed to those that are empirical, logical and analytic. This definition does not privilege a particular form of artistic expression or identify any essential aesthetic sensibility germane to all black peoples. It is useful in describing and clarifying the expressive qualities of art and describing a film's artistic texture.

> It is the perception of stylistic possibilities. It is the perception of those possibilities which broadens the meaning of the term beauty. . . . The aesthetic sense is also the sense of the rightness, of the appropriateness of things. What is appropriate is the completeness of the thing, the sense in the person experiencing that the thing's potential for stylization has been properly exploited. (Fowler, 1981, p. vii)

In black film, a discussion of the aesthetic centers around the actual unfolding of specific creative and expressive strategies used in the filmmaking process. This formulation of the aesthetic gives the viewer a better grasp of and greater access to the internal

conditions and expressive characteristics of film. To acknowledge that a work of art is characterized, first of all, by its aesthetic qualities is not to deny that film is multidimensional or
that the aesthetic represents only one of those dimensions, albeit
a seminal one in art.

Yet, there is a strident critique of aesthetic theory as reac-
tionary because it is rooted too deeply in the problematic of the
Enlightenment and the institutionalization of chattel slavery.
Clyde Taylor, who has written extensively on the ideological pro-
ject of Western aesthetics, explains the major problem with
European aesthetic theory.

> Aesthetics, which is . . . synonymous with Western
> aesthetics, was concocted in the 18th century as an
> instrument of ideological control for the comfort of
> the first-world ruling class. Its principal injury to its
> class victims lies in its doctrine of the autonomy of
> cultural production and appreciation. Through this
> specious paradigm, it appropriated knowledge of
> human creativity for the interests of one social sec-
> tor, alienating those outside the western bourgeoisie
> from their own creativity and the socio-political
> knowledge embedded therein. (1988, p. 80)

Certainly, Taylor's criticism is salient especially in its view that
aesthetic practice is neither innocent nor free of ideological purpose. He argues that even if aesthetics as a doctrine were not
"destructive to the cultural orientation of black people," grounds
would still exist for resistance. Citing William's Styron's *The
Confessions of Nat Turner,* Taylor concludes that aestheticization
involves a certain mischief that distracts "black readers from its
reduction and trivialization of an awesome historical figure . . ."
(1988, p. 80). Mark Reid exemplifies another variety of criticism
in his book, *Redefining Black Film,* when he links aesthetics with
the use of "subjective criteria" in black film criticism (1993, p. 1).

Certainly, there is a damaging critique of European aesthetic
theory because of its development during the Enlightenment and
the Romantic period as part of the movement to establish
European nationalism and commercial exploitation at the
expense of other peoples. Through a narrow reading of history,
European thinkers sought to guarantee the supremacy of
European culture and legitimacy of European imperialist expan-
sion through recourse to a bogus science. "In their discourse,

racial consciousness became a defining category in the politics of European difference. European intellectuals sought to disclose European genius as an explanatory category for the progressive, historical movement of the modern age" (Anderson, 1995, p. 52). The concept of genius is used to refer to superior cultural expression and the creative spirit of a people. When Emmanuel Kant compared the genius of Europeans to Africans, he found little of value in African artistic achievement. For him, the African had no cultural genius. Consequently, he concluded his apology for white racial superiority noting that the African was decidedly inferior to the European.

> The Negroes of Africa have by nature no feeling that rises above the trifling. Mr. Hume challenges anyone to cite a single example in which a Negro has shown talents, and asserts that among the hundreds of thousands of blacks who are transported elsewhere from their countries, although many of them have been set free, still not a single one was ever found who presented anything great in art or science or any praiseworthy quality, even though among the whites some continually rise aloft from the lowest rabble, and through superior gifts earn respect in the world. (1960, p. 110)

However, despite its racist origins and a reactionary aestheticism, which privileges 'art for art's sake,' elements of aesthetic theory remain a useful tool in black film criticism.

AESTHETIC THEORY IN BLACK FILM CRITICISM

Most criticism of black cinema can be described as contextualist, which is opposed to notions of aesthetic isolation and 'art for art's sake.' Contextualism is an umbrella term that includes a variety of critics opposed to the traditional aesthetic attitude. These critics—such as feminists, Marxists, African American culturalists and psychoanalytic commentators—affirm the significance of the social context of art. They reject isolationism and assert the relevance of contextual issues such as race, class and gender in the encounter with art. Contextual critics ask whether the viewer can adequately understand and appreciate black film without knowledge of the sociocultural and historical context of the black experience. Contextualism and isolationism describe the prevalent approaches to the use of the aesthetic in art criticism.

Isolationism is the view that in order to appreciate
a work of art, we need do nothing but look at it, hear
it, or read it—sometimes again and again, with the
most concentrated attention—and that we need not
go outside it to consult the facts of biography, or
anything else.

> . . . Contextualism holds that a work of art should
> be apprehended in its total context or setting, and
> that much historical and other knowledge 'feeds'
> into the work of art, making the total experience of
> it richer than if it were approached without such
> knowledge. (Beardsley, 1972, p. 44)

A sloppy contextualist criticism can devalue the artwork by focusing criticism on secondary issues such as social relevance or
whether the film accurately represents reality, thereby shifting
attention away from film itself as a symbolic construct of the
black experience. An isolationist aesthetics robs black film of its
raison d'etre, which is its ethnic character. Critic bell hooks
asserts that a revitalized discussion of aesthetics is vital for contemporary black arts. She holds the opinion that the lack of critical theories about cultural production and aesthetics serves only
to confine and restrict black art. In a critique of Taylor's essay
"We Don't Need Another Hero: Anti-Theses on Aesthetics,"
she argues that the failure of black nationalist aesthetics or the
cultural imperialism of Eurocentric aesthetic theory should not
cloud the need for an alternative aesthetic theory as a factor to
promote artistic growth (hooks, 1990, p. 109).

A reformulated aesthetic theory should prove valuable for
studying a wide range of artistic and cultural expression produced
in a variety of cultures. Despite the charge that the idea of aesthetics is predisposed to certain kinds of creative expression,
which are believed to be inherently superior to others, using the
term does not necessarily endorse the philosophical position of
aestheticism in Western art that privileges 'art for art's sake.' The
fact that Western medicine has tried to repress and marginalize
other forms of medicine, for example, acupuncture and herbal
treatments in Chinese traditional medicine, does not mean that
some aspects of Western medicine are not valuable. It is possible to utilize what is best in a variety of traditions. Regarding the
aesthetic, there is no need to devalue other varieties of artistic
expression or other important dimensions of the artwork. The

power of African aesthetics was derived from the belief of Africans that aesthetic sensibility permeated all aspects of the individual's life and the community's existence. The aesthetic was believed to inhabit the spiritual and material worlds. It was also articulated in the realm of the living and served as a vital link to the ancestors. A people's aesthetic sensibility is linked directly to their culture and "serves as a vibrant expression or reflection of the ethos of the collective" (Woodyard, 1995, p. 42). Although the concept of the aesthetic arose in the context of Western art, this does not mean that other cultures do not have aesthetic expression or forms to express their unique artistic and cultural sensibilities. Western art historians have had to acknowledge a Eurocentric bourgeois class bias that limited the aesthetic to their preferred forms of artistic expression. Andre Malraux (1974) observed a major advance in cross-cultural aesthetics in acknowledging that art from any society and culture or from any historical period can be inherently aesthetic.

Any progress in African American aesthetic thought must move beyond European provincialism and its narcissistic tendencies to devalue other cultural experiences, especially those that seek to decenter and demystify European modes of analysis and interpretation. Afrocentrism represents one such theory of reading that posits the relevance of an African worldview as an important perspective in cultural studies. Afrocentrism is a critical perspective that places "African ideals at the center of any analysis that involves African culture and behavior" (Asante, 1987, p. 6). Furthermore, black aesthetic theory is viewed as coexisting with other important cosmological, epistemological, and axiological issues. "In this regard the Afrocentric method pursues a world voice distinctly African-centered in relationship to external phenomena" (Asante, 1990, p. 8). For Afrocentric theorists, cosmology provides a sense of place in that it locates the aesthetic inquiry relevant to black art within an African frame of reference. In the African American cultural tradition, forms such as oral narrative and myth become vehicles in which epistemological issues are articulated. Asante's notion of the axiological relates to how black art functions as an institution important to the community's survival.

A reformulated concept of an aesthetic system in black film begins with a view of film as a form of art, and its methodology positions the film as the primary object for critical study. In using the term aesthetic to refer to the creative strategies and the

expressive values the filmmaker uses in filmmaking, we can pose
probing questions that demand specific information about the
characteristics of black film. For example, we can ask whether
there are particular ways that black women write and make films
or whether certain forms are unique to black women's creativity in filmmaking. When studying a black woman filmmaker's
aesthetic, we can ask about the specific choices she makes in the
filmmaking process? In this sense, the filmmaker's aesthetic has
to do with those elements she values over others. Her aesthetic
would refer to the creative and expressive strategies the filmmaker foregrounds in the film to define her preferences for what
she finds valuable in filmmaking. What this means is that our
investigation would proceed from the assumption that the black
woman filmmaker has the possibility of a unique voice, that is, a
unique way of seeing and representation. One of our motivating
questions would be: in what way does the film reflect a black
woman's point of view? Using the recent genre of 'hood' films
about black urban life, we can ask in what way is Leslie Harris's
Just Another Girl on the IRT (1993) different from John
Singleton's *Boyz in the Hood* (1991) or Mario Van Peebles's *New
Jack City* (1991)? The 'hood' genre of films represents a male-
oriented point of view, which seeks the narrative recuperation of
the young black urban male. 'Hood' genre films position women
subordinately and define them in relation to men's needs.
Usually, women are secondary players in plot development; and
the narration tends to emphasize traditional male interests, such
as the use of action motifs, guns as props, and paradigms of war,
that is, winning and losing. In contrast, *Just Another Girl on the
IRT* develops its narrative complication within the terms of a
young black woman's experience: Chantal becomes pregnant and
must decide whether to have the child or not. The narrative
allows its protagonist a sense of agency over her future. She has
a choice. Although women are not demonized in the male genre
of 'hood' films, nonetheless they are not presented as fully developed persons, and they exist in a subordinate relationship to the
male characters. In essence, *Just Another Girl on the IRT* presents
a different view of black women because the black woman functions as a principal producer of meaning in the film. Black women
speak in their own voices and on their own terms. Chantal makes
her own decisions. She does not need a male to sanction her narrative choices.

In a commentary on Asante's thesis, Woodyard extrapolates

a system of Afrocentric aesthetics and presents a model that consists of eight aesthetic elements. These are derived from African American symbolic discourse and reflect African American artistic foundations. This Afrocentric model contains the following elements: 1) polyrhythms, which refers to the simultaneous existence of several major themes, motifs and other rhythmic patterns; 2) dimensionality of an artistic expression, which involves "the sense of a voice behind the voice, that 'help' that comes from preaching and hearing of the 'word';" 3) curvilinear arrangement, which refers to structure and arrangement of ideas; 4) intensification/repetition of images; 5) holism/organic unity, which surbodinates the parts or the individual and elevates the whole; 6) lyrical approach, which emanates from an African cultural experience; 7) improvisation; and 8) storytelling/image-making in which story functions as fully contained idea, not merely as a device to support an idea or as for making a larger argument (1995, p. 42).

Writings that mention directly or indirectly an African American aesthetic sensibility go back to the beginning of the 20th century. The first clear allusion is found in the essay *Of Our Spiritual Strivings* by W. E. B. DuBois (1903), which speaks of a "sense of always looking at one's self through the eyes of the others," and a resulting duality of ideals. Fowler argues that the African American critical tradition has taken root around this problem of double consciousness. It is the problem of how to express the "soul-beauty" of the black experience in an antagonistic social setting that despises it. "The black artist's dilemma is one of expressing his people's authenticity. The need to establish cultural authenticity of black forms of expression leads to a type of criticism bent on ferreting out what is behind the more obvious Euro-American forms" (Fowler, 1981, p. ix).

In what way can the focus on aesthetics be useful to black independent cinema? First, it is a useful point of entry and a mode of critical inquiry into black independent cinema. It allows us to pose critical questions about the value given to special expressive forms and narrative techniques unique to African American film. As a conceptual framework, it establishes the importance of giving primary attention to the text (the film as art), in the first instance; but here it is not being used to close off our ability to establish a relationship between the film and its sociocultural context or its intertextual sources. Rather, the reformulated concept of a film aesthetic sharpens our critical tools so *[handwritten margin annotations: "INTERTEXTUAL SOURCES" (top), ""black art" is too much of a blanket term." (left), "f has been the case" (lower left)]*

that we can better establish the relationship of film to the black cultural experience. A reformulated notion of the aesthetic can be used to enrich our understanding of important intertextual sources and contextual supports that inform black film.

Occasionally, we are confronted with the erroneous claim that a discussion of black aesthetic thought necessarily espouses black cultural nationalist sentiment. However, the paradigm of black cinema aesthetics suggests a plurality of philosophical positions on the issue, so that no one view in particular can claim to have a hegemonic grasp on what we mean by black art. "The term 'the black aesthetic' can be subsumed under black aesthetics. The former is a philosophical stance; the latter attempts to trace the history of philosophical stances. Black aesthetics, because it is historical, is non-exclusive. Under its umbrella can be lumped not only those writers who have argued in favor of a black aesthetic, but also those who have wished, consciously or otherwise, to encourage black creativity along the lines of European art . . ." (Fowler, 1981, p. v). Several philosophical approaches to black film exist, and, often, these may be in competition with each other. As a matter of fact, the paradigm of black cinema aesthetics raises many different questions that may generate multiple answers, such as: What is black film? Is film primarily to entertain, using the black experience to give viewer's pleasure? Should black films be socially uplifting? How does black film relate to the black community? Should a black filmmaker have a social responsibility to the black community? Should a black film be cognizant of the history of negative images of blacks in popular culture so that it does not celebrate oppression, but contributes to social change?

By moving our discussion beyond the aesthetic choices of individual filmmakers and specific films, we can also speak of a larger aesthetic or system of expressive values that provides a context for understanding a body of films. In the history of art, for example, we can identify diverse aesthetic systems such as those of classical Greece, traditional Chinese, Brechtian, or traditional African. The problem emerges when a particular aesthetic system is lionized and put on a pedestal as being superior and embodying universal values. Using the aesthetic paradigm in black cinema foregrounds the issue of how cultural values are reproduced in filmic signification. For example, Spike Lee's *Do The Right Thing* (1989) can be viewed as the product of the filmmaker's creativity; but we can also consider it to be the product

AESTHETIC SENSIBLITY (handwritten annotation)

of a particular historical period, a particular environment and social structure, and specific expressive traditions or a specific aesthetic system. We can view *Do The Right Thing* as representative of the filmmaker's vision as well as the product of the broader African American sociocultural milieu within which it was produced. In summary, a black cinema aesthetic refers to a set of values one finds in black film. These values provide a conceptual foundation for understanding art, and they establish paradigms for the making of narratives and the forms used for storytelling. They also outline the terms of engagement the artwork seeks with its primary audiences and helps establish a critical framework for evaluating art. In this view, aesthetics and criticism as an activity is intimately related to specific historical conditions and social consciousness. Aesthetic sensibility is " . . . more than a philosophy or theory of art and beauty; it is a way of inhabiting space, a particular location, a way of looking and becoming" (hooks, 1990, p. 104). Questions of aesthetics should not be dismissed as a mere intellectual exercise. Rather, it is " . . . an absolute necessity for any understanding of art and our proper evaluation of it. Unless we know what art is, . . . what are its necessary and sufficient properties, we cannot begin to respond to it adequately or to say why one work is good or better than the other. Aesthetic theory, thus, is important not only in itself but for the foundations of both appreciation and criticism" (Weitz, 1956, p. 3). Analysis of the particular formulation of the aesthetic paradigm in the African American cultural tradition provides us with tools and concepts that are invaluable in the study of black film.

THE PURPOSE OF BLACK ART

As an expression that emanates from the heart of the African American community, good black film can represent that which is most unique and best in black culture. A good black film can provide an intellectual challenge and engage our cognitive faculties. It can often present incisive commentary on social reality. The philosopher Schiller (1795) argues that art is an activity that is not critical to survival. It is an undertaking that we choose to do on our own free will and not because of necessity. In this view, art is a form of play, which helps make humans whole and helps develop a well-rounded nature. This concept is in agreement with some aspects of the African American tradition, which emphasize the centrality of play to being human. In the black

ART AS SURVIVAL (handwritten annotation)

cultural tradition, play is often synonymous with the expressivity of style; however, black artistic expression diverges from the view of art as play or an activity that is removed from and is not critical to everyday survival. Whereas Schiller's notion is derived from the Western traditional principle of the aesthetic as a unique experience that exists for its own sake, the quality of playfulness when built into the African American expressive tradition functions expressively as a necessary vehicle for psychic and physical release. We can agree with Schiller that the aesthetic is the consummation of our humanity because we are only human when we play; but the enslavement of Africans in the New World developed a special formulation of play that became critical to African American survival. As an aesthetic value in the black cultural tradition, play is related to the philosophy of African traditional art in which the aesthetic is not an embellishment or extra feature, but is intricately interwoven in all aspects of a community's activities. We find this dimension of play in African American art, particularly the stylistic expressiveness that is so pervasive throughout black cultural expression. Play also functions as a survival device as in the grand metaphor of wearing the mask.

In *The Poetics*, Aristotle presents a system of aesthetic values that give the artwork an organic unity and which function to compensate for certain deficiencies in society. Art, in this view, has a moral dimension in that the spectator identifies with and develops an empathy with the dramatic hero. Through this identification with the hero, the spectator is able to work out emotions vicariously and achieve catharsis, which has a socially beneficial function of dissipating anti-social tensions. In this view, art is therapeutic, a means of relaxation and easing tensions that may otherwise culminate in anti-social activity. In the black cultural tradition, art also has this function, but it operates significantly to maintain black survival by drawing on mechanisms of resistance that stress struggle against hostile forces and perseverance against adversity. On the one hand, African American art displays a superficial mechanism of catharsis, but on a deeper level it often invokes serious elements of resistance in its art forms. In African American culture, art has entertainment and therapeutic value, but it is also a vehicle capable of producing knowledge. While art is affective and offers sensory pleasure, it has a special capacity to foster intellectual activity that can produce insights on black life. In the African American expressive

RESISTANCE TO OPPRESSION

tradition, narrative entertains, but it also conveys a morality. African American folk tales offer captivating experiences for black audiences, who often are familiar with the content and story development of the fable. What is significant about the folk tales is their stylistic rendering of form as produced in the act of narration and their representation of a world-view that extrapolates significant elements of the black experience.

A predominant theme in black aesthetics identifies a necessary relationship between the artwork and its positive relationship to the black community. Although art moves the emotions, good black art communicates and plays a significant social and political function for its audience. In the Republic, Plato endows art with powerful social influences observing that it could inflame the passions and mislead those who seek truth. Plato suggests that art should be censored because in the wrong hands it is a powerful weapon capable of impacting negatively on the emotional development of youth and introducing disruptive political ideas to society. To some degree, African American criticism is in agreement with this statement, especially given the history of the drum, spirituals, and the blues as elements of resistance to oppression. Furthermore, the black cultural tradition finds that notions of responsibility and community are important factors in good art. So long as survival was a key requirement in African American communication, blacks defined art in purposeful and useful terms.

Some black film critics agree with Plato's assumption that art has a powerful social impact. There is no need to contest the thrust of this statement about art; however, there is a common tendency to narrowly assess the cinema's social impact within the framework of a crude empiricism. This type of empiricist criticism overlooks the fact that forms of signification may be more deeply structured at the level of basic perceptions, thereby yielding a greater social impact than is possible by a mere focus on empirical content. A focus on how things mean as opposed to what things mean brings us precisely to the question of the social functioning of signifying processes. This, in turn, is related to questions of ideology and the social system within which meanings are produced. Ideology serves to conceal the fact that the artwork represents the point of view of particular social interests and reflects a particular way of seeing related to dominant social interests. Ideology is part and parcel of the apparatus that establishes the imaginary relations individuals experience to their social reality. Stephen Heath points out that

> This imaginary relation in ideology is itself real,
> which means not simply that the individuals live it
> as such (the mode of illusion, the inverted image)
> but that it is effectively, practically, the reality of
> their concrete existence, the term of their subject
> positions, the basis of their activity, in a given social
> order. . . What is held in ideology, what it forms, is
> the unity of the real relations and the imaginary rela-
> tions between men and women and the real condi-
> tions of their existence. (1981, p. 5)

Without paying adequate attention to the processes of representation and sign-production, the preoccupation with the
empirical nature of film—for example, whether film images of
blacks are positive or negative—implicitly endorses the ideological positions of the dominant society and helps reinforce the
dominant social agenda.

THE LIMITS OF SOCIOLOGICAL THEORIES

What is black cinema? One popular approach suggests a corre-
lation between the film image and black life. In this view, we are
told that a black film can be recognized because its images and
subject matter are identifiably black. This iconic criterion for
defining black film argues that there is an immediate reflective
identification between the image and its supposed referent based
on content. In simple terms, the viewer sees and recognizes black
faces. Thus, the identity and meaning of the film image are readily asserted. Of course, iconic criteria are based on superficial
distinctions, but falter when substantially examined. Iconic criterion for defining black film serves only the ideological purposes of maintaining the dominant system of representation,
principally because it legitimizes traditional cinematic content
and refuses to challenge the prevalent conception of black film.
Being a descriptive formula, it is ever trapped in a vulgar empiricism, which becomes impossible to transcend.

Another approach to defining black cinema might be termed
indexical. Using this operational definition, the sociocultural
background of the filmmaker functions as an index for identifying a film. Because an index is a marker that points to, and is said
to explain its source, it is assumed that a black film is one made
by a black filmmaker. The filmmaker functions as an index or

marker in the same way that an index functions in a book. Whereas iconic criteria limit discussion to the descriptive aspects of content, indexical theories shift discussion away from the art-work to sociological criteria. Since when can a work of art be evaluated principally on the basis of the artist's identity or the artist's identification with a particular ethnic group?

This is not to deny the relevance of the filmmaker's socio-cultural background. However, in contrast to a simplistic index-ical approach, the sociocultural background of the filmmaker functions as the matrix from which creativity springs. It is some-thing the filmmaker lives. It forms the context for the articula-tion of specific cinematic languages. But, at this stage, there is no guarantee of a black film based solely on the mediation of one's sociocultural background. There are moments in artistic expression when the sociocultural background of the artist is superseded by the specific articulation of an artistic language. This complicates the usefulness of indexical criteria, for the music of a black composer who works within the European clas-sical musical tradition cannot be classified as having emanated from the African American tradition. Similarly, Michael Schulz's *Sergeant Pepper's Lonely Hearts Club Band* (1979) cannot be clas-sified as a black film simply because the filmmaker is identified as black. If a black person speaks French, is French then a black language?

The inadequacy of indexical theories as an acceptable means of defining black film can be clearly demonstrated because sev-eral difficulties arise that appear to have no solution. The inva-lidity of the indexical paradigm is most evident when dealing with a film by a white director such as Michael Roemer's *Nothing But a Man*. In my view, what is most important about a film is the film itself. The operators (producer, director and writer) are properly part of the pre-text, in that the text is a product of their work and they exist prior to the text. While their contribution to the making of the text is undeniable, they—in and of them-selves—cannot fully define the film they produce. Often, the film looms larger than its production crew. Although we should not undervalue the significance of having black writers, producers and directors play an important role in black film production, the presence of black filmmakers by themselves are not sufficient to guarantee the production of a black film. Yet, another strate-gy to defining black film is based on what may be termed the filmmaker's intention in that there is some sort of plan to make a black film. Although we often judge the things people do on their intentions, intentionality in art is a complex matter and defies simple solutions. Intentional criterion moves discussion away from the film as text to self-laudatory proclamations that can devalue the work. A proper evaluation of black film centers on how black filmmakers construct their films from symbolic images that emanate or are mediated by a black sociocultural experience.

Films such as *48 Hours* (1982) will not be classified as black films according to this schema of symbolic criteria because they are films produced within the expressive framework of the dominant film industry featuring subject matter involving blacks and characters played by black actors. Diawara observes that although Eddie Murphy "may be the star of the show," certainly he "is not the hero of the story."

> In terms of the Oedipal analogy in the structure of such narrative patterns, the black male subject always appears to lose in the competition for the symbolic position of the father or authority figure. And at the level of spectatorship, the black spectator, regardless of gender or sexuality, fails to enjoy the pleasures which are at least available to the white male heterosexual spectator positioned as the subject of these discourses. (1993, p. 216)

The crucial question is not so much that a film looks like a black film or contains black characters, but how is it that a work qualifies to be a black film; or, how is it that a black film is made? Because traditional cinema functions to reproduce the acceptable legitimate positions prevalent in society, black cinema is conceived in necessary opposition to these dominant sociopolitical structures. There is an emphasis on forms of production and influence over the productive processes of cinema. If the practice of black cinema is derived from that of Hollywood, then it will serve to reproduce the unequal relations characteristic of blacks in society. Hence, the most appropriate strategy is to conceive of black film as a specific signifying practice that proposes a different set of historical relations of production.

THE IMPORTANCE OF THE TEXT
IN DEFINING BLACK FILM

Delineating the scope of black independent film is a most urgent undertaking for black film criticism. There is a need to clarify what critics mean when they use the term black cinema. Is it a reference to all those films written, produced and directed by blacks? Does it refers to only those films whose subject matter deals with the lives of black people or presents recognizable images of blacks on the screen? What other criteria should the critics rely on? Tommy L. Lott describes the complexity of defining black cinema as a "scholarly morass," but makes the point that the definitional process "must be understood in terms of the inherently political context in which the concept of black cinema has been introduced" (1991, p. 221). Most critics would agree that black film has an inherently political dimension. Its mere existence as a signifying process engaged in the production and contestation of social meanings raises questions of oppositional aesthetic practice in relation to the history of Hollywood film. Although the paradigm of black film as art is concerned foremost with questions of how signification and textual practices function in black film, it is unthinkable to deny the relevance of politics to black film practice.

Most definitions of black film tend to be based on sociological criteria and emphasize the importance of contextual factors rather than focusing on the film itself. The issue is not whether contextual criteria are relevant or not to black film, rather the major concern is to establish priorities in our encounter with the text. Hence, should we define black film based on its textual characterization or contextual circumstances? Cripps offers a broad definition of black film that gives high priority to external criteria, which tend to devalue the specificity of the film. He suggests that black cinema would include:

> . . . Those motion pictures made for theater distribution that have a black producer, director, and writer, or black performers; that speak to black audiences or, incidentally, to white audiences possessed of preternatural curiosity, attentiveness, or sensibility toward racial matters; and that emerge from self-conscious intentions; whether artistic or political, to illuminate the Afro-American experience. (1978, p. 3)

The problem with Cripps' formulation is the same we encounter if we defined a game of basketball based on the identity and interests of the audience. Such a maneuver may prove useful in a sociological study of basketball and its fans; but it does not tell us much about the nature of basketball: the rules of the game, dimensions of the court, basketball teams or regulations about the size of the ball. In seeking to establish the identity of a child, can we do so by a simple reference to the child's parents and relatives? Certainly, information about the child's parents is relevant, but in the first instance, priority must focus on the child as a person in her own right before we can make relational judgments. Following this, we can then move on to other kinds of information regarding genetic relationships and so on. Cripps' definition stresses the importance of films about blacks that are produced, written, directed, and performed by blacks primarily for blacks. This leaves Lott to wonder how to account for those films about black people made by white filmmakers. The approach advocated by Cripps would "exclude films such as King Vidor's *Hallelujah*, Shirley Clarke's *The Cool World*, Michael Roemer's *Nothing But a Man*, Charlie Ahearn's *Wild Styles* and John Sayles's *The Brother From Another Planet* from the newly emerging black canon" (1991, p. 221).

In order for a viable black cinema to develop, it is necessary to delineate a broad enough yet succinct theoretical approach based on black filmmaking as a signifying practice. Prevalent definitional approaches, such as the one offered by Cripps, do not provide a strong enough theoretical base for the development of black cinema. The artwork cannot be judged on the basis of who the artist is, or the artist as an individual, the artist's biography, the artist's intentionality, or the audience. The sociocultural background of the authors and their sociological and political aspirations do not guarantee the production of a black film. We can also question whether a filmmaker's intention to produce a black film necessarily guarantees the production of a black film. The use of intentional criteria or the various claims filmmakers make about their art often fail to live up to their promises. This is related to the problem of what precisely a film illuminates about the black experience. Bill E. Lawson questions the opinion that black art communicates the black experience or that we learn something about blacks by listening to black music or viewing black art. He describes these claims as controversial, "that just by listening to the music one can have one's consciousness

Then why study it?

raised or that one can come to know something about black culture" (1994, p. 132). The controversy of whether or not black film illuminates the black experience can be addressed through a focus on how the formal structures of art function to produce signifying practices within the black tradition. Our focus on formal structures shifts attention away from concerns of iconicity and empiricism in black art, the view that somehow there is a direct relationship of the black image in art with social reality. A definition of black film that foregrounds secondary criteria pushes the actual work into the background and necessarily devalues the film.

BLACK GENRE FILM

Black genre film is a useful concept that can be applied to a wide range of films whose subject matter deals with the black experience. Genre refers to a recognizable type of movie, which uses a set of conventions that can be identified in style, subject matter, and values. It is also a convenient strategy for focusing and structuring story material (Gianetti, 1996, p. 510). A definition of black film as genre provides a richer approach for studying these films. Using contextualist criticism, Cripps notes that social and anthropological factors offer a useful approach to defining black genre film. "Genre films, like folk tales and tribal lore, may transmit social meanings beyond the conscious intention of the filmmaker, as well as meaning brought by the audience's own social and cultural history" (1978, p. 9). Genres are based on conventions, ideas that we take for granted and accept as representative of a particular thing. A convention may be described as a commonplace characteristic of something that is, more or less, agreed upon by people in society. Conventions constitute norms of what is appropriate or expected in a particular tradition, and experience plays an important role in the encounter of the viewer with genre film. Genres also derive meaning through expectations shared by members of a culture or audience. In the cinema, genre establishes a set of rules for narrative construction and a framework that is shared by the filmmaker and audience.

In *Black Film as Genre*, Cripps traces the evolution of black film and critiques six black genre films. He proposes the existence of several sub-genres: social drama, black musical film, religious themes, documentary, picaresque hero and heroic black film. The major thrust of the book is to explore and establish a

set of methodical standards of judgment and evaluation of black
film. The concept of genre aids in this endeavor especially as it
points toward a synthesis of ritual, myth, and social meaning,
and to what Cripps describes as "preaesthetic judgments" that
reveal and reflect the world-view of a subculture (1978, p. 156).
The application of genre criticism represented an important step
for black cinema aesthetics. Critics posed a series of new questions that focused attention on the black experience and, importantly, on black vernacular expression in film, especially through
its concern with narrative and stylistic elements that are mutu-
ally understood by filmmaker and audience. This shared symbolic experience is a cultural mechanism that the filmmaker may
use to "make a black film based upon his ability to perceive and
respond to artistic and mythic needs of an audience" (1977, p.
152).

Filmmakers working in the genre of black film incorporate
elements of African American culture in their work. They draw
on a common history, culture and mythology. They use established themes such as a history of oppression and the knowledge
that African American society exists in a disadvantageous social
and economic structure imposed by the dominant white society.
In black genre film, the struggle of good (represented by blacks)
versus evil (which is perpetrated by exploitative blacks and some
whites) can be identified as a common theme. As in Ivan Dixon's
adaptation of Sam Greenlee's *The Spook Who Sat By The Door*
(1973)—a novel about a black CIA agent who uses his training
for the purpose of black liberation—the black hero is often represented as seeking to free blacks. As a result, the black hero confronts the white society, which is responsible for the
marginalization of black life. The conflict of black good over
white-inspired evil is played out significantly in black genre film.
In successful examples of the genre, the black hero wins or comes
out on top in the narrative struggle. The desire for freedom is
basic to the belief structure of black genre film as in Sydney
Poitier's *Buck and The Preacher* (1972), when a group of blacks
set out on a western trek to live as free people. Freedom and
migration function as mythoforms in black genre film. Myths
embody the shared ideals and aspirations of a culture and they
function to keep alive the group's communal memory. The filmmaker becomes a griot, providing psychic links between the past
and the future.

While black film as genre offers a broader canvas for criticism, there are several problems with using it for definitional purposes. Genre is weak when addressing issues of value in black film. It can tell us that a film is a black film, but it cannot tell us what a good black film is. Because of the history of suffering and exploitation, many African Americans are highly critical when anyone exploits black culture. A major problem with black genre film is that it can be imitated easily and become exploitation film. Blaxploitation is a blanket term used to describe a series of films made in the 1970s that featured black themes and were set in African American communities. They featured black actors but were produced, directed and financed, for the most part, by whites. Obnoxiously, blaxploitation films existed principally to exploit and profit from black culture.

In using the broad brush of blaxploitation to describe black film of the early 1970s, we are unable to adequately differentiate between exploitation films and other films such as Gordon Parks' *Shaft* (1971), Michael Schultz's *Cooley High* (1975), Gordon Parks, Jr's *Superfly* (1972) or *Sweetback*. "The nature of exploitation film is defined by the way the economic and psycho-therapeutic mechanisms of film function as palliatives to black and liberal audiences, but operate to reaffirm the political and economic structure of society. Black exploitation films utilize themes of black militancy, black revolt, and black consciousness. In the 1970s, these themes were set against the rise of the Civil Rights movement with a backdrop of urban unrest and explosive black anger" (Yearwood, 1982a, p. 13). Melvin Van Peebles's *Sweet Sweetback's Baadasss Song* (1971)—the quintessential black genre film—represents the most explosive expression of the genre's early phase. Early films in the genre function to blaze trails and play a seminal role in its creation. *Sweetback* is a hard-driving film and its hero is a prototype black, urban outlaw. Sweetback fights against the police and white power structure in the narration. As the narrative progresses, Sweetback positions himself on the side of the black revolution. In the end, he wins, escaping to beat the system. Interestingly, *Sweetback* is a unique film and another like it has not appeared. Characteristic of the early phase of genre film, Van Peebles wrote, directed and starred in the film. As a matter of fact, *Sweetback* helped set the stage for the subsequent development of black independent filmmaking.

The sweeping charge that, in general, black films of the early 1970s constitute blaxploitation cinema tends to erase the differ-

ences between truly exploitation cinema and films using similar
subject matter. Although exploitative circumstances surround
the making and control of films such as *Shaft*, they defy the classification as blaxploitation. A film such as *Shaft* is important
because it is able "to point out the limitations of black cinematic expression within the terms of the Hollywood tradition" and
delineate aspects of a black cinema aesthetic. *Shaft* is a fine example of the classical phase of black genre film. This type of black
genre film usually displays the most salient features of the genre.
The hero is black. The story is set in a black community. It contains a definite structure of good and evil. The good guys are
black and the bad guys are white. The various elements of the
mise-en-scene are all related to the African American experience.
While blacks did not control MGM (the studio that produced
the film), director Gordon Parks imposed an African American
aesthetic point of view on the film through dialogue, performance and music. Interestingly, black audiences seem to enjoy
Shaft better than *Sweetback* possibly because the former tends to
borrow more from commercial cinema, while the latter is more
of an art film.

Stylistically, *Shaft* straddles Hollywood and black independent cinema. Although *Shaft* was made within the Hollywood
studio system, its black genre characteristics function to modify
traditional film parameters. The narrative is motivated by a kidnapping that sets the plot in motion, while symbolically establishing a threat to blacks that must be vanquished to bring about
the narrative's resolution. These narrative mechanisms allow
black audiences to empathize with the hero and his struggle,
especially because *Shaft* is organized around a black hero, a private detective who to some extent usurps the space reserved for
white males in the history of film.

The narration in *Shaft* is driven by a music score composed
by Isaac Hayes, which significantly foregrounds traditions of
popular black music in the cinema and functions as more than
background accompaniment. The film recuperates the figure of
the black nationalist militant, who has been so thoroughly demonized in the Hollywood cinema. An organized group of militants
joins forces with the hero to create a powerful strike force to
defeat the white antagonists in the narrative. Parks uses a performative cinematic ambience to create his film language; but
Shaft demonstrates the problems alternative cinemas encounter
when they utilize the signifying paradigms of the dominant cul-

ture without serious reformulation. Consequently, very much like James Bond, the narrative of John Shaft reproduces dominant sexual ideologies in its construction of women. In the films of this period, "African American women were ill-treated as well, usually assigned a role in which they lounged in scanty clothes being beaten up the by the bad guys or waiting to be rescued by the good guys. Later, black women were updated with their own gun-toting, mini-skirted stereotyped roles like *Foxy Brown* and *Coffy* (Bourne, 1994, p. 22). In *Shaft*, the kidnapping of the daughter of a black mobster initiates the plot, and the dramatic inevitability of the hero's sexual prowess is evident in his conquest of women, which includes the white woman. There are no female villains in the film, but the women exist principally to bolster Shaft's machismo. *Shaft* is symptomatic of the many tensions we find in black genre film that relies too heavily on the Hollywood tradition and utilizes its models of filmmaking. The emergence of a black hero challenges traditional social relations, the dominant society and its institutionalized narratives. Reformulating the paradigm of the hero in black film is not simply a maneuver of replacing black macho types for white ones. Hence, *Shaft* makes an uneven advance in that its narrative helps to break down the dominant parameters of Hollywood film, but because it depends too much on the formal constraints of Hollywood's signifying practice, it is unable to create a new film language and therefore must rely on established stereotypes.

Shaft was an important film to the black male audience of the early 1970s because it depicted the black man kicking ass. The hero wins a personal victory and the narration emphasizes a larger mythic theme of blacks (the oppressed) triumphing over evil (their oppressors). Like most black genre films, the narrator is presented as having a socially conscious voice. However, the problem of the black hero in film remains because the structure of representation, which helps to articulate the filmic signification of gender and racial roles, remains substantially unchanged. *Shaft* is a good example of a film that relies on Hollywood conventions but utilizes the African American tradition to turn around the expectations they arouse. The importance of a film such as *Shaft* is that it produces knowledge not developed in the Hollywood classical narrative and it allows us to observe the way black filmmakers in the Hollywood system incorporate elements of resistance in their work. As a result, although *Shaft* was made within the studio system, it positions itself in defiance of ele-

ments of that tradition. The lesson we bring from these films is
that advances in black film art must include a reformulation of
film language as a signifying practice.

The attempt to transform the genre usually comes with later
films. Spike Lee's *She's Gotta Have It* (1985), which represents
the third phase of black genre film, comments on the traditions
of the genre and sets about to reformulate many of its important
tenets. *She's Gotta Have It* does not work in the same way as
Sweetback or *Shaft*. It does not present a romantic picture of a
black hero or the black community. Its characters are filled with
ambiguity. Lee's breakthrough film narrates the story of a black
woman and her sexual desires. The narrative does not have a
hero. Its theme centers on the sexual life of Nola Darling—the
film's main character. Nola's interest in sex borders on a certain
freakishness and is alienated from the general black genre theme
of elevating the African American community. Furthermore, it
does not position the white power structure as the major source
of conflict. Certainly, it does point to the existence of a larger,
hostile white society; but that is not a major focal point of its narration. Characteristic of Lee's films is an insider's critique of institutions and personalities in the black community. Whereas the
early phases of black genre film are more concerned with black
community restitution, this kind of film tends to focus more on
intellectual issues. Earlier phases treat the black experience with
more reverence. In this sense, Lee's film is meta-critical in that
it looks inward, critically assessing issues affecting the black community. Gianetti describes this stage of genre film as revisionist
in that it is more concerned with symbolism and less certain in
its values (1996, p. 348).

While genre is a useful tool for classifying films about the
black experience; however "Genre film can easily become
exploitation film, through which tastes are teased but no deeper ends are met" (Cripps, 1978, p. 11). Despite Cripps' warning
aimed at separating exploitation film from black genre film, subsequent criticism has used blaxploitation as an umbrella concept.
Bourne explains the need for a more careful application of the
term. "Blaxploitation film was full of contradictions. Most of the
stories in these films took place in a black community and featured a largely black cast. Yet, most of the crews, writers and
directors were usually white. The villains were always white
males, but white males that other whites could be comfortable
with as 'bad guys'—crude Mafia thugs, drug dealers or crazies"

(Bourne, 1994, p. 22). Other black commentators saw blaxploitation as "a way of labeling a film that fails in certain ways to represent the aesthetic values of black culture properly" (Lott, 1991, p. 223). Lott argues that the use of purely aesthetic criteria cannot resolve these issues. He cites *Sweetback* as representative of elements of a black aesthetic. "When *Sweetback* was shown in 1971, it was an immediate success with black audiences because it captured an image of self-defense that gave on-screen legitimation to violent retaliation against racist police brutality" (Lott, 1991, p. 225). Posing a conundrum to black film criticism, *Sweetback* was alternatively hailed and reviled by black film critics. For example, Reid (1993) argues that *Sweetback* is not really a political film and the film's hero does not have a politicized image; while Jim Pines (1988) stakes out a position on the other extreme observing that *Sweetback* went beyond politicization to function as propaganda. Lott states that "To denounce a film, such as *Sweetback*, as exploitative is to suggest that aesthetic criteria provide the highest ground of appeal for deciding definitional questions regarding black cinematic representation, for the charge presupposes that there is some sense in which to produce a blaxploitation film is to have compromised black aesthetic values" (1991, p. 226).

After *Sweetback* demonstrated the enormous box-office appeal of black film subject matter and the purchasing power of the black film audience, "Hollywood then did what it does best, absorb elements from a new, innovative cultural expression and use it to create a bland version of the original. As before, these blaxploitation films, as they came to be known, fulfilled specific economic and psychological purposes on behalf of the notion of white superiority . . ." (Bourne, 1994, p. 22). Lott raises a most intriguing question for black cinema. In the event that a so-called blaxploitation film is made independently by a black filmmaker for a black audience, to whom has the film's aesthetic orientation been compromised, and to what degree do such compromises affect a film's status as a black film? (1991, p. 227). Black audiences warmed to these films because their narratives portrayed blacks as engaged in resistance against their oppression, fighting the system in some form and winning, although their victory involved "beating up only the scum of the white community, exploiting and mistreating women and even selling dope." However, some blacks found the psycho-therapeutic potential of these films useful at that historical moment because it spoke to them as a "people who had seen only 'coon' roles in a steady stream of Hollywood films" (Bourne, 1994, p. 22). Bogle describes this period in the early 1970s as "the age of the buck, a period when a band of aggressive, pistol-packing, sexually charged urban cowboys set off on a heady rampage, out to topple the system and right past wrongs" (1994, p. 232).

EMPOWERMENT THEORIES OF BLACK FILM

A widely held point of view in the black community links questions of aesthetic value—that is, our idea of a good black film—with issues of power and control in filmmaking. The thrust of this argument is to avoid exploitative uses of black culture. Lott advocates a "no-theory theory" of black cinema to address these issues. In order to situate politics and aesthetics within a theory of black cinema, he offers Third Cinema as a model for black filmmaking practice. "What makes Third Cinema third (a viable alternative to Western cinema) is not exclusively the racial make-up of a filmmaker, a film's aesthetic character, or a film's intended audience, but rather a film's political orientation within the hegemonic structures of post-colonialism. When a film contributes ideologically to the advancement of black people, within a context of systematic denial, the achievement of this political objective ought to count as a criterion of evaluation on a par with any essentialist criterion" (Lott, 1991, p. 231). The philosophy of film articulated in Third Cinema sets up a relationship between film and the larger context of socio-economic and political conditions affecting Third World people. The aim of Third Cinema is to empower disenfranchised groups such as blacks, thereby rendering them less susceptible to cultural and economic exploitation. "Film in a Third World context seeks (a) to decolonize minds, (b) contribute to the development of a radical consciousness, (c) lead to a revolutionary transformation of society, and (d) develop a new film language with which to accomplish these tasks" (Gabriel, 1982, p. 1). The 'Cine Liberacion' of Ferdinand Solanas and Octavio Getino (1979), articulated in their influential article, "Towards a Third Cinema," suggests that Third World cinema should produce films of "decolonization," that are opposed to maintaining the power of the neo-colonial status quo and contribute to the decolonization of culture. In this view, film functions as an important arena in the struggle for a full and meaningful independence of oppressed peoples, because art is capable of aiding and facilitating a new awareness

ELEVATED
CONSCIOUSNESS

Disrupt dominant narratives

of how our social world can be transformed and our lives enriched. If black film incorporates Third Cinema theory, it fosters the development of aesthetics within the political framework of an oppositional practice that engages in resistance and transformation. It also seeks to provide the tools to disrupt and challenge the master narratives of the Hollywood cinema. In discussing low-budget films such as Haile Gerima's *Bush Mama* (1974), Billy Woodbury's *Bless Their Little Hearts* (1984), and Charles Burnett's *Killer of Sheep* (1977), Lott argues that they "frequently suffer in the marketplace, as well as in the eyes of critics, when they fail to be aesthetically pleasing." His assumption that aesthetically pleasing filmmaking is synonymous with Hollywood production values does not necessarily hold true because it is possible to consider the slick production values of Hollywood film to be aesthetically uninteresting because of its strong commercialism. A more precise notion of the aesthetic as a system of expressive values does not allow us to restrict aesthetic pleasure to any one model of filmmaking. Lott goes on to describe *Roots* (1977) and *Shaka Zulu* (1983) as examples of films that had commercial success largely because of their aesthetic appeal despite their problematic political orientation (1991, p. 222). While *Roots* may have reached huge audiences, even within Hollywood it was by no means an important aesthetic success.

While critics may find it difficult to distinguish between films that treat the black experience with integrity and exploitation films, Lott contends that black audiences are capable of making these crucial distinctions. Citing the work of commentators such as Teshombe Gabriel and Kobena Mercer who also urge critics to address the politics of black filmmaking, Lott argues that the narrow "essentialist" criteria (e.g., Cripps' definition) and the broad "non-essentialist" approach (e.g., Phyllis Klotman's *Frame by Frame: A Black Filmography*) are flawed because they cannot account for the political dimensions of black film. "Black people have a deep-seated concern with their history of being stereotyped in Hollywood films, a concern which provides an important reason to be skeptical of any concept of black cinema that would include works which demean blacks" (1991, p. 222). Hence, blacks find that raising questions of politics keeps issues related to the control of film production and distribution in the forefront of a black film agenda. Lott distrusts the use of aesthetic criteria for judging black film, pointing out that adding a political agenda to aesthetics would avoid the narrowness of

essentialist definitions. He asks whether "this move toward aesthetics would allow the accommodation of a strictly cultural criterion for the definition of black cinema without invoking a
notion of 'black aesthetics,' upon which some reconstituted version of biological essentialism may again be reinstated" (1991,
p. 222). Needless to say, a black cultural nationalist aesthetic is
but one possibility among several. There is a danger of racializ-
ing the political concern with control so that biological factors
become a sole determinant of authorship in black film. The fact
that the filmmaker is black does not guarantee the production
of a black film.

Although the first phase of black filmmaking was inherently concerned with questions of political control as demonstrated by Micheaux's organizational work, the politics of black film
came to a head much later in the 1970s. At that time, black filmmakers dealt explicitly with political themes in contrast to the
earlier period. Yet, the best work by black filmmakers of the
1970s cannot be described as advocacy films or simple propagandistic work. "These films contain a political commitment to
the liberation struggles of black and other oppressed peoples.
However, these filmmakers are not interested in ghettoizing
black cinema. As filmmakers, they hold a fundamental commitment to advancing the rights of black people; but they never hesitate to speak to larger audiences" (Yearwood, 1982a, p. 12).
Seeking to play a role in the political struggle, black filmmakers
focused on empowerment as an important objective in establishing a viable black independent cinema and in the transformation of popular entertainment and prevalent representations
of blacks in the Hollywood film. The films of Gordon Parks
played a critical role in the political struggle of black filmmakers because they helped change the social expectations the public associated with film, and in the process made black
independent films more accessible to popular audiences.

The issue of political control also played a part in Murray's
concept of black film, which he defines as "any cinema in which
blacks exert significant influence, either by direct input (such as
writing the screenplay, starring in, producing, or directing the
film) or by indirect participation (such as accepting roles in which
no creative involvement is permitted, but in which a black theme
has a decided effect)" (1973, p. xiv). Murray's appeal for blacks
to exert significant influence on black films reverberates throughout black film history. But how do we measure control in a black

film? It can be political, financial or creative. Reid's concept of a "black mode of artistic production" is useful. It refers to "a film-making process in which blacks have written, directed, and produced their films without financial control by major American commercial film producers, distributors, or exhibitors" (1993, pp. 4-5). The financing of Spike Lee's *Get On the Bus* (1996) by 15 black men or the crucial financial intervention of blacks in the film industry to ensure completion of Malcolm-X (1993) is testimony to the role enlightened financial backers can play. When black critics insist on black ownership and control, their arguments are concerned with a best-case scenario, as in the story of Harlem's Apollo Theater, which for more than 60 years has been a premiere national showcase for black performers. The Apollo's "Amateur Night" has served as a coming of age ritual for aspiring entertainers. It is possible that the Apollo would not be in operation today if the Suttons—an African American family prominent in politics and business—had not stepped in financially. It might have become another retail shopping arcade or another abandoned building blighting the urban landscape. In the best of circumstances, black film critics point out that black ownership is capable of seeing the big picture when assessing the value of an investment. In addition to the profit motive, they may stress the social factors of capital, which involve a cultural and political commitment to maintaining institutions in black communities. However, exploitative practices use blacks as a consumer market by removing profits and production activity from black communities, thereby creating impoverished zones. To play the part of the devil's advocate, the brute biological fact of race does not guarantee the success of the final product as a black film. Questions of political control over black film are much more complex than simply reducing the determining factor to one of race. Without a doubt, it is necessary to account for the history of exploitative relations that has characterized relations between blacks and the dominant society. Our history is replete with instances of powerful groups ignoring the interests of blacks for the exploitation of popular cultural resources derived from the black experience. However, the recent success of black musicians in the recording industry would not be possible if we were to extend to music Reid's conceptual criteria, which calls for blanket controls over creative, financial and distribution channels. Black musicians have demonstrated that black culture is resilient and is oriented to survival, and that strategic alliances are vital.

I am not suggesting that blacks have full control of their music
in that industry.

In *Redefining Black Film*, Reid describes prevalent definitional
approaches as "faulty or limited" and suggests that they do not
address the formal aspects of black film (1993, p. 1). Despite his
criticism of the failure of theorists and critics to deal with questions of form in black film, Reid's own analysis does not adequately speak to form. As a matter of fact, he needs to define
more precisely what he means by the formal parameters of black
film. Nonetheless, Reid is on the right track when he characterizes the prevailing approaches to black film as being faulty. Yet,
in his paradigm of control (that is, a process written, directed
and produced by blacks without financial control by outsiders),
he rejects the use of formal parameters in that he locates his critical criteria of control in other factors. Without a proper attention to formal issues, black film criticism will fall easy prey to an
empty formalism and a meaningless historicism. A more critical
understanding of the black community's control over its films
would be better measured through the way the processes of signification inherent in the black cultural tradition function to
interpret, package and express artistic material. Reid bases his
analysis on paradigms (signifieds) of race that have been constructed for us by the dominant society. It is certainly a more
productive undertaking to define black cultural expression formally at the level of its signifying practices, all the while avoiding a narrow tautological definition of signifying practices as
being autonomous and accountable only to the text. Signification
in a text necessarily calls into play several levels of codes, which
are intratextual, intertextual and contextual. Textual signification resonates dialectically through these three levels.
Undoubtedly, the text does not exist outside of the culture within which it is produced and which provides a context for the production of meanings. " . . . It is impossible to grasp the complexity
and multidimensionality of a specific set of artistic practices without relating it to other broader cultural and political practices at
a given moment" (West, 1993, p. 42). Still, Reid's notion that
financial control by major American corporations threatens black
control over our cultural products cannot be ignored, given the
historical evidence available to us.

Many blacks question the usefulness of definitions and paradigms of black film that do not guarantee control over black
cultural production. There is a sense that a definition of black

cinema must somehow guarantee that films should resist being co-opted. James Snead observes that for black American filmmakers, an American identity as such no longer has anything to offer, and as a result, he finds that black filmmakers "are preoccupied with the questions how can I best keep from becoming like white Americans? How can I fulfill my personal aspirations and yet best preserve my distinctiveness, my 'grooviness' in the stultifying square American context?" (1994, p. 127). He urges black filmmakers to move from a narrow usage of the term black, which he finds to be divisive in order to forge new alliances and widen the audience base for their films. "What we might really begin discussing here," he writes, "is the existence of insurgent or alternative cinemas, without mystifying the color of its producers" (1994, p. 125).

Snead argues that the concept of black film has been over-mystified and over-specified, and it "has reached the point where some critics and even filmmakers suggest that a 'black aesthetic' makes films by blacks as visually distinctive a form as say, traditional black music is from white classical music" (1994, p. 123). This skepticism is a function of his predominant concern with questions of race as part of the discourse of the dominant culture. If Snead's inquiry were to proceed using a point of entry that emphasizes the integrity of black cultural expression in a phenomenological sense, a different set of questions would ensue: for example, how do black films relate to the African American expressive tradition? We have no need to search for an aesthetic purity, which in any event does not exist. Mercer clarifies one of the aims of black independent cinema:

> There is no escaping the fact that as a diaspora people, . . . our blackness is thoroughly imbricated in Western modes and codes to which we arrived as the disseminated masses of migrant dispersal. What is in question is not the expression of some lost origin or some uncontaminated essence in black film-language, but the adoption of a critical 'voice' that promotes consciousness of the collision of cultures and histories that constitute our very conditions of existence. (1988, p. 56)

Hence, we can take the history of race relations in the United States as a given because it is impossible to divorce black existence from the dominant white society. Yet, we can still view black cultural expression as an entity in its own right. While blacks are positioned as racial subjects in society, nonetheless there is a phenomenological sense (albeit limited) in which blacks experience values and share preferences that are not completely framed within the larger system of racial positioning. Any important formulation of a black independent film movement needs to make advances not only at the level of a sociology of art and the political control of the filmmaking process, but in control of its signifying practices as well.

The attention to issues of political and economic control of black film was a logical development of the particular history of exploitation blacks have experienced. In the 1970s, Murray declared that the three goals of black cinema were correction of white distortions, reflection of a black reality, and the creation of a positive black image. (1973, p. xiv). To achieve these ends, it becomes necessary for blacks to control important aspects of image production. In presenting his own definition of black film, Reid picks up on Murray's formulation and explains that "American film criticism must be augmented and corrected by descriptions and analyses of films produced by black people and of filmmaking in which black people controlled the key creative aspects of production" (1993, p. 2). Most black writers tend to emphasize the importance of having political control of black film. They point to the history of the Hollywood cinema in which blacks have been marginalized and the dominant paradigm of emasculation and powerlessness that has characterized images of blacks.

Reid finds it useful to distinguish between black commercial and black independent films.

> The black commercial film is limited here to any feature-length fiction film whose central focus is the Afro-American community. This film is written, directed, or produced by at least one black person in collaboration with non-black people. Films included in this category are distributed by major American film companies.

> The black independent film is defined as any feature-length fiction film whose central focus is the Afro-American community. Such films are written, directed, and produced by Afro-Americans and people of African ancestry who reside in the United

States. These films are not distributed by major
American film companies. (1993, p. 4)

His purpose in making this distinction between black commercial films and black independent films is to make the claim that
when blacks maintain control over distribution of their films,
there is a guarantee that positive images will be produced.
Certainly Reid's distinction is valuable in its goal of focusing on
the types of films blacks create when they retain control over
their films.

A CRITIQUE OF EMPOWERMENT THEORIES

There still is a need to ascertain the degree of control blacks must
exercise in order to guarantee the production of a black film.
Commenting on Roemer's *Nothing But A Man*, Cripps success-
fully questions the assertion that simple biological criteria are
sufficient to guarantee production of a black film. He writes, "We
are in a black movie, not only because the themes are black, but
because our point of view is from within black circles in segregated Alabama" (1978, p. 118). For a white American director,
Nothing But a Man is a rare achievement, and black film critics
need to present reasonable arguments as to why and in what ways
it does not exemplify a black film. Reid's guidelines, which
require control of key aspects of film production, would dismiss
Cripps' assessment of *Nothing But a Man* as a black film. A solution to this conundrum can be found by clearly focusing on the
textual characteristics of the film. Developments in the study of
African American music can be used to solve this question. When
we listen to Jazz groups from Eastern Europe or the Jazz orches-
tras of prominent American universities, which may feature several musicians who are not black, we can still make the judgment
that their music is based in the African American tradition. Yet,
some critics state that although white musicians have become a
mainstay of the blues in contemporary society, the music they
produce remains suspect because blacks need to derive some tan-
gible benefit from their art and not only credit for its original
creation.

A solution to the problem can be presented by specifying
that the chain of signification and the signifying practice that
produce these art forms must derive from the African American
tradition. When Wynton Marsalis plays the European classical
composers, in that instance the chain of signification he invokes
happens to be part of a European cultural matrix. At that

moment, we would describe Marsalis as an African American
musician who has mastered a European cultural form. Duke
University chapel, the magnificent Gothic cathedral in Durham,
NC, was designed by an African American architect, Julian
Abele. While this is a proud achievement for many blacks, it still
does not erase the fact that the signifying tradition dominant in
the chapel's design is European, while its construction techniques
are American. In a postmodernist vision of society, it is advantageous to be multilingual. Theorists and critics of the African
American cultural tradition cannot ignore the multilingualism
of a Wynton Marsalis, who is capable of performing in several
different forms of musical signification.

Gates' critique of black literary criticism as being too preoccupied with sociology of art is relevant and can help clarify
these issues in black film theory. In sociological criticism of art,
propaganda becomes a substitute for the textual exploration of
the artwork. Consequently, functional and didactic elements tend
to dictate the value of the work. Art is conceived as a vehicle for
social reform and it becomes an instrument for the social
improvement of black life. Gates argues that the pendulum has
swung too far in favor of the sociological in black art criticism.

> Structure . . . was atomized. Form was merely a sur-
> face for a reflection of the world, the world here
> being an attitude toward race; form was a reposito-
> ry for the disposal of ideas; message was not only
> meaning but value; poetic discourse was taken to be
> literal, or once removed; language lost its capacity
> to be metaphorical in the eyes of the critic; the poem
> approached the essay, with referents immediately
> perceivable; literalness precluded the view of life as
> allegorical; and black critics forgot that writers
> approached things through words, not the other way
> around. (1987, p. 30)

A concern with form in black film contributes to clarifying the
specific interaction and articulation of the black cultural tradition and its expressive values in cinematic expression. Cornel
West finds the promise of a "black formalism" to be valuable.
However, he warns against creating a fetishism of the text, which
would amount to "a religious belief in the magical powers of a
glorified set of particular cultural archives somehow autonomous
and disconnected from other social practices" (1993, p. 42). If

the over-determination of the formal elements of art manifests itself in an aestheticism removed from the currents of African American life, then an abstract formalism is of dubious value in black cinema. "It ignores the way in which issues of power, political struggle and cultural identity are inscribed within the formal structures of texts and thereby misses the implicit readings of the crisis that circumscribes the texts and to which the texts inescapably and subtly respond" (West, 1993, p. 41). Recent developments in African American criticism that examine the formal language of the text have brought substantial improvements to black film studies. But West's caution against fetishizing the text identifies an ever present danger because a black formalism could easily become an overreaction to the more traditional methods of studying texts in the black cultural tradition and only capture select rhetorical features of texts while dehistoricizing their form and content.

Finding an adequate definition of empowerment in black art still needs further clarification. Some critics suggest that political and economic concerns should play a determining role in the making of cultural products. While these play an important role, in my view signification is more fundamental to artistic production. We can find an important formulation of empowerment in black cultural expression in the signifying practices of a film. The emphasis on signification revitalizes the central importance of form in African American art. Many black film critics distrust the attention to formal issues as a device to detract from social and political realities. However, it is a misunderstanding to conceive form as the absence of history and culture, because form is not a Platonic transcendental universal; it only materializes within a particular historical and cultural formation. We should not ignore the advice of Roland Barthes that "a little formalism takes one away from History, but that a lot brings one back to it" (1977, p. 112). The focus on signifying processes opens up the question of form in black cultural expression, which in turn is intricately related to issues of political, economic and ideological significance to black film. This is the path that leads to a true empowerment in black film.

BLACK FILM AS OPPOSITIONAL
AESTHETIC PRACTICE

Throughout her work, bell hooks weaves stories that reveal the way aesthetics permeated the lives of traditional southern black communities. The displaced Africans used cultural production and artistic creativity to maintain connections with their past. They believed that beauty should be integrated into everyday activities, thereby enhancing community survival and development, and they defined their aesthetics as having a political function, for in their art forms, they bore witness and challenged the racist ideology that claimed that blacks were not fully human and were uncivilized. "White supremacist ideology insisted that black people, being more animal than human, lacked the capacity to feel and therefore could not engage the finer sensibilities that were the breeding ground for art. Responding to this propaganda, 19th century black folks emphasized the importance of art and cultural production, seeing it as the most effective challenge to such assertions" (1990, p. 105). The idea of the importance of aesthetic experience in traditional African American life is based on a powerful formulation of an aesthetic that has the capability to function as a resistance tool as well as aid in the social maintenance or transformation of a community. As an oppositional cultural practice, black filmmaking speaks to the complex relationship between black-produced imagery and dominant representations. Empowerment is an integral element of oppositional aesthetics.

Snead identifies three broad categories of black film: films that deal with racism and its legacy, what he terms paradigmatic limitation; films that show blacks fighting the white assumptions of black inferiority that code them in stereotyped terms; and films that use the filmic medium to achieve a "syntagmatic freedom" or "recoding" of the black experience (1994, p. 128). His paradigm accounts for films that are oppositional as well as those that seek to redefine black cinema in its own terms. Taylor refines the notion of oppositional aesthetics, identifying three modes of cultural production used by black filmmakers. Ethiopic portrayals subscribe to the master narrative and fail to challenge the system of power characteristic of dominant representational politics. A second form, which he describes as Cyclopeanism, identifies thoroughly with the values and forms of the dominant society and is unable to recognize the way these contribute to their continued subjugation. The Cyclopean text also looks to the dominant society for legitimation, which it uses as a cultural paradigm and aesthetic criteria for its films. These films seek to be judged by the white film industry without reference to any ethnic criteria. Taylor's third category of black film is Aesopian, which describes a more complex work in which the filmmaker creates from the double consciousness that permeates African American life to formulate "one text for general (majority) consumption and another more subversive level of signification to be appreciated within the 'freemasonry' of the sub-cultural group" (1993, p. 184). The Aesopian mode of black filmmaking, which speaks to the majority without diminishing the interests of the less powerful group, is considered by Taylor to be more effective in generating democratic culture than those that do not engage the mainstream.

Jim Pines and Teshombe Gabriel question the efficacy of defining black cinema principally in terms of oppositional aesthetics. Pines agrees that projecting positive images is important. However, he finds that black filmmaking has a cultural dynamic of its own, and warns that this should not be reduced simply to the exegesis of oppositional practice (1988, p. 36). Gabriel cautions that when black independent cinema is understood principally as oppositional, it can be relegated to a reactive cinema. "However, black independent cinema's search has gone far beyond this, for it is in fact a search for a newly born cinema, one with its own discrete identity, evolving on its own axis. It must be understood as more than a reactive pole—but rather as the development of new, emergent tendencies which are more difficult to categorize in established norms . . . " (1988, p. 72). The mere existence of black independent cinema suggests an act of resistance, which necessarily assumes an oppositional stance to the signification of blackness in the classical cinema. However, Gabriel warns that to succumb to the notion of the other is to be a part of the problem because the other is always that which Western culture excludes through repression and oppression for exploitative purposes.

The concept of black independent cinema has to do with more than merely being oppositional. It allows us to view black film as a cultural product and specify how it emerges from and reflects the sociocultural and historical experiences of blacks. To read empowerment or independence as a reaction to or as simple opposition to Hollywood narrows the psychic space available for the development of black cinema. Snead also questions inde-

pendence observing that dependence has been desired because
it has meant access to bigger markets as well as substantial financial and technical resources, and the so-called independents
depend on "the keenly sought support of private investors, foundations, and public grants" (1994, p. 125). Taylor argues for a
meaningful independence when he suggests that independent
filmmakers who rely on the institutions of the dominant culture
need to rethink their strategies. "This rethinking might begin
with a realization of the present situation of black independence
as trapped within discursive boundaries patrolled by such un-
popular institutions such as the university, the national government foundations, the museums, the western-dominated
international film festivals, the public libraries, and PBS" (1989,
p. 439).

Gerima argues that true empowerment in independent cinema lies in a politically conscious viewer, who understands that
film seeks to manipulate the audience through formal mechanisms—its languages of images and its creation of reality—and
through film structure. Because film is conveyed through a "powerful grammar of visual imagery," in Gerima's view, it is necessary for the black audience to take an active viewing stance
because a whole lot of ideological biases are built into popular
film. "We must understand that Hollywood cinema has always
been escapist. In the pursuit of this escape and entertainment,
blacks and other oppressed social groups have been victimized.
This must be fought by black audiences." Regarding the charge
that black independent film has not been well received by black
audiences, Gerima extends the idea of oppositional practice in
his call for a political viewer, who takes an active role in the film
experience.

> The political audience never sits back and accepts
> the film passively. In my view, films should always
> raise a question. They should not present answers
> as in, 'This is the answer, this is the world.' The end
> of a film should not provide answers but instead pose
> new questions for the viewers. As a filmmaker, my
> interest is not to entertain. It is more provocative
> and argumentative, and to have a dialogue with my
> audience. My interest lies not in whether one has
> seen my film; but where that person goes and what
> action is undertaken after that. (1982, pp. 112-113)

The interrogation of the popular image of blacks and its construction as social reality stand as a motivating premise of empowerment in African American cinema. In this regard, some films implicitly present a muted critique of the problems of racism and sexism in society and hint at the need for social change. Nonetheless, they are incapable of transcending their obsession with what they conceive as true-to-life depictions of African American life to expose the fact that the realism they so carefully construct in their films is itself the result of a social construction. These films take the existing status quo for granted. To escape this empiricism, black cinema calls into question the mechanism that makes dominant social positions possible. It also questions how existing social relations are produced; how it is that these social distinctions are legitimized and reproduced. It also brings to light the conditions under which social relations can be altered. Empowerment in black cinema is at its most creative and insightful when it engages its own symbol-producing mechanisms in a reflexive critique of the social conditions of black life. The problem is that a viable black cinema cannot substantially exist based on dominant film languages, the social definitions, the social positions and relations of the established social order and its cultural manifestations in the Hollywood classical film.

RESISTANCE AS EMPOWERMENT IN BLACK FILMMAKING

As a result, the practice of black cinema can be described as an act of resistance, whose goal is the transformation of the social order. What this means is that a black film refuses dominant social categories and undertakes a reformulation of cinematic languages, so that the film's expressive traditions, formal structure and meanings are filtered through the black experience. We can ask how the practice of black filmmaking reflects the cultural concerns, expressive traditions, peculiar styles and meanings of the black cultural tradition. We find a redefinition of film language within the epistemological terms of reference of the African American experience and the generation of paradigms of signification based on the cultural needs of the African American community. This leads us to inquire how a specific body of films functions as a vehicle of resistance and how these films reformulate cinematic languages to reflect the cultural concerns, expressive traditions, peculiar styles and meanings of the black culture. A focus on black film as a signifying practice provides an illuminating framework for evaluating the film *Menace II Society* and analysis of how political resistance functions in black cinema.

Menace II Society received glowing reviews in the trade press and was acclaimed at Cannes when it opened in 1993. The filmmakers claimed they were presenting the true black reality, which was far more real and truthful than other 'hood' genre movies. When Albert and Allen Hughes, two middle-class siblings from the West coast, inform us that their film reveals the hardcore truth of black life, instead of staking out a new cultural ground for the production of images, they end up playing the cultural politics of traditional cinema. One of the film's major characters, O Dog, is described as representing white society's worst fears: "He's young, black and doesn't give a fuck." *Menace* is a film in which oppressed people celebrate their own oppression. One of its major problems, which is shared by many 'hood' genre films, is that it is too heavily steeped in realist film languages. Consequently, these films carry the ideological baggage and stereotypes of the traditional Hollywood cinema. *Menace* displays little understanding of how politics and ideology pervade social understandings. Although it appears to be articulating a powerful historical moment, it is removed from historical process and seems to possess no intertextual knowledge of the popular cultural stereotypes upon which it draws so heavily. Instead of the filmmakers creating the film, in this case, the tradition of the dominant cinema is the creative force behind the filmmakers, which drives the film. The Hughes brothers remain blind to the fact that film is an important tool in the construction of social reality. Films like *Menace II Society* suggest erroneously that the graphic depiction of the internecine nihilism that pervades a conspicuous section of black urban existence amounts to a deep political statement.

In contrast, seizing the agenda, liberating black voices and creating a space to frame urban black oppression constitute important acts of empowerment. However, these are insufficient because they fall short of providing constructive alternatives and thereby fail to have any significant impact on the system of power or the filmic signification, which often serves to reproduce dominant social relations. Instead of transforming the language of the cinema and reformulating the system of meanings within which social relations are contained, this reactionary filmmak-

ing situates itself within the economics of the popular entertainment industry, aiming to produce marketable images of
rebellious urban black youth who are removed from any serious
rebellion. The X phenomenon is a case in point in so far as the
complex revolutionary life of Malcolm X is reduced to a marketing symbol and packaged for popular consumption on base-
ball caps and T-shirts without the accompanying political
commitment and struggle.

Instead of merely pointing out the conditions for black rebellion and glorifying the visible consequences of social decay, a
progressive black cinema undertakes a critique of social reality
and the transformation of traditional social values and social relations because they help establish positions of power and powerlessness in society. Filmmaking that seeks to empower the black
community questions the way the Hollywood cinema functions
to support the reproduction of traditional social positions in
which black continues to be objectified and defined by the status quo in terms of signifieds of powerlessness. The challenge to
the black film movement in its mission of reformulating traditional social understandings is to proceed behind the facade of
the realism of popular images to expose the way reality is structured and packaged for us through representation and forms of
entertainment.

This is the importance of films such as *Daughters of the Dust*
and *Sweet Sweetback's Baadasss Song*, which exemplify different
but prototypical films of empowerment and transformation in
the African American tradition. In *Sweetback*, Van Peebles rejects
the romanticization of the street lifestyle of the lumpen prole-
tariat for the more important task of politicizing a street blood
and providing linkages with the black protest movement. As a
cinematic document, *Sweetback's* creative uses of film language
immediately set the main character in opposition to the dominant ideologies of traditional cinema. Films that empower the
black community refuse to reproduce Hollywood's cinematic
grammar and syntax. They use the camera not as a simple servant of the film's narrative development, but to reformulate the
question of cinema as a mode of writing. In doing this, they disturb the traditional position of the audience as consumer, forcing a reformulation of the positioning of the viewer in relation
to the film. In contrast, what kind of ideological and political
practices do we find in *Menace II Society*? In what way does this
film develop acts of empowerment and resistance? Does the

viewer encounter the reformulation of new meanings that result from a process of empowerment? Establishment critics describe *Menace II Society* as a profound achievement, a staggering tour de force for a new filmmaker's debut. But the film's orgy of violence serves only to feed voyeurs out for titillation and sexual arousal. Whereas *Sweetback's* violence was explosive, aimed outward at those forces that reproduce the oppressive conditions of the ghetto, the violence in *Menace* is implosive, aimed at destroying the very fabric that has allowed the black community to survive. We know that young bloods in the hood kill each other, that black-on-black crime is a problem and that a meaningless devastation has wasted the black underclass and significant numbers of black males. The visible evidence of these circumstances is all around us. There is no escaping them. In the end, *Menace II Society* is a film that dazzles the eye, but is filled with pessimism. In contrast to films that support the goal of empowerment, it offers no new knowledge of our social condition and sheds very little light on the problems facing urban black youth.

When black film locates itself within the paradigm of the traditional Hollywood cinema and relies too heavily on the language of narrative realism, it inherits particular paradigms of power, social relations and filmic signification that derive from the root signifier of Europatriarchal power in the Western world. It is impossible for a new black cinema to emerge based on the social positions constituted from the dominant system of power. Unless a black cinema challenges these positions through a reformulation of cinematic languages, the historic flood of blackface images and the neo-minstrelsy that is in vogue in contemporary film and television will persist.

In contrast, an important moment for black film is its refusal of the illusion of realism in the cinema, for the illusion of realism reproduces only a limited view of society and its social relations. When a black cinema affirms the illusion, it merely legitimizes the subordinate position of blacks within the social structure and within traditional cinema. *Daughter of the Dust* attacks the illusion of cinema and fosters alternative understandings. In traditional cinema, the viewer is mostly concerned with the narrative action—its causes and their consequences in the progression of the plot. The over-determination of plot dominates the narration and the viewer is encouraged to devote attention to finding answers to unravel the suspense. The narration engages the viewer through its captivating moment-to-moment sequence of plot incidents. But films such as *Sweetback* or *Daughters of the Dust* allow no such luxuries. They forcefully move attention to the uses of cinematic language and other political and ideological questions. In contrast, O Dog—one of the principal characters in *Menace II Society*—brutally kills two Asian shopkeepers, retrieves the video from the store's security camera and makes copies that he circulates among his friends. Some critics are awed by the postmodernist sensibility of this new black cinema. But these kinds of films represent only the uncritical manifestation of an oppressed life.

In *Menace II Society*, we witness the removal of the historical event from history. The circle is closed, and the film offers no escape. We learn of an essential human nature that blacks have always had, which has been passed on through generations and apparently will remain forever. An inventory of the signification of the black male in *Menace II Society* reveals a serious emasculation and very little empowerment: Caine's grandfather is tranquilized by the Bible; his message has no impact whatsoever on the grandson. Caine's father is wasted, having made no impact on his son's life. His alter father-figure, Parnell is imprisoned for life without possibility of parole. Parnell gives Caine the responsibility of being a father-figure to his young son; but Caine introduces the boy to guns and, in the end, shields the boy from death during a driveby shooting. We all know the code of the streets: an eye for an eye. The circle is strengthened. The pessimism mounts and there appears to be no escaping it. Caine (the film's narrator) is killed as he attempts to leave the hood; O Dog survives. His death is a requirement of the gangster genre in the traditional cinema as played out in the nihilism of films such as *Bonnie and Clyde*.

All this points to the need for new black cinema to generate a theory of images and image production. A naive theory of images does not take into account the domination of social intercourse by powerful social classes, but the process of image making in popular culture is intricately related to the system of power in society. The iconic realist image appears to be a neutral articulation of the real world. It claims to be without ideology, to be a simple reproduction of society. Yet, it represses the fact that its pseudorealism mirrors a view of the world in the service of powerful social groups, which functions to reproduce the existing status quo and dominant social relations. A film such as *Menace II Society* demonstrates most vividly the consequences of the oppression visited on the black underclass; but its expressive language is unable to penetrate these problems and produce a new knowledge that is useful to blacks in addressing the severe crisis facing black life in America. In this sense, uncritical "gangsta" films tend to reproduce the worldview of dominant social classes and present their ideologies as a natural way of thinking. Social relations are fixed and not questioned, for it is believed that the essence of things, people and their aspirations do not change. In an Aristotelian maneuver, we are told that film represents reality—as it is, as it was, or as it could be (based on how it is). In this move, there is never a significant questioning of the empiricism of social reality. The knowledge that our world is in itself a transitory sociohistorical phenomenon based on the fixing of social relations, sexual and racial positions and social roles is carefully repressed.

THE PRACTICE OF BLACK CINEMA

The promise of black filmmaking is most fruitful when it challenges the predominant uses and control of the means of cinematic production. Demythification and demystification of institutionalized cinema represent key aesthetic criteria of black independent cinema because the mainstream cinema symbiotically reproduces ideological positions in society. Instead of seeking to emulate the Hollywood tradition, black independent cinema seeks to establish its own ground—its own modes of production and symbolic images. Because cinema is the virtual production and reproduction of aural/visual languages, which are integral to the construction of social ideologies, new black cinema takes into account the transformation of dominant cinematic languages and the construction of its own expressive forms. As a cultural product, black cinema is intricately related to the material and intuitive conditions governing the lives of blacks because the specific articulation of black film cannot be divorced from the larger context of black life. Black cinema is a specific signifying practice emanating from the social relations that proscribe black life.

Because traditional cinema functions to reproduce acceptable, legitimate positions prevalent in society, black cinema is conceived in necessary opposition to these dominant socio-political structures. Black cinema incorporates a historical consciousness through its emphasis on the black experience as a mediating force in the process of cinematic production. The social formation of institutionalized cinema is, itself, a moment of this historical process. It seems that Hollywood is permanent, the essence of film; however, Hollywood is but one instance of cinematic production, one frame of film history, although a very dominant and important one. The Hollywood cinema, itself, is subject to the law of process, the law of change and transformation. If the practice of black cinema is derived from that of Hollywood, then it will help reproduce the unequal relations characteristic of the position of blacks in society and the nature of representation in the cinema.

Instead of conceiving and evaluating black cinema outside of a framework of Hollywood, film theorists and critics too often use the Hollywood tradition and its system of ideological supports as the basis for evaluating black filmmaking. Any black cinematic tradition is viewed in terms of Hollywood. Hence, a popular judgment of many film critics is that black film is a low-grade B-Hollywood product. In essence, the development of a black cinema that refused Hollywood's tight narrative conventions and its editing patterns that produce a limited realism is completely misunderstood. What could possibly be used to forge a black cinema tradition is glossed over as technical and artistic liabilities. In contrast, black cinema is at its most productive when these factors are used, not to make a Hollywood film in black-face, but to build a black cinema tradition.

Because filmmakers and commentators assessed the possibility of black film within Hollywood parameters, there was very little understanding and, furthermore, very little development of a black cinema aesthetic. This has been the historical albatross around the neck of black filmmakers. Early black filmmakers functioned to reveal the limits of Hollywood and were able to identify the systemic ideological operation at work in institutionalized cinema. Yet, at the moment when black film begins to mark off its special ground, that is, its character of difference from Hollywood, critics refuse these possibilities. Although a black cinema, by its mere founding precepts, reveals the ideological boundaries of the dominant cinema, nevertheless, in black film history, many black genre films have remained within the problematic of the institutionalized cinema.

Without significant influence over the cinematic means of production, only partial advances can be made in the development of a new black cinema. Black filmmakers must answer a fundamental question: whether black film will set up its own terms of exchange or become simply another item of exchange in the consumer system? To establish its own ground, the process of black filmmaking is built on a series of activities—economic, political, ideological and signifying practices that speak to its cultural specificity and define its relationship to the black community. Practice refers to "a particular form of productive activity by which the social formation is produced and transformed" (Coward and Ellis, 1977, p. 63).

The history of black independent filmmaking is testimony to the centrality of economic practice to black cinema. Economic practice refers to the functioning of the productive capacity and the series of relations that undergird filmmaking. From the work of early black filmmakers such as Micheaux and the Johnson brothers to Melvin Van Peebles during the 1970s resurgence, Haile Gerima and even Spike Lee in the 1990s, the need to exercise significant economic influence over film production and distribution has been firmly established in black filmmaking. "Political practice produces the 'mutual relations' of social groups, the forms of social organization, and the relations of dominance and subordination between these forms" (Coward and Ellis, 1977, p. 64). In American cinema, political practice refers to the way the existing status quo functions to reproduce institutionalized film, especially the way powerful social groups establish particular modes of power and influence over film activity. Ideological practice produces a framework within which the activity of individuals and groups play out social roles they find acceptable to themselves and to the status quo. In so doing, it also relates to how the cinema as a cultural apparatus works to represent and support the political and economic relations that govern the status quo. Ideological practice in mainstream cinema confers social legitimacy for officially sanctioned forms of knowledge and social organization. It also seeks to ensure the smooth interaction of various participants in the playing out of their social roles. Ideology involves the system of representation that defines our activities and social positions. It conditions definitions of who we are, our relation to the institution of cinema as well as to society. Hence, ideological practice is related to the positions that are scripted for actors in the film (for example, heroes and villains) as well as the relationship between the viewer and the film. Ideology helps to produce social definitions and meanings that justify the dominant system of social relations. Black cinema can help redefine and transform the system of social positions.

So far, black cinema has been described as being constructed on a series of practices that challenge the system of exchange and the social relations it establishes. As a socio-political force, it seeks to transform established paradigms of power and prevalent ways of seeing that characterize the dominant cinema. Signifying practice is a fourth concern of equal importance. We can describe it as the process that reproduces and orients subjectivity to specific legally sanctioned social relations and social positions. Signification is related to the semiological impulse of culture. It is, in turn, derived from the symbolic, which functions as a metaphor for the Unconscious. Julia Kristeva argues that the semiological harbors a revolutionary potential if it confronts the symbolic thesis of meaning and structure. "Politically revolutionary acts must open up politics to the presymbolic, to what came before structure and socialization" (Turkle, 1978, p. 82). Signifying practice describes the process we use to make our films, the sum of cinematic languages, aural and visual languages, languages of color, and languages of imagery. It is through various language systems that existing social relations are represented and reproduced. Consequently, a viable black cinema cannot survive within the shadow of Hollywood reproducing cinema's dominant signifying paradigms.

SIGNIFYING PRACTICE OF BLACK CINEMA

Although theories of signification feature prominently in contemporary film aesthetics, like much of Western thought these developments have proceeded with scant attention to the existence of the black experience. However, in a groundbreaking study of African American aesthetics, Gates reminds us that signification has been a term in the black vernacular tradition that is approximately two centuries old. It is a theory of reading one finds in the black cultural tradition. Within the black tradition, tales of the "Signifying Monkey" had a wide currency among the slaves. Since the 19th century, folklorists have recorded these tales, and in the 20th century many black musicians have recorded songs called "Signifying Monkey" or simply "Signifying." In the black cultural tradition, signifying is "a rhetorical act that is not engaged in the game of information giving. Signifying turns on the play and chain of signifiers, and not on some supposedly transcendent signified . . . As anthropologists demonstrate, the Signifying Monkey is often called the Signifier, he who wreaks havoc upon the Signified" (Gates, 1989, pp. 236-238). Although the term 'signifying' shares some use with its Standard English

meaning, its use in black discourse can be traced in African
rhetoric and it incorporates meanings that go beyond interpretations identified in dictionary entries for words. In black usage,
signifying "generally means intending or implying more than
one actually says" (Kochman, 1981, p. 99). The concept of signifying in the black tradition has a precursor in the trickster figure from Yoruba mythology, Esu-Elegbara in Nigeria and Legba
among the Fon in Dahomey, who also exists in New World fig-
urations in Brazil, Cuba, Haiti and in the United States. The figure of the Signifying Monkey "speaks eloquently of the unbroken
arc of metaphysical presupposition and patterns of figuration
shared through space and time among black cultures in West
Africa, South America, the Caribbean, and in the United States."
In all these versions, Esu is a messenger of the gods: "he who
interprets the will of god to people, he who carries the desires
of people to the gods. Esu is the guardian of the crossroads, master of style and the stylus, phallic god of generation and fecun-
dity, master of the mystical barrier that separates the divine from
the profane worlds. He is known as the divine linguist, the keeper of ase (logos) with which Olodumare created the universe."
Gates argues that this moment can stand as the metaphor for a
critical tradition in black cultural expression, equivalent to the
Western figure of Hermes on which hermeneutics—the study
and process of interpretation—is based (Gates, 1989, p. 237).

Because we are concerned with black cinema as a signifying
practice, Gates' formulation helps to lay the foundation of how
signification works in the black tradition. But we also need to
seek out strategies for studying signification in the cinema.
Semiotics—the study of cultural phenomena as signs—provides
a useful tool for studying signification in the cinema. It is based
on the assumption that the things human beings do, make, say,
and surround themselves with signify—or they mean something.
Semiotics is concerned not so much with what things mean, but
how they mean. In other words, it is the study of how meanings
come about and are constructed in society. This is why semiotics
is spoken of as the study of cultural processes. What is of particular importance to us is that signs function very much like language systems. Furthermore, a primary understanding of
linguistic systems is that their only reality is in their realizations,
that is, in their particular use; and that the meaning of the sign
is only possible in its realization or its particular use. For example, Robert Townsend's *Hollywood Shuffle* (1987) uses the low-

comic image of blacks as a critique of Hollywood film and not as a celebration or uncritical representation of its use.

Semiotics is important to the study of black cinema as a signifying practice because it helps account for the text and its signification. It is precisely in the focus on the productivity of the sign that semiotics proves valuable for witnessing signification in emerging forms of cinema, such as black independent film, and for opening up mechanisms for understanding forms of cinema that utilize signifying practices that differ from the mainstream Hollywood cinema. The premise that all signs and languages are cultural phenomena informs us that a black independent cinema is at its most creative when it engages the symbol-producing mechanisms prevalent within the African American tradition. The problem is that a viable independent cinema cannot substantially exist based on the social definitions, positions and relations of the traditional cinema. Semiotics exposes the knowledge that signification is a social construct and cinematic languages are forms of signification. Herein lies the significance of the semiological analysis; for we are not so much concerned with the empirical nature of the film image, but with delineating how it is that the image means and the circumstances within which meanings arise. Semiological analysis shifts our attention from an obsession with subject matter and the iconicity of images of blacks to expose how blackness is produced in the cinema as the product of a chain of signifiers, and not as a simple reflection of social reality. This is especially important for independent cinema because it keeps our focus on how film language is produced, thereby allowing the possibility for new and insurgent approaches to cinema to emerge.

What we learn from semiotics is that because signs are cultural phenomena, the criteria for understanding the signs within a particular culture are properly located within that culture. Different cultures use different rules for sign-producing activities. This is why it is in error to rely too heavily on the conventions and criteria of the Hollywood cinema to evaluate black independent film. A proper understanding of black independent film needs to take into account the cultural context of African American history and culture, its signifying processes and its idiosyncratic strategies of narrative construction. This cultural context helps to ground critical activity by focusing on the material conditions of a culture especially as they provide formal parameters for the production of meaning. Umberto Eco argues that

"The laws of signification are the laws of culture" (1976, p. 28). In their book *Film Art: An Introduction,* David Bordwell and Kristin Thompson further clarify the importance of culture to artistic production when they write that, "In the arts, . . . there are no absolute principles of form which all artists must follow. Art works are products of culture. Thus, many of the principles of artistic form are matters of convention" (1993, p. 55).

Semiotics allows us to question the institutionalization of the Classical Hollywood cinema as the yardstick against which all other films are evaluated. We are privy to the knowledge that these aesthetic standards are by no means universal, the best to which all other cultures must aspire. The problem with the classical film narrative is that it utilizes only a limited range of signification, which in turn reinforces and helps reproduce existing social, political and economic relations of the dominant society. Semiotics opens up the plurality of the signifier-signified relationship. It provides favorable ground for understanding the black experience because its methods better allow us to explore filmic expression in terms of symbolic representation and transformation. Film transforms actors into characters and other items from the real world into images. Undoubtedly, a hermeneutic process is involved. A semiological framework provides a good point of entry for examining the process of transformation and resistance in cultural practices. The knowledge that film is transformational is dangerous to the maintenance of social order and social stability. Semiological analysis bears witness to the functioning of artistic codes of production and performance, that is, it exposes the means whereby transformation is achieved. Using semiotics, we can view black film as a text (in its own terms), in its context (in relation to social and historical forces), and in intertextual terms (how it relates to the African American tradition or to Hollywood cinema). Importantly, this approach is capable of establishing how the cinema functions as a player in social negotiation, and we can glean intimate knowledge through the somatic exploration of deeply embedded forms that inform intellectual, psychological and affective states.

Semiotics is relevant to black film criticism because it addresses the aesthetic dimensions of a film without restricting analysis to a reactionary aestheticism. Hence, black film can be viewed as a signifying practice, a textual discourse that calls into question contextual issues involving the social, cultural and political significance of film. The semiological approach informs us that to talk productively about an object, we need to establish its intrinsic characteristics. To determine the distinctive forms and textures of a film, it is necessary to have a clear idea of its textual elements. It is important for the critic to listen to the work and let it be. To do justice to black art, the best criticism utilizes a definition of the artistic as determined by the black cultural tradition. The search for a tradition is not to suggest that black art can be evaluated using pre-established ideas of what it should be. In African American cultural expression, tradition is always in motion. It is a dynamic process, which is constantly being reworked and redefined through a cultural mechanism that encourages exploration and change. Semiotics is, therefore, very valuable to studying the African American cultural tradition because it is inherently concerned with examining signs-in-process, and it is capable of recognizing new or emerging creative forms precisely because of its focus on the ever-shifting relationship between signifier and signifieds. When film art is viewed as a semiological discipline, we gain access to powerful conceptual and methodological resources that are custom-made for studying artistic texts in relationship to their cultures.

In our paradigm, black film is located within the black experience and the black cultural tradition. The tradition conditions the decisions we make about what we eat, the clothes we wear, the way we dance, the way we walk, the way we talk, and the artistic expressions we create. Whether we wish to acknowledge that there is a cultural milieu surrounding important aspects of the lives of all African Americans is beside the point. An examination of cultural manifestations such as religion or music, for example, reveals the existence of a sociocultural and historical experience that in critical ways impacts on the lives of blacks. This tradition encompasses the individual but may be described as having an existence independent of any one person, because it functions very much like a language. We don't create it, but we are born into it and live it. We use it to negotiate our day-to-day living. Some blacks can deny the relevance of the African American cultural experience to their lives, but their denial does not erase historical fact.

In defining black film, Diawara focuses on the mediation of cultural criteria drawn from the African American experience. He describes a black film as " . . . any black-produced film outside the constraints of the major studios. The filmmakers' independence from Hollywood enables them to put on the screen black lives and concerns that derive from the complexity of black communities. Independent films provide alternative ways of knowing black people that differ from the fixed stereotypes of blacks in Hollywood" (1993, p. 7). Diawara's emphasis on films that provide alternative ways of knowing is most perceptive. To focus on the way that filmic signification produces knowledge derived from the complexity of black culture is to locate one's definitional criteria precisely in the formal mechanisms of the culture. He demonstrates how an initial focus on formal criteria can be broadened to address important political concerns.

> Black independent cinema, like most independent film practices, approaches film as a research tool. The filmmakers investigate the possibilities of representing alternative black images on the screen; bringing to the foreground issues central to black communities in America; criticizing sexism and homophobia in the black community; and deploying Afrafemcentric discourses that empower black women. The narratives of such films are not always linear; the characters represent a tapestry of voices from W.E.B. DuBois, Frantz Fanon, Toni Morrison, Malcolm-X, Martin Luther King, Jr., Karl Marx, Angela Davis, Alice Walker, and Zora Neale Hurston. (1993, p. 5)

Using a semiological framework, a definition of black film would be cinema whose signifying practices are derived from a black cultural tradition and whose mechanisms for image production use these traditions as a means through which artistic languages are mediated and expressed. The film is conceived as having its own organizing laws and rules, that is—its own system. At this point, we are concerned simply with making descriptive statements, and not evaluative judgments about whether a particular film is a good black film or not. The important consideration is that a black film must develop out of a black sociocultural experience, which is not only formal but also substantial. By specifying formal as well as substantial criteria, we can address the reservations of those critics who demand that blacks have significant control over black film. In the final analysis, black film represents a different point of view, a different way of seeing American society, and this point of view is produced through the signifying practices of the black experience, which cannot be isolated from other pressing issues of black existence.

A good black film helps us to see society and historical events through fresh eyes, and good black film criticism can help make black film more accessible and meaningful to viewers. The assumption here is that the film is primary because without the film, there is little to discuss. The activity of defining black cinema is but one step in a larger process. Definitions help clarify basic concepts. They are formulated simply to clarify methodological and conceptual issues and not to establish the essential characteristics of a 'true' black cinema. Ultimately, definitions are inadequate and fall short of determining or dictating the criteria of black film. Only the films themselves can determine what is black cinema.

However, there is no urgency for black film theorists to definitively settle the issue of what constitutes a black film. If we seek an exhaustive definition that establishes a set of criteria, then frustration sets in when attempting to account for films as diverse as *Just Another Girl on the IRT* (1992), *Sankofa* (1993), and *She's Gotta Have It* (1985). The philosopher Wittgenstein's discussion of theory (1953) provides a useful insight to solving the problem of defining black film. He posed the question: what is a game? A common answer would posit a set of exhaustive features common to all games. Wittgenstein suggested that what is important in a theory of games is not all the things that various games have in common, but the ways in which they are alike, that is, the similarities and relationships between them. In defining black art, all that is required is a working definition that gives us enough information to recognize new examples. The purpose of a definition is not to establish universal criteria for black film. In contrast, it seeks to address "the solution of certain problems arising out of the situation in which artists find themselves here and now" (Collingwood, 1938, p. vi). Black film is a dynamic concept. It is characterized by a dialectic of change as new works and critical strategies emerge and extend established boundaries. This insight opens up productive ground for black film theory. For example, developments in black feminist aesthetics in the work of writers such as Toni Morrison, Margaret Walker and Alice Walker permit critics to embrace Dash's *Daughters of the Dust* as an important groundbreaking film in the African American expressive tradition. Without this contribution, the avant-garde cinematic techniques used in *Daughters* would have been read as simply an art film about black life.

Chapter Four
Narration as a Cultural Process in Black Film

There are many different perspectives from which we can study the movies. As an industry, we examine the cinema through its modes of production and organization. As a business, we analyse its financial structure and the management of creative resources. As a social institution, we consider its impact on socialization and its influences on culture. As history, we investigate the development of film as a medium and its relationship to social, political and economic events. As technology, we focus on the tools and techniques of the cinematic medium. We also invest personal meaning in films. Experts often discuss this aspect of the movies in terms of theories of audience reception, that is, how viewers respond to particular films. They may also focus on uses and gratifications in relation to audience members. To many people, the cinema has a powerful entertainment function. It may be used for leisure, relaxation or amusement. Some even claim to derive therapeutic benefits from movie going. The question is not to isolate any one of these dimensions of the cinematic experience because the multiple modes of knowing film are related and symbiotically feed off each other. To be dogmatic about the superiority of any one method is futile because "every kind of knowing is in process, not only because of its historicity but also because of the inexhaustibility of its object...." (Dufrenne, 1987, p. 11). The cinema is truly multi-dimensional. While these various perspectives emphasize different objectives and often use distinct approaches, their aggregate impact gives us a fuller understanding of the cinema's broad cultural influences. However, there is one seminal discipline that plays a primary role in the filmmaking process. At its most basic level, filmmaking is the art of narration. Narration in film is what makes possible all the other perspectives that we use to discuss the movies. The art of narration constitutes the fabric and texture of filmmaking. In black culture, the act of narration manifested in the oral tradition is an integral part of everyday activities. It is simultaneously ritual, ceremony, communication and celebration. It finds its greatest triumphs in its participatory, social and communal aspects, and it is evident in day-to-day pursuits from mundane modes of communication to forms of religious activity.

THE FUNCTIONING OF CULTURE IN NARRATION

Stories play a key role in our lives. We use them for entertainment, to transmit important cultural information, to teach moral lessons and to provide a frame of reference for communicating new ideas. As a fundamental mode of artistic and social expression, narrative helps define a group's existence and reveals vital clues about its world-view. It tells about the kinds of knowledge a society foregrounds and what it marginalizes. As a cultural process, narrative helps group members construct existential meaning of the mythic structures that govern their existence. Bordwell and Thompson (1997) argue that narrative is a fundamental way through which humans make sense of the world. In childhood, we learn fairy tales and myths and we are lulled to sleep by bedtime stories. As adults, we read short stories, novels, history, and biography. Even religion, philosophy, and science present their doctrines through stories. The Bible, the Torah and the Koran are key collections of narratives. Our art and cultural forms—plays, films, TV shows, comic books, paintings, and even dance—are often structured around stories. In our leisure time, our conversations are mostly based on stories. News reports are called stories. When we go to sleep, we often experience our dreams as little narratives. sometimes. . .

Narration is a cultural system that elaborates basic social values and provides social legitimacy for a culture's beliefs and world-view. At its most primary level, narration is a form of communication intricately related to a culture's mythic consciousness. It is part of the basic human need for self-expression and creativity, and it is integral to the poetic impulse represented in a culture's founding myths. Stories of origin seek to explain who we are, where we come from and our purpose in life. In the Bible, God created the earth and then there was the word. We con-

[handwritten: narration as a of articulation of symbol.]

struct narratives that make meaning out of our lives and create
signifying processes that reveal the deep structures of our experience. Narration is a type of discourse through which people
create a symbolic world. It is through the basic symbol system
of a culture that a society's knowledge of law, history, art, philosophy and politics are articulated.

To study film narration is to emphasize how film stories are
told, paying close attention to questions of technique, form and
structure. Stories fundamentally involve creativity, image making, and symbol construction, which are forms of signification
that distinguish culture from the natural world and from each
other. We create symbolic structures—mythic religious, artistic—to help us understand and articulate our experiences in the
attempt to find meaning in our lives. Symbolic activity plays a
key role in the construction of our world through its impact on
the making of images and storytelling. Aesthetic sensibility is
inextricably interwoven with the art of narration because art is
the product of a creative process involving the use of sensory
perception and expression. The art of narration serves as an
excellent point of entry to the study of film. It offers a useful vantage point for observing the values of a culture because in the
creation of symbolic structures, people articulate fundamental
epistemological and ontological concepts of their experiences.
Through the study of film narration, we can evaluate the special
ways in which the black experience uses the cinema as a means
for expressing its values.

We can observe the values of a culture through the artistic
and creative work its people produce, through the forms a people use to record and preserve their response to historical, social,
physical and psychological circumstances. In so far as narrative
is an expression of a specific culture, it represents the semantic
structure people use to construct judgments and articulate their
experiences. When we foreground the narrativity of an art work,
we are better able to observe its expressive forms and the way
these function to reproduce the sense of an imaginary, which is
so critical to our notion of self. The imaginary is not so much
our imagination; rather it is defined as the representations, points
of view, cultural assumptions and basic values people use to develop their identity and to negotiate their day-to-day living.

Narration offers a useful point of entry to the study of signification in the cinema. We can study black film narration
through a focus on subject matter, or in terms of how a particu-

lar film represents the black experience. This strategy focuses on
whether the representation presents an accurate picture of black
life and whether it presents stereotyped depictions. It pays little
attention to the important activity of image production. Popular
images function as a primary vehicle for the propagation of dominant ideologies, and images, imaging and image making are all
related to the political-economic bases of power. When our focus
is on the empiricism of the image, we may overlook significant
questions regarding its production. In addition to examining narration as a discourse in which images and stories are produced,
the semiological project is especially equipped to study narration as a process. Bordwell refers to this view of narration as "the
activity of selecting, arranging, and rendering story material in
order to achieve specific time-bound effects on a perceiver"
(1985, p. xi).

In studying black film narration, it is important to examine
the process of narrative in the larger framework of black cultural expression. Black film narration is a cultural process that is
based on the priorities and epistemological categories of the
black experience. The analysis of black film narration focuses
specifically on how the African American tradition informs the
use of space and time in storytelling and how this shapes narration. In focusing on the process of narration, less attention is
given to subject matter as the dominant element in storytelling
and more is given to how the formal structures of the black experience inform subject matter and how modes of storytelling function in relation to the black expressive tradition. In so doing, we
view subject matter in a more productive light because special
attention is paid to how the black cultural tradition shapes the
process of narrativization and storytelling practices.

The strategy of focusing on narration as a cultural process
offers an alternative to the preoccupation in black film criticism
with issues of representation and image studies, and it excavates
new ground for black film aesthetics. It moves beyond the predominant view in criticism of black film that the cinema merely reproduces or represents reality rather than being involved in
the construction of it. By focusing on narrative as cultural
process, we can observe how categories of knowledge are established and constantly reproduced in social discourse. We can also
reflect on the forms of knowledge that we foreground and those
things we deem unimportant and commit to the background.
We get to examine how narrative functions in the social con-

CULTURE, EXPERIENCE, NARRATION

struction of reality. Using narration as a point of entry to the study of black film strengthens black film criticism, especially through its explicit attention to issues of form and the process of narration in the black expressive tradition. The process of narration refers to the special way that the African American tradition utilizes its own vernacular space and time for storytelling.

Different cultures use approaches to narration that are derived from their own historical experiences. Let us use the example of bread—as a cultural product shared by many groups—to examine these issues that arise in relation to the specific uses of narration in the black cultural tradition. We are foremost concerned with the way cultural mechanisms shape raw material to produce an artifact or an experience that has meaning for a group. The raw materials of bread include ingredients such as flour, water, edible oil, salt, sugar, etc. The content has to do with the particular definitions and meanings people in a particular culture give to bread. The formal elements are derived from the culture's definition of bread, the structures that govern its production and use as well as the specific vernacular practices of bread making. The technical elements would comprise the tools and techniques (baking pans, ovens or other heat-producing devices) used in the processing (baking, cooking, frying) of the bread.

Although the basic ingredients can reveal a lot about bread as a cultural product, nonetheless a proper understanding of the basic ingredients needs to be considered within the context of how they are utilized specifically in various local bread making practices around the world. In most cultures, the raw materials tend to be very similar. Generally, grain is ground into a powder. Occasionally, flavors such as potato, pumpkin, carrots or banana are added according to local cultural requirements. Some people use yeast to improve the texture of the bread; while others may use baking power. These may be added to the raw materials. However, processing is the most critical step in bread making. Processing is the transformation of the raw materials using the culture's specific formal values to make a cultural product. Particular forms of mixing, kneading, settling, shaping in addition to frying, baking or cooking are used to produce a unique bread product in different cultural settings.

The end product varies according to its cultural setting. The French baguette is long and crusty. Some bread is dome-shaped. In Mexico, the end product is a wafer-thin tortilla. Middle

Easterners and North Africans may favor the flat, pocket bread called pita. In India, there is naan. Jamaicans prefer a hard-dough bread or a small flattened cocobread. Lefse is a variety known among Scandinavians as potato bread and Norwegians as wrapping bread. West Africans eat a corn-based product they call moi-moi. In parts of the Southern Caribbean, the dough may be fried into small round balls for use as a breakfast food. "Brioche, biscuit, corn pone, scones—the very names conjure up cultures that produced breads as characteristics of their makers" (Rombauer *et al*, 1973, p. 553). Many North American consumers prefer sliced white bread made of bleached flour. In recent years, there has been a proliferation of flat breads and wrappers in American supermarkets. Although the raw materials are very similar or may even be the same in different cultures, the final product takes on a local vernacular form. In this instance, we can witness the way that the formal practices of a culture transform raw materials using indigenous traditions and cultural preferences to produce a unique cultural product.

The analysis of bread as a cultural product helps clarify significant issues relating to black cinema. The raw materials and technical elements of the bread making process tend not to vary too widely; and interest in these may provoke intense discussions among scientists, nutritionists and anthropologists. Similarly, whereas advanced technical issues may be of interest to film experts, a wider group of people encounters the film more through the functioning of formal and content elements. The functioning of technical elements to shape raw material and the corresponding influence of raw material on how technical elements are used play a key role in structuring basic perceptual processes. The functioning of form and content are also interrelated because the one cannot exist without the other. This underscores the importance of having a clear idea of the use of raw materials, technical elements as well as formal and content issues in film analysis.

"A film is not simply a random batch of elements. Like all artworks, a film has form. By film form, in its broadest sense, we mean the overall system of relations that we can perceive among the elements in the whole film" (Bordwell and Thompson, 1997, p. 66). We can use *Daughters of the Dust* to better illustrate how these elements function in black film. The narrative focuses on an event—the Peazant family's decision to move from the Sea Islands off South Carolina to the North. The film's style is the product of the specific use of cinematic elements, such as mise-en-scene, camera framing and movement, editing and sound. Form has to do with "the system of patterned relationships" the viewer encounters in the film. "Artistic form may cue us to make expectations and then gratify them, either quickly or eventually. Or form may work to disturb our expectations. We often associate art with peace and serenity, but many artworks offer us conflict, tension, and shock. An artwork's form may even strike us as unpleasant because of its imbalances or contradictions" (Bordwell and Thompson, 1997, p. 70). The formal elements in *Daughters of the Dust* involve the narrative's loose plot structure, which is related to a black woman's aesthetic sensibility as opposed to a male-driven paradigm that emphasizes competition in which there is a winner and a loser. They include improvisational techniques based in the black cultural tradition, which are more concerned with the spatial and existential articulation of narrative elements in contrast to the linear temporality that propels Aristotelian-based forms of narrative. In addition, the narration is also shaped formally by the use of multiple points of view representing a variety of black women's voices. Form is a set of principles within a cultural setting that provide structure for the viewer's encounter with the artwork and in the production of meaning. When first released, the predominantly white-trade press found little value in Forest Whittaker's film adaptation of Terry McMillan's novel *Waiting to Exhale* (1995). In contrast, the film found significant support in the black community. This apparent difference in how diverse audiences value films informs us that artistic form and content are interrelated, and are generated within a particular cultural framework, which conditions and provides cues for the film viewer. The varying responses of the predominantly white trade press and black female audiences to *Waiting to Exhale* inform us that cultural background plays a key role in the production of meaning. "Our activity cannot be in the artwork itself. A poem is only words on paper; a song, just acoustic vibrations; a film, merely patterns of light and dark on a screen. Objects do nothing. Evidently, then, the artwork and the person experiencing it depend on one another" (Bordwell and Thompson, 1997, p. 66).

SIGNIFICATION IN BLACK FILM NARRATION

In studying black film signification, a focus on narration lends itself to a critical analysis that can speak to aesthetic concerns and textual criticism without removing the film from its grounding in the black experience. The focus on narrative is able to satisfy those critics who demand textual specificity and accountability in criticism. At the same time, the study of black film signification is able to address the concerns of those critics who foreground contextual issues in black film criticism. In semiological criticism, a film is considered a text, that is, it is a network of meanings and a site through which signifying forms are articulated. Semiotics informs us that analysis of textual systems involve questions of meaning, which are properly studied through a hermeneutic process or a system of interpretation. In emphasizing narration as a point of entry to the study of signification in black film, we can observe the special ways filmmakers use cinematic images and construct their films using the black experience as a mediating language.

The aesthetic is central to the process of narration because it plays a key role in artistic production and receptivity. A focus on the aesthetic in black film narration foregrounds those forms that occupy a special place in the black cultural tradition and pinpoints expressive values important in black expression. Studying the aesthetic sources of the black experience leads directly to the folk roots of the black cultural tradition; the influence of orality and performative elements associated with improvisation in black cultural expression; as well as an ethos of style and expressiveness that permeates black life. When black film is linked to these intertextual sources, we have better tools for exploring the richness and depth of films as diverse as Burnett's *Killer of Sheep*, Dash's *Daughters of the Dust* and Gerima's *Sankofa*.

Narration in black film is best examined against the historical background of the black cultural tradition, which produces a system of aesthetic values that are articulated in its expressive forms. The history of black aesthetic thought and ideas provides a context for black film studies. When we view film narration from the perspective of art or as poetic language, we are better positioned to study signification in black cinema. Because issues of signification always require appropriate interpretative methods, semiotics provides powerful conceptual and methodological tools for examining black film as a signifying practice. By locating black film criticism within the project of semiotics, we can savor the richness of the film as text. We can also account for its intertextual and contextual relationships. "In reinserting the signifying process into the social process as a whole, critical

invented culture

practice allows the reader to see not just the way in which a . . . text is 'made' but also the manner in which culture, as well, is produced and invented—rather than being 'natural,' absolute, or eternal" (Hogue, 1986, p. 36).

A viable black independent cinema cannot substantially exist based on the structures of signification articulated in the narratives of the dominant cinema because black film reflects a series of social definitions and relations that are contextualized and legitimized in the black cultural tradition. Film is revealed to be the product of a particular culture and chain of signification. The focus on signification is not so much concerned with images of blacks in film (as in a content analysis or a journalistic report), but with how these images as signs are endowed with meaning and the historical circumstances that provide a context for the construction of meaning. We are most interested in the discursive activity of the cinema and the activity of producing meanings in the black cultural tradition. Narration offers a unique vantage point from which we can examine the symbolic forms and unique perspectives of the black experience expressed in black film. By using narration as a point of entry to the study of black film, we are focusing on the black experience as a phenomenon in and of itself, and specifically, the unique philosophical perspectives of the African American experience as expressed in film.

By examining black film narration, we are compelled to pose several questions that address the specific practice of black cultural production, for example: In what unique ways do filmmakers in the black tradition use the raw material of film? In what special ways do these films provide a structure for producing meaning? Does the black experience provide organizational cues to the filmmaker? Are there expressive and stylistic elements unique to the black cultural tradition that filmmakers use?

VERNACULAR INFLUENCES ON BLACK FILM NARRATION

The black cultural tradition functions like 'langue' (the larger language system) to provide a broad structuring and mediating influence for particular expressive forms. The formal constraints and aesthetic sensibilities of the African American tradition help define what is an important story and mediate the way these stories are told. It is not that subject matter is irrelevant and unim-

portant. Rather in this instance what is most crucial is how subject matter is rendered cinematically and expressed according to
the filmic possibilities of the medium as it is understood through
the African American experience, and not so much according to
the conventions of the dominant cinema. The over-determination of subject matter can lead us away from a richer understanding of the unique expressive forms of the African American
experience and the development of black independent culture.
In his work on black genre film, Cripps explains how issues of
style and signification reflect an inner black world that was inac-
cessible to Hollywood filmmakers: "A look at any early black film
reveals a self-evident segregation from white life. A closer look
reveals, whether in a roughly shot Micheaux film or the polished
Scar of Shame, flat and grey interiors lacking visual reference to
a world outside the tiny sets, internalized, looking at themselves,
without the need of a peephole into the white world" (1978, p.
153). He argues that a black point of view was reflected stylistically in the 'race movies' through signification that proclaimed
"this movie is about us." Cumulatively, we can trace this sense
of an interior black world throughout the history of black film.
Cripps writes, "In this sense neither MGM nor Gordon Parks
made *Shaft;* he emerged from a sub-culture whose parents had
seen or heard of Ralph Cooper in *Dark Manhattan*. In so far as
art draws its life blood from a dynamic relationship with its cultural context, it reflects the vernacular energy and mythic consciousness of its culture" (1978, p. 154).

Black folk culture provides the matrix from which African
American vernacular expression springs. It has had an immense
influence on the development of contemporary black art and on
how black artists approach questions of form and style in their
work. "In addition to the continuities of African culture in black
America and the Euro-American concepts and values as they are
manifested in art and artifacts, black Americans possess the culture of our slave heritage. It is a survival culture in which our
responses are conditioned by oppression, repression, coercion
and alienation" (Fowler, 1981, p. xiv). Any discussion of African
American aesthetics needs to acknowledge the rich reservoir of
source material that informs the culture's folk sources.

Black folk culture was seminally influenced by the encounter
of Africans with the system of plantation slavery, and its quintessential expression, found in the blues form, functions as a key
aesthetic value in African American cultural expression. The

blues form emphasizes the activity of the signifier and it involves the exploration of how form shapes narrative. It is not to be confused with a popular signified that defines the blues as a song of despair. In its fullness, the blues form reflects the resilience of the black experience. It is a lament as well as a celebration.

> ... The most astonishing aspect of the blues is that, though replete with a sense of defeat and down-heartedness, they are not intrinsically pessimistic; their burden of woe and melancholy is dialectically redeemed through sheer force of sensuality, into an almost exultant affirmation of life, of love, of sex, of movement, of hope. No matter how repressive was the American environment, the Negro never lost faith in or doubted his deeply endemic capacity to live. (Wright 1963, p. 9)

Houston Baker (1984) explains that the blues is a synthesizing form. It combines eclectic elements including work songs, group seculars, field hollers, sacred harmonies, proverbial wisdom, folk philosophy, political commentary, ribald humor, elegiac lament, and much more. He emphasizes a notion of the blues as process in so far as it reveals a sense of motion in the black experience that he describes as always becoming, shaping, transforming, and displacing the peculiar experiences of Africans in the New World. The blues as incorporated in African American cultural expression reflects the way particular art forms are organized using key elements of the black experience.

The blues form functions as a key aesthetic value in African American cultural expression and it reflects the way particular art forms are organized using key elements of the black experience. The blues form is intricately linked to black women's cultural expression. It is not surprising that women—such as Ma Rainey, Big Mama Thornton and Bessie Smith—played central roles in forging blues as an expressive form and helping Americans find meaning in the emerging urban industrial landscape in the early years of the 20th century. Similar to black women's cultural expression, the blues form has retained its character and potency as a key signifier of the African American experience because it developed outside the constraints of dominant cultural expression. It did not have to conform to this or that stylistic convention or the imposing mores of the middle classes. In a man's world, women's activities and cultural expression

were not considered that important beyond their reproductive
and family nurturing roles. As a result, these forms had to be
resilient for their continued survival. In its urge to survive, the
blues is about celebration; it is about accepting oneself, one's culture and the dialectical ebb and flow of life. Black women's cultural expression mirrors the blues in the way it celebrates core
cultural elements hand-in-hand with resistance and social protest
within the formal concerns of the artwork. Protest and testimony are neither appendages, nor an afterthought. They constitute
an integral part of black women's cultural expression in 20th century America. Writers such as Margaret Walker, Alice Walker
and Toni Morrison, who have shifted from a direct reportorial
style to a more syncretic form of expression that incorporates
myth, fantasy and folklore, utilize the blues form. It confirms
Morrison's argument that realism does not insure authenticity
in black art (McDowell, 1987, p. 23).

The focus on the blues form as a signifier allows artists to
celebrate African American roots while simultaneously engen-
dering a sense of empowerment through their art. It reveals the
strong mediating influence of the oral tradition and illustrates
the use of creative strategies germane to the blues. John Michael
Vlach maintains that, "If the blues can be understood as a cultural endowment, . . . a way of thinking about the world, then it
is more than a source or a stimulus for an art form. The blues
provides the rules for creating art in several modes beyond song
as well" (1989, p. 67). The spirituals and the blues emanate from
African American folk experience and function as key signifiers
of the black experience. Gates (1989) finds that the spirituals play
a central role in black poetic language, and Baker (1984) argues
that the blues functions not merely as formal inscription, but
exists as a forceful condition of Afro-American cultural signifying itself.

Essentially, these fundamental forms of black folk culture
invoke vast dimensions of experience, interconnecting and
informing other codes of the African American experience. The
recognition of black folk sources as a key element in African
American cultural expression directs our attention to how the
vernacular as a mode of expression functions in contemporary
black arts and culture. The material conditions that marked black
life in plantation society and the subsequent development of
African American expressive forms helped spawn a unique and
dynamic aesthetic sensibility. This aesthetic fashioned from

African influences and their adaptation to the social and economic conditions of the New World has produced creative
strategies that continue to permeate black cultural expression.
These creative strategies are autobiographical in that they speak
directly and personally as vernacular expression in African
American arts. Important writers such as W. E. B. DuBois (1903),
Alain Locke (1936) and Arna Bontemps (1966) were aware of the
richness of black folk expression and the potential it held for the
development of new expressive forms and new technical traditions. Undoubtedly, great art usually draws on the folk sources
of its culture and incorporates contemporary vocabularies to
produce new insights. Fowler confirms the importance of folk
culture to 20th century black artistic expression. She points out
that the black aesthetic of the Harlem Renaissance "looked for
the echo of folk culture, for the use of a folk ethos and folk forms
as the raw materials of art, for the reinterpretation of the community's myths . . . " (1981, p. ix).

   Good black film contains expert and intimate knowledge of
the black experience, which precisely describes the terms of the
vernacular. The vernacular exists as a mode of communication
that is more directly, more intimately linked to sensuous perception. In black music, the vernacular is more dynamic, more
in touch with black life. In literature, we also find the exciting
exploration of African American expressive forms. There is a
somatic aspect to these forms of black art in that they elaborate
deeply embedded structures that inform intellectual, psychological and affective states of the black experience. The cognitive structures found in African American religion also contribute
to a sense of self and help define ontological relationships for
black Americans. Mechanisms of redemption, psychic release
and a culture heavily influenced by oral communication operate
to condition expressive forms, which manifest themselves in performative utterances. As a result, black expressive forms such as
oratory, music and dance display peculiar structures of feeling,
a particular vernacular expression that should prove useful to
understanding black film. Unlike music, dance and literature in
which the peculiar imprint of the black experience is most evident, the development of black cinema has been hindered by the
uneven development of its own vernacular language. However
Bill Greaves' 1967 film, *The First World Festival of Negro Arts* represents a critical milestone in its successful exploration and use
of African Diasporic vernacular forms as the basis for con-

structing its narration. Because the cinema is a relatively recent
art form, a vernacular style is not highly developed in black film.
African American filmmakers have tended to stay within the
expressive parameters of the dominant cinema, and critics have
been unable to account for the difference in their films. As a
result, criticism of black cinema has, for the most part, remained
within the linguistic parameters of the classical Hollywood cinema to the disservice of black independent film.

THE AUDIENCE IN BLACK CULTURAL EXPRESSION

When we universalize art works, we rob them of their specificity and their social, cultural and historical relations because art is
a specific symbolic act that occurs within a particular cultural
context. Black film narration is best characterized as a dialogue,
a symphony involving visions and viewers. So as not to devalue
black cinema, we need to present appropriate hermeneutic models that allow viewers to see film as part of the problematic of the
black experience, in which we relate art to the cultural roots of
the tradition. Although the nature of film does not lend itself to
the direct affective relationship that exists between artist and
audience in black musical forms, nonetheless, it would be an
error not to explore how these elements of the tradition impact
on black film. It is impossible to analyse black cultural expression without reference to its social, historical context, its sense
of community, modes of address, Afrocentric aesthetics stances
and the special values the tradition foregrounds.

Because black filmmakers operate out of a unique aesthetic
and sociocultural tradition, we can surmise that any criticism of
black film must acknowledge how that tradition permeates the
text. There are several important implications for black film criticism. In addition to the play of signification in black expressive
forms, we also encounter a particular formulation of the role of
the audience in the black cultural tradition. Several forms of black
expression provide intertextual reference points useful for understanding the activity of the viewer in black film. By taking into
account forms of black cultural expression—such as the church,
musical performance, forms of oratory including rap—we are
better able to explain the position created for the viewer in relation to black artistic expression. In the black cultural tradition,
the audience takes an active role in the production of meaning.
Black cultural expression is constructed in such a way as to provide a space for the audience who is expected to share in the pro-

duction of meaning. It incorporates the audience in a dynamic call-response relationship, creating a circle that bonds participants in a unified movement (Smitherman, 1977, p. 108). Ceola Ross Baber explains that "Call-response performances and expressions are highly symbolic 'signals' or cultural cues with a meaning shared among Afro-Americans" (Baber, 1988, p. 97). Using a performative model of black cultural expression, the audience relationship in the best examples of black film is constructed in such a way as to require the viewer to engage the text as though it were a sermon or a musical performance. Abrahams makes the point that in the black cultural tradition the performer is not only concerned with the performance as a product, but emphasizes performance as process. The performer functions "not to make a thing but to bring about an experience in which not only his creative energies but the vitality of others may find expression" (1976, p. 9).

In his book, *The Power of Black Music*, Samuel Floyd examines the African American folktale of *Brer Rabbit in Red Hill Churchyard* to demonstrate the cultural basis of performance-based expressive forms and improvisation in African American music. The folktale, which is about a ceremony involving Brer Mockingbird and Brer Rabbit, provides us with important intertextual information about improvisation useful for the analysis of narrative form in a range of black art.

> (They) had chunes floatin' all 'round on de night air.
> Dey could stand a chune on end, grab it up an' throw
> it away an ketch it an' bring it back an' hold it; an'
> make dem chunes sound like dey was strugglin' to
> get away one minute, an de' next dey sound like
> sumpin' gittin' up close an' whisperin. (Floyd, 1995,
> p. 95)

Improvisational techniques stress fluidity of form and tend to work against the permanence of an artwork's structure. They are foundational elements in the African American tradition and are elaborated in other art forms as demonstrated in *Daughters of the Dust*. Whereas in the Western cultural tradition enormous currency is given to the presumed originality of art and the sacredness of the artwork, in the black cultural tradition some important kinds of art tend to be fluid and actually change from time to time. Art historians the world over are engaged in hot debate about the issue of restoring the works of the Renaissance masters. Some view it as sacrilege; others as necessary to allow the artwork to continue to exist in its original splendor. In the black cultural tradition, especially in music, value is placed on the performance and not so much the original work. Contrast the different aesthetic contexts that help explain Michael Bolton's remake of Otis Redding's *Sitting on the Dock of the Bay* and Chantal Savage's remake of Gloria Gaynor's Disco classic, *I will Survive*. Bolton's rendition is a cover in the traditional definition (a term used to describe a white performer's recording of a black singer's work for white audiences), so it remains almost faithful to Redding's original. The listener can find value in Bolton's cover of Redding's song in the quality of his voice and in the beauty of the song. In contrast, Savage's version seeks to make strange or to alter Gaynor's well-known work. Not only is there an emphasis on vocal techniques, there is a major focus on a new and different *I Will Survive*. In the black expressive tradition, orality and performative values strongly influence the structure of texts. The phenomenon of the 'remix' in rap music also supports this observation. Whereas in the Western aesthetic tradition, an artwork is complete and held almost sacrosanct, in the black tradition art often functions as a work in progress. Black musicians may release several different remixes of any one work. What is critical is the apparent existence of a cultural mechanism that operates in black expressive forms all the while striving for a call-response relationship or searching for its completion in the audience. Interestingly, there is an instance of this activity in black film involving Micheaux, who because of his close relationship with black audiences would occasionally recut his movies, actually changing scenes, while on the distribution circuit.

The paradigmatic narrative of the Signifying Monkey and the notion of signifying in black culture help clarify the importance of improvisational techniques to black cultural expression. These refer to figurative speech and the use of rhetorical devices that privilege vernacular forms such as playing the dozens, testifying or rapping. There is a cultural basis for signifying in the black tradition. Floyd argues that it "is a way of saying one thing and meaning another; it is a reinterpretation, a metaphor for the revision of previous texts and figures; it is tropological thought, repetition with difference, the obscuring of meaning—all to achieve or reverse power, to improve situations, and to achieve pleasing results for the signifier" (1995, p. 95). This cultural

shifting
signifiers

(referential)

mechanism of signifying, which is a central feature of black artistic expression, informs improvisation in African American music through its emphasis on the play of the signifier. "In African American music, musical figures Signify by commenting on other musical figures, on themselves, on performance of other music, on other performances of the same piece, and on completely new works of music" (Floyd, 1995, p. 95).

Geneva Gay describes this cultural creativity as "an ethos of expressiveness" stressing the importance of an aesthetic of style and the existential power of performance (1987, p. 5). Baber explains that "Unable to use their indigenous languages to talk freely among themselves or to their captors, the slaves were forced to develop a different form of communication that was part African, part American. The slaves devised a language that was rich in allusion, metaphor, and imagery, and prolific in the use of body gestures and non-verbal nuances" (1987, p. 87). Through time, a formal mechanism privileging performative values and the existential playing out of events in space evolved as an integral part of the black cultural tradition. This mechanism originally linked to survival focuses our attention on the act of signification and the play of signifiers in black communication. Its impact on black cultural expression would be to pay less attention to the immediate narrative requirements of the signified while emphasizing the existential playing out of the signifier (that is, the process through which signification is coded). The slaves used the spirituals, for example, to communicate important information about their resistance struggle, shifting attention away from what was being said to how it was being expressed. In the black cultural tradition, the audience has always known that signifiers such as 'wait in de water' could have multiple signifieds: as a reference to the Christian religion or as a message to runaway slaves to remember that rivers and streams help to throw dogs and trackers off track. The slaves used the knowledge of shifting signifiers in communication as a means of protection and often rebellion.

The existence of these survival mechanisms, which have had a powerful mediating influence on black cultural expression, does not suggest that the black tradition is conservative and reactionary, in the sense that it more or less tends toward the solution of past problems and is ill-equipped to deal with the future. Some political conservatives claim that this mechanism is no longer useful for black progress and serves only to keep blacks in a disadvantaged position relative to whites. In contrast, the element of change and cultural mechanisms for adjusting to change stand as enduring and successful features of the African American tradition.

Fundamentally, black cultural expression always outstrips mimesis (a concern with merely reproducing or imitating existing reality) in that it is more presentational than representational. We find that the performance unfolds in space and reformulates the notion of time most associated with classical Western narratives. While classical Western narratives progress temporally, African American narratives tend to expand, taking the form of a quilt or a mosaic. Goal-oriented narratives do not seem to be as important as experiential, existential, that is, spatial narratives. In black cultural expression, we can observe a mechanism of estrangement at work, which often takes the form of improvisation. Although these narratives may point to the existence of a goal, however, the moment-to-moment narration is preoccupied with other things. There is movement, but not in the linear manner of the Classical Hollywood cinema. We should remember that in the African tradition improvisation plays a central role in oral narratives. It is possible to argue that having to adjust one's life style and day-to-day behavior to the vicissitudes of life during slavery and segregation led to the development of social mechanisms that favored constant redefinition of one's situation as a means of survival. Achieving direction through indirection has become an important element of the African American performance aesthetic. A related point is made by Diawara, who identifies a particular use of space in the work of some black filmmakers. He makes the observation that black films use spatial narration to reveal and link black spaces that have been separated and suppressed by the dominant culture and to validate black culture (1993, p. 13).

In the black cinematic experience, the spectator brings knowledge of black expressive forms and an aesthetic sense developed through these intertextual experiences. The viewer not only constructs story information, but also brings an emotional content to the film experience. These emotions are influenced by the larger social history of political and historic relations and the accompanying need for self-expression. This idea of emotional content is not of the melodramatic sort. It is more primary, more related to our sensory perceptions in that it developed as a survival mechanism in early African American culture. As such, the

[handwritten marginal note: SPATIAL NARRATION and meaning]

emotions the viewer brings to the film encounter fosters a discriminating kind of intellectual activity, which has to do with reinforcing acts of resistance and developing day-to-day strategies to counter cultural information at odds with the African American experience. This was exemplified in the cultural strategy of wearing the mask when slaves presented an acceptable image that was non-threatening to placate the slave master's assumed superiority while camouflaging their true feelings. They might have played the role of a helpless, dim-witted, banjo-playing roustabout in order to poke fun at the master, to facilitate an escape or gain some small advantage. This strategy of constructing one pattern of behavior for the master and another behind his back is related to improvisation as a seminal survival mechanism in the black cultural tradition. Given the fluidity of social expectation, in which fortunes could change dramatically at any time for blacks, improvisation was important for survival purposes. "Despite the environmental, psychological, and sociological constraints imposed by the institution of slavery, the Africans first endured, then abided, and in the end remade themselves culturally to accommodate the circumstances of their existence in the New World" (Gay, 1988), p. 2).

In the viewing encounter, the black cultural tradition functions like a framing device that provides basic parameters for filmic narration and the activity of the viewer. There is an inherent expectation based on the protocol of call-response in the African American tradition. In black cultural expression, the audience exists in a dialectical relationship, which is more readily observed in those arts that favor interpersonal performances and involve oratory, music and dance. However, like the black performer, the filmmaker creates his or her performance (the film) with a space present for the viewer. Many black viewers are therefore literate in different modes of cultural experience, being familiar with the Classical Hollywood cinema as well as African American cultural experience. Unfortunately, the same is not true for many film scholars and critics.

EXPRESSIVE FORM AND THE BLACK CULTURAL TRADITION

Free form plays an important role in the aesthetic sensibility of the African American experience. Instead of foregrounding the regulation of a linear temporal change as in the Hollywood classical narrative, there is a tendency to explore space and its dimen-

FLUIDITY

sions. History is not viewed as being teleological, correcting itself; rather it is necessary to engage in struggle for space in order to bring about change. In the black cultural tradition, style is fluid and is constantly shifting. There is less emphasis on fixing limits or imposing closure to restrict how a narrative or song must be delivered. "The alert songster or story teller exploits the context to achieve not only immediacy but also some variations on old themes. . . The oral tale lives in the telling (and) draws its vitality from the context it is told in" (Harrison, 1972, p. 7). We also observe this mechanism in African American instrumental music in which the black tradition places more emphasis on modernist use of form than on representational aesthetics. As a matter of fact, we desperately need more informed terminology to talk about these mechanisms, which represent hallmarks of the black cultural tradition. When Picasso encountered a new use of form in the African mask, he went on to create a radical breach in the Western visual arts tradition. We also witness a different use of form in popular Jamaican music of the 1960s—toasting, for example. In the development of black film, filmmakers have been striving to make film do what its intertextual supports such as forms of black oratory and African American classical music do. This is why it is an error and a severe devaluation to evaluate black film as a poor imitation of Hollywood cinema. Therefore, the most successful films in the African American tradition are those that go beyond dominant approaches to film and use black cultural expression to transform the cinematic medium. This helps explain the importance of Spike Lee as a filmmaker within the African American tradition. Although Lee borrows freely from the language of Hollywood films, he grounds black film within the intertextual space of the black experience. Like African American classical music, the black cultural tradition is a hospitable one that is open to change and welcomes new ideas. Examples from this musical tradition include Cool Jazz and Latin Jazz. The Jazz ensemble itself often features a contrast of timbres and distinct voices. Whereas the symphony seeks to blend, Jazz is constructed so as to allow difference. It is not a conformist, hegemonic form, but is readily receptive to innovation.

Although film is conceived as embodying a basic illusion on which the traditional cinema is constructed, black cinema has other interests. Instead of constructing an art form on the illusion, an important strategy of black cinema is motivated by punc-

the illusion of what?

SPACE-BASED
NARRATIVES

turing it. This is the mechanism through which the African American tradition will often select a melody or narrative with which we are very familiar and then rework it, paying more attention to the fabric of its *écriture* and the process of making it 'strange.' Jamaican music of the 1960s and 1970s, rap sampling of the 80s and 90s, even John Coltrane's various recordings of *My Favorite Things* display concerns with reworking the narrative process and exploring the feature of estrangement. Classical European-based narratives tend to develop through time, while the African American tradition as expressed through forms such as music, oratory and film explores and develops the spatial dimensions of its narratives. *Daughters of the Dust* uses a paradigm of narration that unfolds in space, paying greater detail to existential detail than to a linear temporal detail in which the present follows the past and leads into the future. While D. W. Griffith's *The Birth of a Nation* (1916) represents itself as historical in the bourgeois sense of the term informing the viewer that the film's events are real and that even the sets are facsimiles of real ones, *Daughters of the Dust* does not. Griffith's film privileges the signified—a particular conception of race relations—and as a result is a slave to a racist reading of history, which is conceived as having the structure of a classical narrative. Within the classical European narrative, it is important to specify a motivating incident, which sets a series of actions in motion and justifies the entry and subsequent action of the hero in the name of law and order. In a film such as *Daughters of the Dust*, history is a device that unites. It brings both the past and future into the present. Although *Daughters* utilizes a narrative structure that is heavily influenced by improvisational techniques, the stories it tells are intelligible and make sense to the viewer. However, making sense does not mean that the film must construct a realism based on a slavish mimesis that merely regurgitates the official history of a particular era. Rather it is able to demonstrate that any notion of reality can be shown to consist of multiple dimensions. The metaphor of the quilt or the mosaic provides an appropriate description of these space-based narratives.

NARRATIVE STRATEGIES IN BLACK CULTURAL EXPRESSION

In *Ways With Words*, Stanford ethnographer Shirley Brice Heath (1983) examines the style and function of storytelling practices among blacks and whites in North Carolina. Heath compares the distinct traditions of storytelling in two working-class communities—Roadville and Tracton, which are a few miles apart in the Piedmont Carolinas. "The Piedmont includes the area West of the Atlantic Coastal Plain and east of the Southern Appalachian Mountains" (Brice Heath, 1983, p. 19). Roadville is a white community built around generations of families who have worked in the textile mills. Tracton is a black community whose older members worked the land, while younger ones work in the mills. Heath's study is instructive for our discussion of narrative traditions in black culture. Although one must be careful in generalizing from the experiences of these two North Carolina communities to the national experiences of blacks and whites, comparative study reveals information that resounds with other cultural expressions reflecting black and white cultural experiences.

Although storytelling is an important social activity in both communities, the stories of the two groups differ in form, content and function. Roadville stories tend to be factual and are subject to very little embellishment or exaggeration. In contrast, reality functions as a starting point for storytelling in Tracton, but the actual stories are highly fictionalized based on the creative power of the individual narrator. However, on serious occasions, straightforward accounts are used in a traditional journalistic sense. Stories in the white community tend to be more formulaic. They develop according to a strict chronological time frame. Their structure allows little commentary on behavior of the characters and no direct statement of meaning in the narrative act. The ending of the story invokes a summary statement of a Biblical passage or proverb. Narratives in the black community are less formulaic and usually reflect the personality of the storyteller. Little attention is paid to strict chronology. These stories tend to be episodic and feature observations and commentary on the morality of characters in the story. Tracton stories do not have formulaic endings. They may include boasts to boost the personality of the main character and may even serve as a transition to another story not intended initially.

While both communities use their stories as a form of entertainment and to celebrate verbal skills, Heath concludes that storytelling techniques differ in the two communities. As a result, children in Roadville and Tracton grow up listening to different conceptions of narration and therefore develop different kinds of competencies in storytelling. She finds that the white and black communities structure their stories differently, value different approaches to storytelling and hold distinct expressive criteria for judging good and bad stories. "The patterns of interaction surrounding the actual telling of a story vary considerably from Roadville to Tracton. One community allows only stories that are factual and have little exaggeration; the other uses reality only as the germ of a highly creative fictionalized account. One uses stories to reaffirm group membership and behavioral norms (Roadville), the other to assert individual strengths and powers (Tracton). Children in the two communities hear different kinds of stories, they develop competence in telling stories in highly contrasting ways" (Heath, 1983, p. 184). Whereas the Roadville storytellers place a premium on the factual value of narrative events and a strict chronology, Tracton storytellers emphasize the truth of the message underlying the story and de-emphasize an accurate rendering of empirical fact. "Tracton folks see the truth and the facts in stories in ways which differ greatly from those of Roadville. Good storytellers in Tracton may base their stories on an actual event, but they creatively fictionalize the details surrounding the real event, and the outcome of the story may not even resemble what indeed happened. . . Straightforward factual accounts are relatively rare in Tracton and are usually told only on serious occasions" (Heath, 1984, p. 166). Whereas in Roadville, storytelling is didactic and functions principally to reinforce the community's moral codes, Tracton stories illustrate a key feature of the black expressive tradition in which form often becomes a significant determinant of meaning. Heath comments that, "In Tracton, stories have no point; they may go on as long as the audience enjoys the storyteller's entertainment" (1983, p. 186). For example, the storyteller gauges audience interaction and may extend what was initially a single story and introduce new ones, based on the receptivity of the audience.

Another significant feature of storytelling in the black community illustrates the importance of the play of signifiers in the black expressive tradition. Heath explains, "In Tracton, various types of language play, imitations of other community members or TV personalities, dramatic gestures and shifts of voice quality, and rhetorical questions and expressions of emotional evaluations add humor and draw out the interaction of storyteller and audience" (1983, p. 186). Regarding the aesthetic criteria that mark a good story, Heath states that the "best stories" in the

audience improvisation

it is referential

black community can be open-ended and lead to diverse stories
that deal with different themes. Fluidity of form, which is a powerful technique grounded in the improvisational quality of narration in black cultural expression, describes the performance
aesthetic so important to the African American tradition.
Kochman suggests that as blacks move into the middle class and
adopt more of the culture of middle class whites, their communication patterns begin to reflect the cultural norms of the dominant society. He cites a study of white and black first graders in
a South Florida school, which found differences between poor
black children (whose contact with the dominant culture was
limited) and white children along with well-to-do black children
(who had more contact with the dominant culture). The performance of the white and the well-to-do black first graders
reflected the cultural norms of the dominant society. Those children repeated details verbatim; they did not deviate from the
instructions given; they were modest in their expressive gestures;
and there was little to distinguish one child's performance from
that of another. In contrast, "the poor black children were literally performing, emphasizing both individuality and vitality,
which because of their cultural background, blacks have come to
regard as essential to successful performance" (Kochman, 1981,
p. 154-5).

SYSTEMS OF FILM NARRATIVE

In *Narration and the Fiction Film*, Bordwell (1985) presents four
paradigms of narration: classical, art-cinema, historical-materialist, and parametric narration, and he examines how style functions in each of them. Each paradigm has its own conventions
and use of stylistic patterns. Variants of the historical-materialist and parametric narrative can be found in black film. In historical-materialist narration, we find a dual emphasis on poetic
and rhetorical devices as organizing principles of narration.
"Narrative causality is construed as supraindividual . . .
Characters also lose the uniqueness sought to some degree by
classical narration and to a great degree by art-cinema narration;
they become prototypes of whole classes, milieux, or historical
epochs" (Bordwell, 1985, p. 235). Instead of elevating the individual character, a mass hero in the form of a group of workers,
for example, takes his place. Stories—drawn from history, myth
and contemporary issues—are generally well known and provide
a limited range of options for narrative development. In black

cinema, the Cuban filmmaker Sergio Giral's, *The Other Francisco*, represents a powerful variant of historical-materialist narration. It emphasizes an interrogative cinema as opposed to psychologically driven and individual-centered narration.

Daughters of the Dust is a film that is propelled significantly by artistic motivation within the black cultural tradition. Bordwell's conception of parametric narration is useful in studying films of this sort. In this paradigm, style is elevated to the level of a shaping force that dominates the film, thereby functioning principally according to its own aesthetic and cultural logic. In other words, the plot (the decision of the Peazant family to go North and their eventual crossing to the mainland) is subordinated to the internal progression and stylistic logic of cinematic elements. In African American narration, the story is so heavily charged with extra-narrative and historical information about the larger black experience that it gives the film its ethnic flavor and functions very much like a cultural voice that permeates the narration.

Classical narration conforms most closely to the 'canonic story,' which places a premium on character-centered causality and the presentation of the narrative in terms of a goal-oriented action that drives the logic of the film. A linear causality motivates the use of time in Bordwell's paradigm of classical narration and the organization of space is based on realist uses of mise-en-scene. Classical narratives tend to be Aristotelian in nature in that they emphasize the unities of space, time and action. Technique and style are used to motivate the dominant logic of the story. For example, "classical editing aims at making each shot the logical outcome of its predecessor and at reorienting the spectator through repeated set-ups. Momentary disorientation is permissible only if motivated realistically" (Bordwell, 1985, p. 163). The overall thrust of narration in Classical Hollywood cinema is to foster the creation of a story that is coherent and consistent with a particular conception of time, space and social positions.

This aesthetic system owes a debt to Aristotelian poetics, which is built around notions of spectacle. In this system, the viewer is positioned as a spectator who delegates a certain power to the filmmaker to act, to create the world for him. Augusto Boal describes Aristotelian poetics as the poetics of oppression in that they foster a set of reactionary values. "The world is known, perfect or about to be perfected, and all its values are imposed on the spectators, who passively delegate power to the characters to act and think in their place. . . A catharsis of the revolutionary impetus is produced: Dramatic action substitutes for real action" (1979, p. 155). Spectacle in the cinema has its own ideological and commercial requirements. It creates a rigid narrative space that does not encourage the viewer to become active in the viewing process. "Narrative as spectacle reaches back to the problematic of 19th century art in which the space for the audience fosters a passive consumer whose interest in making history is arrested because history can be read in the history book" (Solanas and Getino, 1976, p. 51). In this paradigm, audience members become spectators who consume art rather than create it. In contrast to the Aristotelian model, which presents limited possibilities for a new kind of viewer, other aesthetic systems create a space for a more active viewer who is encouraged to act on the circumstances surrounding his or her social existence. For example, the Brechtian aesthetic system encourages activism and motivates the audience to use the narrative to develop information that could help them break out of a social malaise and a world of illusory escape. Importantly, it seeks to deny the catharsis effect, which is a device used in forms of classical narrative to vicariously diffuse social tension. The viewer is refused the pleasures associated with the classical cinema. These are the pleasures of looking, identification with the hero, containment of the other and narrative closure. As films begin to utilize elements of the black cultural tradition, it becomes increasingly difficult to classify them within the classical system. Bordwell and Thompson present an analysis of Lee's *Do The Right Thing* (1989), which argues that the film departs from classical narrative to some degree, but they find that "it has the redundantly clear action and strong forward impetus to the plot that we associate with classical filmmaking. It also fits into a familiar genre of American cinema—the social problem film. Moreover, closer analysis reveals that Lee has also drawn upon many traits of classicism to give an underlying unity to this apparently loosely constructed film" (1997, p. 393). Lee's films straddle the boundary between Classical Hollywood cinema and black independent film in very unique ways. However, we cannot reduce his body of work to Hollywood conventions as Bordwell and Thompson imply in their analysis of *Do the Right Thing*, or fully accept Wahneema Lubiano's view that critics uncritically praise Lee's films. In all fairness, Lubiano's critique is a broad interrogation of Lee's work which she describes this way:

"I examine Lee's evaluation of his work (specifically *School Daze* and *Do the Right Thing*), others' evaluations of his work, the problems raised by Lee's place in film production and discourse, and the films *School Daze* and *Do the Right Thing* " (1991, p. 255). My difficulty with this criticism is the tendency to lose sight of the film and pay more attention to Lee's persona and his self-promotion. This is not to devalue Lubiano's critique of the politics of Lee's filmmaking, the relationship of his films to Hollywood, or the "masculinist representations" in these films. ⟶ v. true .

To make this broad critique of Lee's work, it is necessary to proceed carefully delineating the method of our critique and properly specifying our object (text). How do we find signification in Lee's work and what particular elements and parameters do we use? Any close reading must begin by engaging the text in its specificity, that is, its narrative elements. Then we can make connections with the larger contextual questions of ideology and politics. Barthes' textual analysis of Balzac's *Sarrasine* (1974) still remains quite useful as a critical tool for the close reading of texts. The *S/Z* method not only examines the artistic texture of a work, but also importantly addresses a film's multidimensionality through explicit evaluation of its political, sociological and historical context. In a close reading, we focus on the film's narrative elements, which is "the moment-by-moment process" that allows the critic to construct the story out of the plot information (Bordwell and Thompson, 1997, p. 102), so that our judgments are made using sound criteria. Within the framework of semiotics, the viewer does not come to the text in order to find ready-made meanings. In contrast, the textual encounter is active because the viewer is encouraged to engage the text. Lee's films often utilize techniques from the classical film narrative. With a focus on the structuration of the film text, we are in a better position to witness the way the filmmaker violates conventions of the classical cinema and invokes elements of the African American tradition in his signifying practices.

Bordwell's paradigm of art cinema narration cannot be adequately applied to black film because it does not address the cultural specificity of the text. Art cinema narration is most intelligible within the context of European art history and its related art forms. While art cinema analysis can reveal some interesting information about *Daughters of the Dust*, it robs the film of its raison d'etre, which is its location in the black experience. Art cinema narration appears to be inadequate for study-

ing black film. Although *Daughters of the Dust* utilizes elements
of art cinema narration, it is not really an art film. Similarly *Killer
of Sheep* develops outside conventional narrative conventions. It
is not a Hollywood classical film and although related to neo-
realist film defies art cinema classification. Burnett's narration is
most intelligible within the African American expressive tradition. Its exposition develops through a careful decentering of the
subject in the narration, and it exemplifies a notion of the blues
as a philosophical stance and cinematic statement. The film is
not driven by a structure of suspense and conflict governed by
the traditional enigmatic codes of the classical cinema. Its narrative structure is reminiscent of improvisation in African
American classical music, which develops moment-to-moment
instead of building toward a major climax. *Killer of Sheep* is the
story of a black family in South-central Los Angeles. Stan, the
father, who works in a slaughterhouse is engaged in a constant
struggle to retain a sense of humanity and manhood in the inner
city. Burnett's narrative deals with several themes that are marginalized in film dealing with the black experience: the transition from rural to urban existence by blacks; ordinary black
people and their daily lives; non-traumatic relationships among
black men; and the treatment of working-class whites as human
beings who inhabit some of the narrative spaces with blacks. The
cinematography emphasizes the existential, appearing to linger
as though savoring each moment and occasionally favoring
unusual camera angles, for example, from a child's point of view.

Both classical and art cinema narration are culture bound
and tend to be endowed with European aesthetic sensibilities
that are specific to that cultural history, much more than the historical materialist and parametric forms of narration. When we
apply Bordwell's narrative models to black independent film, we
find that black film narratives may utilize some elements of his
four narrative types, but do not fit neatly any of them. However,
when black film narration is considered part of the African
American expressive tradition, the critic finds a rich framework
for looking at black film.

BLACKS AND THE CLASSICAL
HOLLYWOOD CINEMA

The term Classical Hollywood cinema refers to a consumerist
model of filmmaking associated with the American Studio system during the first half of the 20th century, which featured

approaches to narrative development and cinematic style that
were based on an industrial form of organization that focused on
pleasing the consumer. "Like the industry-based, assembly-line
process innovated by Henry Ford and his peers in the business
world to make the production of automobiles and other consumer goods as streamlined and as economical as possible,
American movies rapidly evolved during the 1910s and 1920s
into a highly efficient mode of telling stories" (Belton, 1994, p.
22). The Hollywood film studios were organized to deliver a film
product that presented audiences with stories that were easy to
follow and featured identifiable characters. These films offered
a highly selective and romanticized larger-than-life image of
social reality.

The creation of a unified narrative for the satisfaction of the
spectator played a major role in guiding the selection of story
ideas, use of formal elements and the development of the aesthetic system in Classical Hollywood cinema. Although the
method of filmmaking involved the use of multiple camera positions, the action appears to unfold seamlessly for the viewer.
Narrative elements such as technique and story are developed
for a viewer who is positioned as a spectator. The cinematography is often referred to as invisible because it does not call attention to itself. An easy-to-follow linear plot functions as the
central pivot of the film, and technique operates as an almost
invisible framework for the narration. The attention of the viewer is directed toward plot development and on-screen action, and
the knowledge that the film represents a make-belief world is
not considered important. In the classical cinema, the system of
continuity operates to direct the viewer's attention, seeking to
establish a closed narrative that represses elements not conducive
to its narrative point of view. The viewer experiences the film as
though real events were unfolding before one's eyes. The film
appears to be a slice of life, a picture window from which the
viewer gets a most opportune view of society that ironically
appears not to have been produced by cinematic means.

As a result, the narrative is delivered so effortlessly
and efficiently to the audience that it appears to have
no source. It comes magically off the screen as if
spontaneously creating itself in the presence of the
spectators in the movie theater for their immediate
consumption and pleasure. But, in fact, it is creat-

> ed; it is made according to classical principles of clar-
> ity, simplicity, elegance, order, economy and sym-
> metry (Belton, 1994, p. 22)

Hollywood cinema is the product of a specific culture that has
its own narrative traditions. In the mythic world of classical
Hollywood, blacks have been defined as the other. For most of
its history, blacks were rendered invisible and exiled to the margins of American cinema. When blacks are represented in the
Classical Hollywood cinema, the range of signification has been
objectified and restricted to signifieds of powerlessness or evil.
This signification is constructed on an imaginary that has coded
blackness as "the nuclear fantasy in opposition to its polar cog-
nate, whiteness, the two being symbolic abstractions of a human
vision of a world that in reality has no such absolutes" (Kovel,
1971, p. 62). Film historians generally agree that conventions in
the Hollywood cinema reflect the ideological positions and the
elite class interests of white patriarchy. Knowledge, the dominant value system, forms of social organization and artifacts
reflect these values, which are reinforced through subsidiary economic and ideological institutions such as mainstream cinema.

We often use the term dominant culture to describe this series
of power relations in American society. Dominant culture refers
to the group that has "historically or traditionally had the most
persistent and far-reaching impact on culture, on what we think
and say, on what we believe and do in our society" (Folb, 1994, p.
134). The dominant culture is reflected in the cultural, social, legal,
economic, and political institutions that operate to maintain the
status quo and sustain the system of power. The Hollywood cinema is part and parcel of the cultural apparatus of the dominant
society. Accordingly, elements of the Classical Hollywood cinema
such as stars, narrative action, conflict, and settings all tend to flow
from this matrix. In the history of Hollywood film, the heroes are
white males, and those groups occupying the position of the other
exist to support the structure of heroism in its narratives. The classical phase of the Western genre, for example, articulates a reactionary paradigm of social relations and constructs a peculiar
iconography of color in which white is a signifier of goodness and
black functions as its opposite. The mythic structure underlying
the Hollywood cinema produces a way of seeing within which the
black body is constituted as the object of the look, thus helping to
reinforce the traditional system of social relations in which black
functions as the subordinate term.

In the development of Hollywood classical narrative, the representation of blacks was subject to careful control: blacks were either a threat to society or a castrated being. In *Birth of a Nation*, the extent to which the blacks are presented as grotesque savages out to rape white women and overcome the established order reveals a rampant primal fear. The actual darkening of the face with blackface makeup and the use of white actors to play black villains are related to the same psychoanalytic problem in Western culture which led to women being represented by young boys in the theater. The problem is really the inability of the dominant white, male culture to deal positively with the position of women and blacks in society. Even the classic *King Kong* (1934) represents the dramatization of this problem. There is Africa, known in European mythology as the 'Dark Continent.' There is the looming threat of the beast and the eventual domination and death of it. And there is the helpless white woman whom the savage craves.

Hollywood's dominant narrative system has been equally fascinated by the castrated figure in the representation of blacks as low comics. From the beginnings of cinema, the dumbwitted, castrated figure provided comic relief for film audiences. A distinct comic tradition arose in Hollywood in which white comics derived their comedy through confrontation with the environment and eventual success in overcoming obstacles. However, the representation of blacks as comics was constructed around a contrary narrative device in which the comic situation facing blacks was their sheer lack of intelligence to comprehend the environment. Therefore, the tradition of comedy in which blacks were represented was not one of strength and resilience in the face of adversity, but one of cowardice and fear. Blacks existed in an irrevocable comic proportion to the environment. They were neither masters of their environment nor their fates. Characteristically, it seemed that the film only 're-presented' social relations, commonplace social truths which after all existed in society. There was a certain common knowledge in the West—based on racist ideologies—that blacks possessed subhuman capacity. It was easy to transfer these social understandings to the world of film within the realist model of film language, which claimed that the film image only reflects existing circumstances and social relations.

UNDERSTANDING BLACK FILM NARRATION

A major problem facing black film—as well as other insurgent cinemas—is that most people base their idea of a good film on the Classical Hollywood cinema. Because of its success, glamour, easy availability and its emphasis on consumer-friendly narratives, Hollywood has become synonymous with the dominant paradigm of cinema. Films that do not fit the narrative system established in the Hollywood film often are overlooked and neglected. Because black films tend to use different systems of narration, critics schooled in the Hollywood paradigm tend to misread black cinematic expression. Filmmakers whose work is produced within the framework of the black experience emphasize a different set of values in their film practice and use alternative strategies of representation. Their films may not develop the traditional unified story line bequeathed to classical narrative by Aristotelian poetics or the true-to-life style of realism created through cinematography and editing that is found in most Hollywood cinema. While Hollywood puts a premium on entertainment, other models of filmmaking, such as Latin American *Ciné Liberacion*, stress a model of film as a tool for social, political and economic development, thereby paying greater attention to issues of education, social cohesion and history as well as entertainment. In the same way that not all American music sounds alike, why should all films look the same or use filmmaking techniques to produce the same type of images?

Certainly, black film culture cannot be properly understood without reference to Hollywood; but it is important not to limit discussion to the characteristics of the dominant cinema as manifested in black films. It is wrong to establish critical criteria that construct a master narrative and then proceed to see how films by black filmmakers fit into such a schema. Some critics assume that the aesthetic criteria of what we consider a good film are cross-cultural or universal. This view assumes that art works invoke essentially the same responses in a variety of audiences and are constructed on the same emotional and intellectual supports regardless of their cultural context. Take the popular criticism made by Daniel J. Leab in his article, "A Pale Black Imitation: *All colored film 1930—1950*," that black film represents a low-grade *B-Hollywood* product.

> Hollywood has produced a large number of stinkers
> over the years, but few of the movies turned out by

the studios have been as bad as the ghetto-oriented films made by both black and white filmmakers. Whether these people were in the industry or only on its fringes, their productions were of poor quality both technically and artistically. These cheaply produced, quickly made Jim Crow movies were inferior to almost everything produced by the industry. Despite their overall shabbiness and many technical imperfections, the genre persisted well into the 1950s. (1975, p. 57)

Leab's criticism misses the mark because early black film emphasized textual systems related to the cultural needs of the African American community that defy the disparaging "ghetto-oriented" characterization. David Nicholson, founder of the now-defunct *Black Film Review*, echoes this kind of criticism in a retrospective article on black film in the 1980s.

In their quest for 'art,' or some mistaken ego fulfillment, black filmmakers seem to have forgotten (or perhaps think themselves above learning) elementary rules of plot, character development, and story construction. Some offer as an excuse that their films are made for the people. It is interesting to me that this excuse is offered for shallowness and inconsistencies in plot, character, and story and for films that are so densely convoluted they require explication by professors of semiotics to be comprehended. (1995, p. 444)

a new cinematic language.

In response, filmmaker Zeinabu Irene Davis argued that this negative criticism refuses to take into account that "What independent black filmmakers are creating is a new cinematic language in our films. We are asking the audience to see things anew." She noted that recent Hollywood filmmaking cannot boast of significant new explorations of narrative style or innovative content. However, "recent black independent film takes on new subject matter and often brings interesting perspectives to old themes that we as a community don't care to discuss: sexuality, sexism, slavery, migration, religious fanaticism, the color line, science fiction, and campus politics" (1995, p. 450-51).

If we use the Hollywood classical film narrative as the standard against which to measure developments in black cinema,

then the criticism of black independent film as deviant and technically imperfect cinema can be made. However, are critics so
blinded that they are unable to conceive the possibility of a different narrative system at work? In the same way that folk artists
create a different aesthetic that defies the realism of figurative
painting, why is it not possible to consider black film as the con-
figuration of an aesthetic that reflects its own cultural point of
view. The emergence of nonrepresentational and abstract painting early in the 20th century led some critics to conclude that it
was farcical. One critic was "absolutely skeptical as to their having any claim whatever to being works of art" (Cortissoz, 1924,
p. 42). However, others agreed that the new works could be considered art. A review of the first exhibition of modern art in the
United States observed that, "the real meaning of this Cubist
movement is nothing else than the total destruction of the art of
painting . . . Now the total destruction of painting as a representative art is a thing which a lover of painting could hardly
envisage with entire equanimity, yet one may admit that such a
thing might take place and yet an art remain that should have its
own value" (Cox, 1913). This new approach to artistic expression was not viewed in terms of shabbiness and technical imperfections; rather, it was conceived as the exploration of a new
frontier through the use of different artistic languages.
   When critics examine narrative within its proper cultural
context, a more enlightened criticism results. Audiences vary in
their narrative expectations, textual reading and cultural experiences. So do the signifying practices that characterize different
systems of film. The problem with universalist aesthetics is the
assumption that filmmaking across cultures is at base the same
phenomenon. All films share common elements in that the technology is basically the same. However, the specific uses to which
technology is put varies. Black filmmakers employ film technologies and cinematic techniques to achieve ends that often differ from Hollywood cinema. Micheaux's films, for example, do
not reveal the rampant negative stereotypes that existed in
Hollywood films, and D.W. Griffith's *The Birth of a Nation*, for
example, reveals an ideological terrain that could not exist in
black cinema. Pearl Bowser and Louise Spence comment that
"In his silent films, Micheaux chose themes that were contentious
or explosive in their time. By responding to such contemporary
social issues as concubinage, rape, miscegenation, peonage, and
lynching, he created a textured and layered expressive response

to the social crises that circumscribed African American life"
(1996, p. 57). Diawara argues that this cinema "puts black people and their culture at the center as subjects of narrative development; in these films, black people are neither marginalized as
a problem, nor singled out as villainous stereotypes such as
Hollywood constructs in its films" (1993, p. 7).

Part Two

Criticism

Chapter Five

Myth and Narrative in
The Harder They Come

The Classical Hollywood cinema presents a limited range of formal options in its narration, which delineate particular formulations of power relations in its discourse and prescribes definitions of gender and race. This practice raises several central issues for black film criticism. First, there is a question of whether a viable black cinema can be constructed using the political and ideological categories of the dominant culture as these relate, for example, to the structure of heroism developed in the narrative and the empathic identification of the viewer with the hero. Reception theory suggests that black viewers establish different relationships to traditional film heroes than most white viewers. A second issue has to do with the fundamental relevance of the mythic structures of narrative in the Classical Hollywood cinema to the development of black film. A third concern recognizes the dangers that arise when a less powerful social group uses the mythic traditions of a dominant culture without serious reformulation or redefinition before incorporating them into its cultural traditions. The problem is in the adoption of a particular narrative paradigm that contains a series of mythic structures based on a series of ideological prerequisites that position those who are different as the other. This narrative paradigm also fosters the repression and marginalization of the views of less-powerful groups in social discourse and imposes a sense of closure that functions to reinforce dominant social understandings.

MYTHIC CONSCIOUSNESS AND FILMIC NARRATION

Joseph Campbell (1968) suggests that myth has both metaphysical and psychological implications for humans. Its significance is to be found in the way it informs empirical events, how these events are communicated and the meanings their internal values hold for adherents of the myth. Through their reproduction of archetypes and mythic structures, film narratives convey basic cultural information that often goes unquestioned because it is embedded deeply in our consciousness. A people's culture and their world-view are codified in their stories; and the basic elements of a culture are reworked and repeated in its narratives. Narration involves the writing of history or the telling of a people's story in their own words and images embodying their own unique perspectives. In mythic terms, the narrative traditions of the Classical Hollywood cinema speak to those fundamental issues that have confronted white American society. Its narratives tell of the founding of a nation and the struggle of white settlers to build a legal and political system within their own cultural and ideological terms of reference.

The way the formal mechanisms of myth (as a structuring device for narrative activity) mediate and influence the story-telling traditions of the black experience is of fundamental relevance to black film criticism. The particular problem of narrative expression that arises in relation to the black experience and the conventions of classical narration is that the ideological preoccupations of the dominant cinema operate to reinforce the history of unequal political and economic relations in American society and often mitigate against meaningful social change. The mythic system in classical narration is at odds with the historical experiences of blacks.

Myth provides key symbolic forms or deep structuring principles for a group's existence, helping to establish a society's cultural priorities and its world-view. It organizes experience in deeply symbolic and sacred ways. Myth is an often silent means of maintaining a group's rules and regulations, mitigating against social disintegration and seeking to perpetuate a sense of an ordered purposeful existence. It functions as a mechanism to preserve a group's integrity amidst the uncertainty of the encounter with new and unknown phenomena. Myth, then, is a primary form of communication—a cognitive mechanism—that facilitates our ability to understand the world around us and seeks to anchor our place in it. It helps to establish a map of our world, a compass for safe passage through unknown, uncharted seas. Film narratives are capable of dialectically impacting on social consciousness and can be instrumental in the construction of new social meanings. In fiction, the way the hero surmounts narrative obstacles, or is overcome by the superior power of the established social order, plays a key role in harnessing or liberating the potential for social change. As myth, film is intricately related to our sense of social possibility and social change.

The problem is that popular narratives appear to be deceptively easy and readily understood by the viewer. Barthes would describe them as a contemporary form of myth.

> What allows the reader to consume myth innocently is that he does not see it as a semiological system but as an inductive one. Where there is only equivalence, he sees a kind of causal process: the signifier and the signified have, in his eyes, a natural relationship. This confusion can be expressed otherwise: any semiological system is a system of values; now the myth-consumer takes the significance for a system of facts: myth is read as a factual system, whereas it is but a semiological one. (1973, p. 142)

Signification in the classical cinema appears to be so innocent and so true to life that we tend to displace the knowledge that these images are fabrications controlled by powerful social interests. We are entranced by the parade of magical, wonderful images that talk and move, that appear to so thoroughly mimic everyday life. In addition to entertaining us, these narratives also propagate and reproduce dominant ideologies. Seldom do films remind us that their narratives contain an inherent political dimension that represents institutionalized modes of social organization and social reality.

As myth, the classical narrative is constructed around the continued ratification and recuperation of the status quo of existing social relations. It locates its legacy in Aristotelian poetics, whose narration emanates from the vantage point of dominant social classes. It acknowledges the existence of social problems and social tensions in the text and in society, but does not encourage the viewer to question the nature of society or its social relations in any fundamental way. Furthermore, although it proceeds through the creation of social crisis and the eventual return to social equilibrium, the options for solving a crisis within the narrative usually represent solutions acceptable to the dominant status quo. A seeming social crisis that threatens to destroy society is resolved through affirming the superiority and resilience of the political system. It is in these terms that the classical narrative is said to present threatening but harmless entertainment that feeds on our social dissatisfactions, but ultimately fail to address them. As a paradigm, the classical narrative is capable of challenging our imaginary social stability by placing the audience in fictional situations of risk. Its mechanisms encourage us to dissipate social anger not at the unequal political and economic structures of society that seek to maintain control over our lives, but through the vicarious escapades of the film's actors and actions as escape and entertainment.

Boal argues that Aristotle's poetic system presents the first extremely powerful poetic-political system that could be used for social repression. In his opinion, it remains today an important model still used in the theater, soap operas and cinema (1979, p. xiv). If we accept the proposition that these mechanisms in the Aristotelian-based narrative film provide reactionary orientations in relation to social change and do not fundamentally challenge the relations of power that characterize the dominant status quo, then it becomes clear that this type of entertainment is incapable of introducing new social models in its discourse. Any important formulation of narrative in black film needs to extricate itself from an aesthetics based on the pleasure of subservience to create an aesthetics based on the pleasure of liberation.

FILMIC SIGNIFICATION IN
THE HARDER THEY COME

The Jamaican film *The Harder They Come* (1971) provides an excellent example of the way mythic consciousness influences narrative choices in the cinema. *The Harder They Come* is the story of a mid-20th century Jamaican folk hero Ivanhoe 'Rhygin' Martin, whose fight against the established order parallels the day-to-day struggle of society's disenfranchised. In the film, Ivan is trapped between two worlds—the persistent poverty of Jamaica's suffering underclass and an alluring metropolitan North American lifestyle. Within the ideological system of the narration in *The Harder They Come*, the hero transgresses proscribed social positions in his struggle against the established order and consequently must be punished for it. *The Harder They Come* provides an opportunity to observe the way the system of filmic signification characteristic of the classical film narrative is inadequate as an expressive language for the development of an alternative cinema that foregrounds the aspirations and experiences of marginalized peoples. Although filmmaker Perry Henzell is able to push *The Harder They Come* to the limits of classical narrative cinema as an expressive form, its ideological baggage limits the narrative power of the hero, the narrative functioning of the female, and the film's ability to transcend its conservative perception of social reality. The signification of the hero in *The Harder They Come*, his narrative development and narrative destiny, raise serious questions about the capabilities of the classical narrative to formulate new possibilities for emerging forms of cinema. Within the ideological system of the film's narrative, the hero transgresses proscribed social positions in his struggle against the established order and consequently must be punished for it.

Ivan comes into conflict with the law because he refuses to live out his prescribed social role and seeks to develop his potential outside his subordinate social position. His heroism is pre-revolutionary, but the prescribed structures of the classical narrative sabotage his potential. Ivan's eventual downfall occurs precisely because he seeks his freedom in a system of values that has sought to guarantee his subordination. In the classical narrative, the social possibility of the black hero and his narrative fate are already predestined according to its ideological requirements. "Black tragedy differs from the classical European in that it is undeserved. The tragic flaw is in the Other; but human volition, in its tragic grandeur is with the black victim. This aesthetic experience cannot purge, in the sense that the classicists argue. Instead, the person experiencing has accepted the weight of facing, spiritually and creatively, man's-inhumanity-to-man. One goes away from the theater, the sculpture, the painting, the novel or poem not drained of emotion and at peace, but troubled, and with no place to go" (Fowler, 1981, p. xxiv). In its most incisive and progressive moments, classical narrative is able to dramatize certain faults and deficiencies in the status quo; however, it stops short of producing a new knowledge of these conditions. Classical narration is based on the acceptance of the dominant social reality and the prescribed social positions it reflects. Certain political mechanisms are built into it, which mitigate against any important social transformation. In that *The Harder They Come* uses classical narration, it is capable of dramatizing the unequal nature of social and political power. However, the Aristotelian system is built on system maintenance, and through its mechanism of catharsis draws in the viewer emotionally as it works out the narrative conflict. We empathize with Ivan's dream of escaping poverty by becoming a successful musician, and we want him to win his gallant fight against those oppressive forces that seek to contain him in a life of poverty. But although the film points to the existence of a fatal flaw or weakness in the social order, the narrative ultimately reinforces the same corrupt system because it functions as a purgative for the elimination of emotions that may prove subversive to the interests of the status quo.

Ivan is a hero from a different time, who inevitably finds himself in conflict with society's enforcers because he refuses to live out his prescribed social role and seeks to develop his potential outside his powerless social position. Immediately, Ivan's narrative desire seeks to violate the laws of his social existence. His heroism contains the seeds of his revolutionary development, but the filmic vehicle within which his narrative is played out sabotages this potential. His is a quest for freedom; but it is the freedom based on an illusion. Ivan identifies with the cowboy heroes of the Old American West. His eventual downfall occurs precisely because he seeks his freedom in a mythological system that has sought to guarantee his subordination. Schooled in the entertainment genres of the Hollywood cinema, we know that the cowboy lives a dangerous life, on the edge, on the fringes of society. Ivan's narrative fate is tragic because there can be no symphony orchestrating the expressed hopes and struggles of the oppressed and society's refusal to allow any significant challenge to its symbolic order or social change.

In Ivan's transformation from poor country boy to slick city hustler, instead of gaining the control over his future and the freedom he yearns for, he loses both progressively. In the course of the narrative, Ivan has neither the personal freedom that marks a revolutionary character, nor the freedom of mobility in the narrative that is characteristic of traditional heroes. The filmmaker skilfully builds a structure of visual images that poignantly clarifies political and economic contradictions in Jamaican society; and grasps several important insights concerning the plight of the poor and the constitution of power in society within the approach to film language he uses. Henzell's presentation of the country boy-hero and Ivan's subsequent downfall within the jungle of the city does not devalue the strength and character of rural life, but offers a powerful critique of the brutal and immoral vicissitudes of urban existence. Without a doubt, the filmmaker deplores the massive flow of humanity from the rural areas into the degradation of the city. This motivating premise of the narrative is crucial to the film's signification as evidenced by Ivan's arrival in town. All hell breaks loose in the city, and the hero is placed in an alien environment, which he does not understand and cannot control.

As the bus arrives in the city, visual signifiers emphasize the modernity of urban life city. Billboard advertisements claim: "Talk with Phillip Waite for a Better Life." The motion of moving from the country to the city is complete when the overloaded bus disgorges its load. Ivan, carrying his possessions on the street, encounters a pushcart vendor who tricks the newcomer and steals his possessions. In contrast to the city slicker, the people from the countryside are noble characters. On the bus to the city, Ivan displays a mango. A fellow passenger asks him whether he has more. Ivan tells the man it is the last one, and it's for his mother. "Put it up," the man replies. In the city, this kind of compassion does not exist, for Ivan is given a rude welcome. As soon as he arrives, he is impoverished further when the pushcart vendor cons him out of all his worldly goods.

Ivan is a dreamer. He dreams not of spiritual fulfilment in the search for God, but of a crude material gain. The nature of his dreams is just as idealistic as the 'pie-in-the-sky' variety he condemns so vehemently. The narrative presents a view of religion as having a socially equilibrating and cathartic function in contrast to Ivan, who believes that religion is a futile waiting game for some future utopian promise. Ivan wants his future now, in today's life and at this moment. However, the structure of his desire and his struggle to fulfil it turn out to be, ironically, of the same variety as that which he condemns. This is a major flaw in the structural possibilities of filmic signification in the classical narrative. It makes no distinctions between concretely different historical circumstances, but merely informs us that the actions and desires of the individual will remain essentially the same, because human desire and actions reflect certain core truths that, more or less, prove intractable through historical time. This view of the world implies that members of various social classes share the same interests, for example, to attain social advancement or the good life, and they will abuse power and incur social corruption in the same manner as social elites. A dialectical reading of history avers a different understanding. The poor do not have dreams of this sort, for these are a middle-class luxury. The poor have forthright realities to fulfil. Yes, the poor do have dreams, but the filmic signification in the classical narrative refuses to differentiate between the dreams of the powerful and those of the powerless.

Upon arrival in the city, Ivan goes to the movies. In the framed film narrative that features a Western being screened at the Rialto, a lone gunman is besieged by a score of hostile masked men. As they approach menacingly, the audience cringes in fear for the lone man's life. The odds are against him. But Jose, who brought Ivan to the cinema shouts out: "You think de hero can die till the last reel." In what appears to be his final moment, the gunman grabs a Gatlin gun and mows down his enemies. In this film within the film, the hero does not die; but in the framing film, Ivan's fate is sealed within the system of narrative realism so long as he opts for the outlaw lawlessness of the Western outlaw. The film within the film (which is a Western) and Ivan's fixation on the Old West play an important role in his narrative motivation. When these are coupled with the intertextual references to the urban outlaw Rhygin (a real-life mid-20th century Jamaican folk hero-outlaw), the narrative signifies a double failure for the hero: in so far as he seeks out and utilizes the cultural models of the oppressor without transforming them, he reinforces his own oppression. But the system of classical narration tends to glorify the hero, and a rebellious hero who seeks to alter the scheme of social relations in opposition to the reproduction of traditional social positions cannot be fulfilled within its narrative system.

Within this variety of narrative, the hero's motivation, his desire and the structure of his quest are related more to the cosmopolitan aspiration of Jamaica's middle classes because the poor are not the point of production of these views in *The Harder They Come*. The narrative system claims implicitly to be a neutral articulation of various voices in social discourse. It appears to speak for all social classes folding their consciousness into its own and masking the fact that there is a dominant perspective from which the narration speaks, a perspective that is concealed or repressed to generate a facade of democratic discourse. The articulation of poverty and the struggle that the hero undertakes against it all emanate from the position of society's advantaged classes, which guarantee its expression in the cinema through the system of narrative realism. The sensitivity with which Henzell handles his filmic material should not be devalued, but it is constrained by his mode of expression. His filmic language plays tricks on him: it unilaterally determines the structure of desire of his hero and his hero's destiny.

Ivan's heroism is rendered futile within the filmic signification of the classical narrative. The connections between the lives of the poor, their need to survive and their inevitable transgression of the law as a means of rectifying their powerless social position are carefully elided from the space of the narrative. The film does present the cultivation of ganja (marijuana) as a means of survival, and characteristically points out the nature of foreign and local exploitation of the trade. Most of the profits elude the farmers, those who produce it and take the risk in the first place. When Ivan challenges this system, he is isolated and must be put in his place. He becomes a man on the run. His eventual capture hinges on an increasing isolation through a deepening of the economic crisis the farmers are experiencing. They cannot earn a living because the police have put a halt to the trade until Ivan is caught. Surely, the cultivators of the crop will suffer; but the narrative carefully avoids the question of the effects of the ban on the local elites and international distributors, for so long as the trade is halted, the international connections also experience the drought.

All this leads us to question the speaking voice that controls the narration, for it is necessary to interrogate the system of biases it incorporates and the ideological interests it seeks to protect. Signification in the classical narrative suggests that individual characters speak from their individual and social class interests. But this understanding only masks the fact that the filmic world in the traditional cinema is constructed by dominant social forces and speaks to their concerns. Out of necessity, the voice of the poor resonates in opposition to that of dominant social groups. Thus, although Ivan's dream of removing himself from the yoke of exploitation and poverty is concrete and necessary, the manner in which he pursues this dream through the glorified life of the star and the illusory fame of the entertainment world is more the creation of the speaking voice of the narrative than of the poor. Within the narrative, Ivan is transformed from a pre-revolutionary peasant-type into an urban street hustler, whose revolution centers on the acquisition of a cosmopolitan lifestyle and consumption of North American consumer goods. Here, we witness the way the genre contains the

revolutionary potential of the film. As a result, when Ivan begins
to live out his dream, he loses touch with the social realities of
his life. Ivan appears to be a crazed man, driven into a stupor of
insatiable insanity. Hence, the narrative creates a space for Ivan's
rebellion, but it structures his revolutionary potential within the
context of a fantasy, a world within which the hero is destined to
die. This kind of rebellious hero, who challenges the status quo
must die within the system of classical narrative because his winning creates a crisis for the dominant system of values and the
narrative meanings they seek to justify.

NARRATIVE REALISM IN
THE HARDER THEY COME

In the narrative, although Ivan appears to have acquired the trap-
pings of power, such as guns, money and mobility, the filmic signification does not confirm their traditional meanings; rather it
contradicts them. When juxtaposed with Ivan's flamboyant cloth-
ing and conspicuous urban manner, the concept of lack anchors
these signifiers. Ivan acquires the form without the substance.
There is the acquisition of material goods, but he does not control the power that society associates with having such possessions. Ivan is thereby an increasingly vulnerable and dangerous
figure within the system of social signification, for the development of his character seems a fullness where in fact there is
absence. Ivan's narrative transformation from country boy to city
slicker is constructed intertextually upon a filmic signification
developed in the Hollywood cinema that stereotyped the black
male as a Zip Coon-type character. Within this delineation, castration and powerlessness mark the Zip Coon signifier especially in its low-comic zeal. Based on the symbolic codes of our
culture, the flamboyant coquettish attire of the street hustler signifies an absence, the lack of power. In *The Harder They Come*,
Ivan is transformed from square country boy to city slicker who
wears fancy, colorful hats, jeans, suede outfits, wet-look vests,
leopard-patterned shirt and dark glasses. Ivan becomes the
Johnny-Too-Bad signifier—a thug—from a song used in the
film's soundtrack. In the Johnny-Too-Bad scene, Ivan turns on
the radio and the song "Johnny-Too-Bad" provides a backdrop
to this encounter in the preacher's workshop.

Longo
Hey, pretty boy . . . , pretty hat. Johnny-Too-Bad,
bring me the hammer.
Ivan
What happen, yuh can't get it yuhself?
Longo
No man, you bring it for me.
Ivan
Bring the hammer!
Longo
You have on pretty hat this morning.
Ivan
Yuh like it?
Longo
You really look like Johnny-Too-Bad. You only need
to have a gun to look like Johnny. But before you
get a gun, get the broom and go sweep out de shop.

The signifier of Johnny-Too-Bad is already loaded with a question mark. The lyrics of the original song signify the 'rude-boy'
culture in the signifier *Johnny-Too-Bad*. He is the urban gangster
predator "walking down the road with a pistol in the waist," who
is looting and shooting while his victims are wailing. The song
informs us that his judgment day will come, and there will be no
running, no hiding place for Johnny. The misreading of Ivan's
rebelliousness in terms of the gangster compromises the filmic
signification of the narrative. As the lyrics of the song indicate,
this is a strident critique of the glorification of gangster elements
in contemporary urban Jamaican culture:

> *Walking down the road with a pistol in your waist,*
> *Johnny you're too bad;*
> *Walking down the road with a ratchet in your waist,*
> *Johnny you're too bad;*
> *You're just robbing and stabbing and looting and*
> *shooting . . .*

But whereas the sound image undertakes a sophisticated critique
of a social problem, its juxtaposition with the visual image of Ivan
wanting to break out of his poverty and oppression engenders
new meanings. Apparently the narrative is unable to separate
righteous rebellion from thug life. It presents us with a loaded
signifier: a hero with whom we can empathize, whose act of resis-

tance we invest in emotionally, but whose rebellion is linked with signifieds of urban gangster terrorists who prey on their own community. What we glean here is that a reformulated hero cannot be developed within traditional narrative signification, for the ideological baggage of narrative realism tends to support conservative cultural models more than give shape to the narrative potential of a reformulated heroic tradition.

Henzell's narrative presents a sophisticated paradigm of social change coded in the form of transportation technology, which is used to propel the narrative. Ivan is in control when dealing with forms of transportation that are integrated into his social existence. As the newly arrived country boy, he harnesses and masters the technology of the bicycle, which he actually builds from bits and pieces retrieved from the rubbish heap. The bicycle is also the vehicle for his romantic encounter with Elsa. Later in the narrative, he even manages to escape on a bicycle from the soldiers who close in on him. When Longo claims the bicycle after Preacher orders Ivan to leave the church premises, there is a moment of uninhibited violence and bloodletting. Given the structure of the incident, Ivan's choices are limited because the one moment when he is about to have control over his life is being snatched away from him. Ivan strikes out violently. Fanon (1968) writes: "He of whom they have never stopped saying that the only language he understands is that of force, decides to give utterance to force."

Ivan plays out a Fanonian theme of violence as purgative for the oppressed. His swift and spontaneous anger against Longo is less the result of the narrative's claim of a suitor's rivalry over Elsa between the two men, but the result of Longo's attempt to deprive Ivan of the creative moment when he has mastered his environment and constructed the bicycle. In a garish, exhibitionistic display of violence, Ivan mutilates the man's face. This incident propels Ivan into a life of crime in which his ambitions to become a famous singer preoccupy the major interest of the narration. But a more important reading locates these events within a vantage-point of the paradigm of power relations within the narrative. Ivan's swift response to Longo's attempt to seize his bicycle is his most important stand in the course of the narrative. By building the bicycle from the rubbish heap, Ivan has engendered some modicum of control over his life. One cannot simply take this away from him without a serious fight on his part. Ivan's punishment is just as violent. He receives eight strokes with the tamarind switch. The legally constituted violence of the system is brutal in its execution. It sheds its humanistic ideals in order to maintain the legal order. The liberal humanist ideology characteristic of narrative realism avers that violence in all its forms begets only violence. There is an apparent condemnation of all forms of violence through the genre's structuring of crime and punishment, and the futility of resorting to violence is underscored given that the forces of the law control and exercise more overpowering means of violence. The ideology of this system of narrative suggests that to struggle against the dominant order leads only to futility.

The filmmaker fashions his narration around the encounter of the individual with technology. Using the form of a riddle, Henzell codifies the problems of social development in relation to the acquisition and utilization of forms of technology. This theme is developed in the Jamaican context through the metaphor of forms of transportation technology that the hero confronts in his struggle for survival. The technological option he chooses, given the state of social development of his environment, contains the seeds of his survival or his narrative death. Ivan's encounter with various forms of transportation technology fuels the complications of the narrative. The more advanced forms of transportation technology—the motorcycle and the motor car—lead eventually to the hero's downfall and are linked in the narrative with various kinds of lawlessness. A discarded automobile is where Ivan sleeps. Preacher finds in it various signifiers of death and decadence: space-age toy gun, *Two-Gun Kid* comic book, *Playboy* magazine and pin-up posters of nude women. The motorcycle is the means for transporting ganja; it even becomes an accessory to the murder of a police officer.

Throughout the narrative, Ivan yearns for the freedom signified by the automobile. As the film opens, we see him as the outsider inside the bus looking longingly and excitedly out the window at a white convertible Mustang that zooms by filled with fun-loving riders. The recording studio mogul, Mr. Hilton, drives a white convertible Mercedes Benz. Hilton drives up as a group of unemployed musicians wait for a quick audition. He listens to their song, turns them down and drives on as Ivan stands in the background looking on. The signifier of the white convertible, whose drivers seem to possess the power and success for which Ivan craves, becomes a central factor in understanding the film's narrative structure. When Ivan's opportunity arrives finally, he too must be in the driver's seat of the particular automobile. At the hotel parking lot, he commandeers a white convertible Chevrolet Impala, holding the hotel attendant, who wears a white suit and white hat, at gunpoint. The white convertible is a signifier that Ivan is forbidden to express; however within the film's narrative system, he is destined to possess it. Possession of the white horse within the system of narrative realism can signify only his death. When Ivan transgresses the fixed social positions and relations of society and seeks to reformulate the structures of the Unconscious by moving from the position of the onlooker—that is, the passive object of power, to intrude upon a seemingly sacred rite; that is, the power and control of the white convertible—he must be punished. The signification of whiteness in *The Harder They Come* functions as a prominent hermeneutic feature of the film's structure of suspense. Upon Ivan's arrival in the city, he asks for directions to get to Milk Lane, which we learn is his mother's address. But when we read Milk Lane within the context of the other signifiers of whiteness that emerge throughout the film and which help determine its narrative outcome, we witness how social signification influences filmic signification, for Ivan's narrative quest is structured within the codes of power and powerlessness and dominant ideological positions of society.

The repeated shots of Ivan as the outsider pushes the narrative along a structure of social relations based on a system of social signification equivalent to the paradigm of powerful-powerless. The film utilizes windows, fences, natural barriers and other boundaries or demarcations to forcefully construct this visual motif. As the outsider, Ivan (the country boy) is unskilled and suffers constant rejection. When he seeks work at a construction site, he is kicked off and pushed further into the underground. The urban environment is cold and alien, with scenes of raucous poverty and human scavengers who survive off the dump heaps of Kingston's shanty towns. Ironically, the soundtrack appears to plays a wicked game actually inspiring Ivan to his fated confrontation with the law.

> You can get it if you really want;
> But you must try, try and try, try and try;
> You'll succeed at last.
> Persecution you must bear;
> Win or lose, you got to get your share,

> *Got your mind set on a dream,*
> *You can get it though hard it may seem now.*
> *Rome was not built in a day;*
> *Opposition will come your way.*
> *But the harder the battle you see,*
> *It's the sweeter the victory.*

In the film, the sound signifiers are highly developed and sophisticated in their signification of the plight of the powerless in society. The soundtrack points to and actually presents a complex and progressive commentary that the film's visual language has not mastered. For example,

> *007, Oceans eleven*
> *Dem a loot, dem a shoot,*
> *Dem a wail, Shanty town.*
> *Dem rude boys gone pon vacation.*

When the lyrics of the sound signification are juxtaposed with Ivan's struggle and the concrete circumstances of his existence, the result is irony, as in *Many Rivers To Cross*. The soundtrack proclaims: "Stop that train, I want to get off." But the narrative refuses to stop; rather, it drives Ivan deeper into the life against which the sound signifiers caution. The soundtrack informs: "You can get it, if you really want it." Ironically, Ivan really wants it, but he can't get it. The only sweet victory for him in the end is the manner of his death—he dies fighting. But his death is a setback because he dies as a result of delusional hallucinations interspersed with scenes from a Western movie, an illusory reality. In this sense, the filmic signification plays a cruel game, for it lifts the hopes of society's sufferers, but offers no consolation and they make no gains. The system of narrative realism draws on diverse sources, which in themselves may offer a progressive social critique. But when they are incorporated within the filmic signification of the narrative, their meaning is redefined within the ideological structures that reproduce realist film language.

WOMEN IN CLASSICAL FILM NARRATION

So long as Ivan remains within the strictures of his prescribed social position, a certain social equilibrium is maintained. Dominant political and economic relations are reaffirmed. But Ivan is a rebel, who is in conflict with established authority. When Preacher takes in Ivan, he demands his soul for God.

Preacher is a signifier of authority, he is a possessive figure, the keeper of the moral and legal order and the controller of sex. Ivan's quest for sexual and political freedom is met by Preacher's wrath. Preacher is disgusted with Ivan's lifestyle and warns the young rebel that he "should be reading the Bible and praising the Lord." Preacher finds Ivan in the church late at night rehearsing a secular song. Ivan's act is a desecration of the church. Whereas Preacher has bought what Ivan describes as pie-in-the-sky religion, characterized by orgiastic services, heart-rending sermons and rhythmic music, Ivan's religion is the expression of his freedom and the search for social justice. Although the narration develops the differences between Preacher and Ivan in terms of a conflict of social values and religion, when preacher finds Ivan in the church singing popular music late at night, immediately he storms into Elsa's room. Preacher wakes her up and interrogates her seeking to find out who let Ivan into the church. Yet, the narrative shifts attention away from Ivan's entry into the church to that of sex and control of the female.

> **Preacher**
> You gave him the key to my church, why?
> **Elsa**
> I had to give it to him.
> **Preacher**
> What else did you give him?
> **Elsa**
> Nothing! . . . I gave him nothing.
> **Preacher**
> You're lying.
> **Elsa**
> No.
> **Preacher**
> You've been fornicating with him.
> **Elsa**
> No.
> **Preacher**
> You gave him your lips.
> **Elsa**
> No.
> **Preacher**
> You gave him your body.
> **Elsa**

(Weeping)
No . . . No . . .

Whereas the narrative offers concrete issues over which the men argue and fight, nonetheless, the significant tension arises in relation to the position of women especially when men negotiate the lives of women. In an early scene, Longo tells Ivan that Preacher has been tending Elsa's garden for a long time, and if Preacher does not pick the fruit, he will, because implicitly he is entitled to possess women. Later, Ivan mutilates Longo's face. When Preacher confronts Elsa about giving Ivan entry to the church, his exchange disintegrates into charges about fornication.

The representation of women in *The Harder They Come* provides another example of the way the classical narrative is an ineffective means for reformulating an alternative film language. The film actually reproduces a reactionary ideology regarding the social positioning of women in its narrative. Who are the women in *The Harder They Come*? The plot is motivated by the death of Ivan's grandmother, which functions as the motivation for his move to the city. The hero's mother opposes his desire to emancipate himself from a life in the country for a dead-end life in the city. Ivan's encounter with his mother Daisy upon his arrival in the city is characteristic of the tension involving the representation of women in the film.

Daisy
What happen to de place?
Ivan
Grandma sold de place before she die.
Daisy
And what happen to de money?
Ivan
She say she wanted a big funeral.
Ivan gives her the remaining money from the property.
Daisy
Tis only this leave . . . ? How you going get back tonight?
Ivan
I not going back.
Daisy
What you going to do then? Yuh can't stay here, yuh know . . . because I can't help yuh.

Ivan
I staying in town.
Daisy
Yuh think town is easy? How yuh going to live?
Ivan
I could make a record. I can sing, yuh know mama.
Daisy
Yuh tek this thing for joke.
Ivan
Well, I can get a job then.
Daisy
What kind of job you can get outside of turn criminal.
Ivan
Why you say a thing like that? Why you say a thing like that 'bout me?
Daisy
. . . . Go back to country.

At best, we can say that Daisy is pragmatic and displays a maternal urge to protect her son. However, pragmatism is more concerned with adjusting to the practical problems of everyday existence as opposed to seeking out opportunities for change.

Another female is presented in the character of the suburban middle-class housewife who lounges in a verdant social setting oblivious to the poverty that pervades the world around her. She is isolated, insulated, dependent and romanticized. She has no sympathy for the suffering of the poor. Ivan approaches as she relaxes in an easy chair. He is positioned outside the hedge and is physically separated from her.

Ivan
How do you do?
Woman
What you doing here?
Ivan
I'm looking for work, ma'am.
Woman
I don't have any work to give you.
Ivan
I can wash your car, you know ma'am.
Woman

My husband gets the car washed downtown.
Ivan
I can do the gardening, you know ma'am.
Woman
We have a gardening service to do that.
Ivan
I can do anything you know ma'am . . . anything.
Woman
Look, there's nothing you can do for me . . . nothing.
Ivan
Give me ten cents ma'am.
Woman
What's the matter with you young, healthy boys. All you know is beg, beg, beg. That's all you can do is beg. How did you get in here anywhere?
Ivan
The gate was open.
Woman
Well, when you go outside, you make sure you lock the gate behind you.

The spectrum of female characters is completed with Pinky—Jose's companion—who lures Ivan into a police trap by granting him sexual favors. The police close in on Ivan as the couple enjoys sex.

A summary of the representation of women in *The Harder They Come* reveals how the death of Ivan's grandmother throws his life into crisis by catapulting him into the jungle of the city. His mother cannot help him in his time of need. Ivan pleads for help from a well-to-do housewife, who turns him away and berates him for his poverty. Ivan falls in love with Preacher's ward, Elsa; she gives him the key to the church where the Preacher catches him rehearsing a "profane" song. While on the run, Jose's companion leads him into a police trap. Finally, Elsa turns Ivan over to the authorities, and he is surrounded and killed by the army. The women in *The Harder They Come* function to legitimize the very status quo the hero sets out to overcome because their signification either thrusts Ivan into crisis or is developed in opposition to his struggle for freedom. What we learn about women in this film is that they are pragmatic, unquestioning of their social dependence and God-fearing.

The problem with the filmic signification of women in the classical narrative is related to the way we conceive of film: does the film reflect life and its social relations objectively? Or does it provide a critique of society in an attempt to produce knowledge with which we can change our social reality? The filmic signification of women in narrative realism reifies their political marginalization and functions as fodder for foregrounding a male-oriented narrative and the protagonist's heroic struggle. Ivan's conflict with Elsa illustrates the problem:

> **Ivan**
> You want me to go and beg work for $10.00 a week for the rest of my life. I tried that. I'd rather die. I don't want to. I'm going to make it.
> **Elsa**
> Ivan, . . . You're a dreamer.
> **Ivan**
> Me, a dreamer? Who's a bigger dreamer than you? . . . Always talking 'bout milk and honey in de sky. But no milk and honey no in de sky. Not for you, not for me . . . (It's) right down here, and I want mine now, tonight.

The dramatic requirements of the narrative position women in subordinate and in stereotypical terms. Toward the end of the narration, Elsa reveals to the Rastafarian Pedro that, "Every game I play, I lose." This certainly is a fitting epithet to describe the position of women in *bourgeois* society and their representation in the narrative realist film. Although this paradigm of filmic signification contains some progressive tendencies, it fails to proceed beyond stereotypes and the limitations imposed by the dominant world-view. The classical narrative seems incapable of radically transforming the popular signification of women. As an expressive form, it does offer elements of resistance, but it is extremely limited in its ability to reformulate new meanings and social positions.

IDEOLOGY IN CLASSICAL FILM NARRATION

Filmic signification in the classical narrative cinema conditions a limited view of the world and of social relations, which then ironically masquerades as truth; not ideology, as fact, not fiction. Although some Hollywood films present a progressive critique of society, it is through the use of a vulgar realism that the 'real' is removed from its proper historical context and is used to reproduce the world-view of dominant ideologies. Witness the way that movements and institutions of the socially disadvantaged are appropriated either intellectually or commercially by powerful social classes, thereby rendering mute important moments of social critique. Popular cinema may tend to use forms of social realism as a means of cinematic expression because it is believed that this narrative realism provides the most poignant expressive language for communicating political ideas and helping to bring about social change. The concern with realism exemplifies but one moment in a political critique of society. It dramatizes social conditions and may point to the need for resistance, but it steers clear from the more important task of reformulating meanings. But we must ask: how a system of signification that emerged within the problematic of contemporary Western society to meet its ideological needs can also serve as a vehicle for those who have suffered as a result of the rise of the West without any serious transformation? When filmmakers use narrative realism, it is imperative for them to question its system of filmic signification. It becomes crucial to undertake a reflexive critique of realist signification itself, for film not only reflects the conditions of social reality, but also functions to help create and alter reality through the production of its signification and its creation of alternative modes of perceiving, organizing and structuring reality.

Fundamentally, realism in the classical narrative is a descriptive cinematic form, which concerns itself with the visible and visual empirical effects of oppression as good subject matter for filmic signification. In so doing, it does not speak to the causes of oppression and the conditions that reproduce it. It visualizes suffering, but offers no perspective of society's oppressed. Henzell is able to push the genre to its limits in *The Harder They Come*, but in so doing aptly dramatizes the limits of narrative realism as an expressive language for the development of an alternative cinema. The use of film language within *The Harder They Come* is driven by the requirements of the narration. The cinematography and editing are lucid and lyrical. There are some brilliant visual sequences, such as the romantic interlude with Ivan and Elsa on the bicycle along the waterfront, that point the way to an alternative filmic signification. But the film relies primarily on realist framing and compositions, shot-reverse shot patterns and poignant documentary vignettes of urban life. The camera follows the narrative attentively, but does not push it or seek to redefine narrative concerns.

When the system of the classical narrative is pushed to its limits, it is possible to acknowledge the existence of a counter-cultural hero, but a new hero cannot be developed within the terms of this type of filmic signification. Ivan's exhibitionism and fatal confrontation with the law are tantamount to irresponsi-bility, and his acts of resistance take on the intertextual glamour and romance of Hollywood film genres, instead of locating the film's violence in the historic motivation of society's sufferers to redress their deprivation. Without a doubt, the filmmaker offers no sympathies for social elites: they are seen as corrupt and oppressive. In turn, the film also offers no strong sympathies for the oppressed. But the film is most cynical in its refusal to sep-arate the violence of the victim in response to his social condi-tion from that perpetrated by powerful social classes maintaining their social power. Ivan's narrative fantasy desire for the Old West elicits little sympathy for his fate. But the nature of his choice is where the problem lies. According to the ideology of the narra-tive, the oppressed will aspire to the conditions and lifestyle of dominant social classes if they are given the opportunity. At best, we live in a world gone mad, in which the victim, no matter how glamorous and romantic, is just as bad as the oppressor.

REFORMULATING THE PROBLEM OF BLACK CINEMA

There has been a strident modernist critique that realism in the classical narrative is a fabrication, that it is a way of seeing based on the established conventions of traditional social classes and dominant ideologies. It is not that realism cannot be a produc-tive means for an independent black film movement; but classi-cal narrative realism and its representational aesthetics are based on the institutionalized modes of perception and organization of social phenomena based on dominant paradigms of gender and race. It does not question the basis for its imagery, nor seek to transcend existing empirical social circumstance. This type of realism is a conservative social force.

Black independent cinema is most productive when it priv-ileges the expressive traditions it utilizes in its filmmaking prac-tice. By focusing on the expressive traditions through which a black cinema speaks, we emphasize the process of production of the film above its subject matter. When our principal concerns are with subject matter, it is easy to displace blacks in the film-making process. During the third wave of black films in the 1970s, a series of films emerged that ostensibly were labelled black films because they dealt with black subject matter. These films were produced for the most part by whites, within the Hollywood tradition; and many of them were exploitation films. Because audiences and critics were foremost concerned with the sociological and therapeutic values of these films, little attention was paid to the process of production.

Why is this important to black cinema? Inasmuch as tradi-tional cinema falls within the problematic of Aristotelian poet-ics, its paradigm of the relationship between the film and its audience presents limited possibilities for a new kind of viewer. Epistemologically, the world is revealed as subject to change, and cinema provides an excellent arena for helping to produce new knowledge and social transformation. The viewer refuses the tra-ditional positioning of a spectator, refusing to delegate power to the screen hero to act vicariously for him. Hence, this cinema is a catalyst for activating the viewer out of a social malaise. Unlike *Menace II Society* or *New Jack City*, a new black cinema is not so much concerned with graphic representations of a limited social reality, whose realistic depiction of events and dramatic situa-tions are based on a stereotyped urban pathology. The preoccu-pation with realism can turn into a fetish, hijacking the narrative and shrouding the knowledge that social change is possible or even necessary. Any important formulation of black film refus-es to celebrate a frozen moment in black history as the defining black experience; rather it returns that moment to a historical understanding that penetrates the captivating realist image, sub-jecting it to a process of transformation.

It is not surprising that the narration in an important film such as *Sankofa* engages questions of film form and film language as integral elements of its reformulation of African American his-tory. *Sankofa* explores cultural memory and historical fact begin-ning from the assumption that not only is it necessary to transform subject matter to reformulate meaning in the cinema, but the filmmaker must take into account narrative form as well. In the practice of black filmmaking, we ask that film produce new knowledge, help forge new relationships, afford some plea-sure and help change our world for the better.

Chapter Six

Narrative Transformation in *Sweet Sweetback's Baadassss Song*

C ontroversy has surrounded Melvin Van Peebles's *Sweet Sweetback's Baadassss* Song since its first screening in 1971. Some of *Sweetback's* detractors base their criteria of black film on the aesthetics of Classical Hollywood cinema, emphasizing middle-class values over the unvarnished tension characteristic of working-class urban images, such as those found in *Sweetback*, early blues singers and in forms of rap music. They also use a definition of black film that values wholesome content, a sort of Afrocentric Disneyesque criterion. Some critics find that *Sweetback* represents the epitome of misogynist thinking. To some, it is exploitation cinema par excellence. Yet others, including myself, consider the film an important work in the history of African American cinema.

THE SWEETBACK CONTROVERSY

Black establishment critics like Lerone Bennett rejected the film's revolutionary activism and considered it as sexual propaganda, stating that "fucking will not set you free" (1971, p. 106). Nelson George observes that "Sweetback defied the positive-image canon of Sidney Poitier, dealing openly with black sexuality, government-sanctioned brutality, and the arbitrary violence of inner-city life. Its refusal to compromise still sparks black artists from Ice Cube to Matty Rich" (1992, p. 4). Cripps writes, "In contrast to the upstanding, prim, overtrained characters played by Poitier, *Sweetback* set forth new outlines of heroic behavior. He killed remorsely; swaggered; lived off black allies in a squalid, neon-lit streetscape; wore the cool mask behind which black youngsters carried their private selves; performed feats of sexual athleticism" (1990, p. 238). Diawara makes the point that *Sweetback* "is the paradigmatic text for the 1970s blaxploitation films" (1993, p. 9). Huey P. Newton, Black Panther Party minister of defense, found *Sweetback* refreshing and an important political film (1972, p. 116). The black cultural nationalist arts group, the Kuumba Workshop (1978) viewed the film as lewd and sensational. In their opinion, it failed to advance the cause of black revolution. Bowser found that criticism of *Sweetback* did not really get at the heart of the problem, which she describes as being "a very painful experience for the black community to look at . . . for the first time, on that 10-foot screen – in a public movie house – one is looking at very, very painful characters in our community" (1982, p. 57). Michele Wallace characterizes *Sweetback* as "fantastically mysogynistic" (1993, p. 260). Cade Bambara wanted to know: "Was *Sweetback* a case of Stagolee Meets Fanon or Watermelon Man Plays Bigger Thomas?" (1993, p. 118). Taylor commented that *Sweetback* "remains a powerful evocation of police-state brutality against the black community" (1988). While Reid does not include *Sweetback* in his canon of black independent films (1993, p. 82), others find it to be a "landmark film, . . . a seminal work in the search for a black cinema aesthetic" (Yearwood, 1982, p. 75).

The *Sweetback* controversy presents a prominent example of the need for greater methodological clarity in black film studies. Although *Sweetback* has been one of the most intensely discussed works in black film history, most of the controversy has skimmed the film's surface and has not adequately addressed the film as text. The problem of methodology in black film studies remains significant because most critics do not articulate the methods they use for film analysis and drawing conclusions. Black film critics use a variety of methods, approaches and strategies, which are often unstated and difficult, if occasionally impossible, to replicate. Their criticism is too often unsystematic, anti-method and riddled with excessive subjectivity. A lot of black film criticism overlooks the text. This has led to many misunderstandings about *Sweetback*. How do we understand a film like *Sweetback*? How do we resolve the widely divergent responses of critics? To do so, it is necessary to focus on the textual system of narration by using a close reading to examine filmic signification and narrative choices. Fundamentally, *Sweetback* is a critique of cinema, representation, and social reality. The film's narration raises several issues: Does film "re-present" the real world or does it create signification of that world? Should film "re-present" the established conventions and dominant understandings of society or should it undertake their transformation? *Sweetback* seeks to alter traditional ways of seeing by presenting new possibilities for the development of filmic signification and creating an alternative "popular" cinema outside the conservative ideological parameters of the traditional Hollywood cinema. Van Peebles opens his narration with a quotation from a medieval saying:

> *Sire, these lines are not a homage*
> *To brutality that the artist has*
> *Invented, but a hymn from the*
> *Mouth of reality.*

SWEETBACK'S ALLEGORY OF REVOLT

Sweet Sweetback's Baadasssss Song is not only a landmark film in African American cinema, it stands as a seminal work in the search for a black cinema aesthetic. Because *Sweetback* was made outside the studio system, it effectively established methods of popular filmmaking defying traditional boundaries. As cinema of transformation, it rejected the glorification of urban street culture for the more important task of the political development of a street hustler and linkage with the black protest movement. As a cinematic document, Van Peebles' creative uses of film language immediately set him up in opposition to the dominant ideologies of the cinema. *Sweetback* represents a significant formulation of the political uses of non-documentary cinema.

The intervention of politics in non-documentary cinema takes place precisely at the moment when the filmmaker uses prevalent cinematic paradigms as a means of expression. The use of the classical narrative and its accompanying star system imply acceptance of the ideological system it supports. Black cinema, as a cinema of difference, cannot assert itself when constructed upon the very ideologies that maintain its oppression. In *Sweetback*, there is a refusal to reproduce Hollywood's cinematic grammar and syntax. Van Peebles uses his camera not as a simple servant of the film's narrative development, but to reformulate the question of cinema as a mode of writing. In doing this, he disturbs the traditional position of the viewer as consumer, forcing a reformulation of the viewer in relation to the film.

The refusal of the illusion of reality in cinema functions as the basis for development of black cinema because the illusion of reality reproduces a limited view of society and its social relations. When a black cinema affirms the illusion, it merely legitimizes the subordinate position of blacks within the social structure and within traditional cinema. *Sweetback* attacks the illusion of cinema; and as a result fosters alternative understandings. In the classical narrative, the viewer is preoccupied with the progression of the narrative and becomes engaged in a pursuit of the story through the enrapturing moment-to-moment unraveling of the story line. However, *Sweetback* allows no such luxuries; it forcefully moves attention to the uses of cinematic language and other political and ideological questions.

Black cinema fosters this movement against traditional understandings. To underscore the point, traditional positions, prevalent cinematic languages, and classical narration are all constructed within an ideological paradigm based on the subordination of blacks. If a black cinema consciously locates itself within these racial and sexual paradigms, it digs itself deeper into a state of non-existence. Thus, in *Sweetback* a chain of change is triggered, and we are confronted with the transformation of cinematic illusion, which does not allow the viewer to experience the film as pastime. In so far as *Sweetback* reveals knowledge of cinema as a mode of production, we can clearly see film not as slice of real life unreeling before our eyes, but as the result of a process of production. It is a narrative world that is manufactured and fabricated according to ideological, political, symbolic and economic constraints.

Claims are often made that *Sweetback* set back the black movement through its explicit exploitative themes and main character. In contrast to the character *Sweetback*, a middle-class heroic type is generally advocated as an exemplary black film hero. This argument locates itself within a historical bias of the black middle class, which has viewed itself as the leaders of the black community. This historical bias centers on the emulation of cultural standards and values approximating those of dominant social groups and the repression of vernacular expressions derived from black folkways. Many black middle-class critics saw the intrusion of folk styles and black working class urban cultural expression as coercive, destructive elements. Ironically, the finest expressions of an Afro-American cultural tradition are to be found in these very sources that have had to struggle for their survival. As a result, these cultural expressions are, in fact, tools of resistance because they present a clear and fundamental formulation of the position of blacks within the social structure and keep alive the African American expressive tradition. In black film history, *Sweetback* continues a tradition of black resistance. In its allegory of revolt and its sophisticated symbolic delineation of a black hero, *Sweetback* takes its place in black folk history along with the mythical folk-tale tricksters who embody our survival. In *Sweetback*, there is a necessary refusal of the fixed relations of power that function as supports in traditional cinema. The film informs us that Hollywood's language of imagery, its negative ideology of color and its star system all emanate from a series of primal ideological supports, which at their base foster the political subordination of blacks and women and the symbolic oppression of these groups in social intercourse. In the system of the classical narrative, fear, suspense, chaos, savagery, for example, are all signified in a matrix of darkness and femininity. In contrast to the signification of darkness and blackness in a film like *Star Wars*, its delineation in *Sweetback* or even *Shaft* takes place within a different range of meanings. The history of popular culture and of the cinema as a commercial and political complex finds its greatest successes on these ideological constructs. When a black film enters the system of exchange, it must be on *Sweetback's* terms. Otherwise, it will be edited and distributed to meet the commercial requirements of the status quo.

THE POWER OF NAMING – 'RATED X BY AN ALL-WHITE JURY'

The notion of struggle permeates several aspects of *Sweet Sweetback's Baadasss Song*. When the film was rated *X*, Van Peebles included a statement in the film's publicity that it was "Rated *X* by an All-White Jury." The filmmaker initiated a struggle over who has the right to name and validate the social reality of African Americans. The contestation of meanings and the challenge to traditional social perceptions serve as important organizing principles of the film.

 Sweetback also presents new possibilities for the development of visual and sound elements in filmic signification and succeeds in creating an alternative popular cinema outside the conservative parameters of the traditional Hollywood cinema. In his motion of refusing the system of established conventions, the opening credits of the film read: "Starring . . . The Black

Community, Brer Soul." Essentially, the star of the film is all of us and none of us. Movie stardom elevates the hero to the status of the gods. Thus, in contrast, this film has performers but no stars. Sweetback is its hero because the multitude of narrative acts clusters around him, but not in the way we associate with the world of traditional film heroes. Van Peebles avers that what we know as reality is really the point of view of particular social classes and is, therefore, open to contestation and questioning.

It is not possible to understand the signification in *Sweet Sweetback's Baadasssss Song* by isolating the film's images from their filmic context through an antihistorical, non-contextual critique. In the cinema, the single image functions similar to the way a word functions in sentence. Cinematic images are properly understood as part of a chain of filmic signification. The pivotal force of the film is the moving image. A filmic signifier is very much like Barthes' lexia in *S/Z*, rather than an independent frozen image that stands alone. In filmic signification, one image can effectively nullify, neutralize, reinforce or accentuate another.

The filmic strategy Van Peebles uses is motivated from the use of the familiar stereotype, which initiates a progressive defamiliarization of the image so that a process of Brechtian distanciation is enforced. This becomes the driving force of the film. The familiar stereotype is then deprived of its regime of pleasure and its conventional enjoyment. The task that Van Peebles sets for himself is doubly difficult for it involves the use of popular stereotypes as a motivating premise for a political analysis of society and a fundamental concern with challenging traditional perceptual modes of experience.

The subsequent series of images that initiate the narration exemplify this particular approach to filmic signification: cut from a shot of a coquettishly dressed woman wearing dark glasses and a feather shawl to a shot of the behind of a woman who wears a red house dress and has her foot raised on to the edge of a bed. The woman entices a young boy whom she undresses, and pulls him on top of her in a sexual position. But the soundtrack refuses to confirm the popular meaning of the visual image. The chorus chants the African American religious song "Wade in de Water". The woman tells the boy, "You ain't at the photographer's, you ain't getting your picture taken . . . Move!"

While the visual image features a sexual encounter between the obviously older woman and the young boy in a house of prostitution, the sound image presents religious music. First, we hear "Wade in de Water," which is followed by "This Little Light of Mine, I'm gonna Let It Shine," and a woman's climactic screams. Whereas the separate sound and visual signifiers suggest a variety of signifieds, the clustering of these images suggests new meanings that arise only with the juxtaposition of the visual and sound. The boy, who has now come of age, is taken in by the matron of a whorehouse where he was mothered, nurtured and initiated into adulthood. The religious music of the soundtrack counterpoints the sexual scene by injecting meanings of purification, baptism and initiation.

The separate, disparate elements comprising the filmic signification are, in themselves, contradictory. On the one hand, the visual signification implies sexual exploitation and statutory rape of the child/adult for the pleasure of the woman. However, to get a better grasp of this image, it is necessary to assess the metaphors of irony used by the filmmaker in the film's chain of signification and not focus only on its separate units. Undoubtedly, our common knowledge tells us that the visual image is perverse; but the larger context of the filmic signification within which that image arises provides a commentary and critique of the image. Let us contrast this "Initiation Into Manhood" scene with a similar one from *The Learning Tree*, which develops its sequence of events within a mystical aura. Newton Winger, the film's protagonist is lost as a storm approaches. Big Mabel, an adult woman who works as a prostitute helps Newton out of the storm. The woman seduces the boy who is dazed. The sexual scene is full of the forbidden pleasures, which the classical narrative hints at but conceals. Its representational style plays to the viewer's voyeuristic curiosity. The sex scene ends with a brilliant pregnant orange balloon of a sun poised against the landscape of the American Southwest. While some critics find Sweetback's "Initiation Into Manhood" scene despicable, very little comment is made about the corresponding scene in *The Learning Tree*. Interestingly, Parks' film is usually recommended for young viewers, while *Sweetback* is not. Whereas *The Learning Tree* creates the mystification of sex, *Sweetback* demystifies it. The representation of sexuality in *The Learning Tree* is a glorification of traditional romantic notions of sex. *Sweetback* rejects this romanticization by offering a certain reprehensible reality in the filmic signification that refuses to be seen as simple object for our consumption as pleasure.

Throughout his work, Van Peebles examines the bases of popular entertainment and analyses how the sound image and visual image are used within traditional stereotyped entertainment functions. The melodies of the film's soundtrack may be captivating; but the lyrics offer no compromise. Van Peebles finds reality to be a complex business, which defies simplification. The filmmaker does not merely accept and pander to these common understandings, he initiates a polemic against them. Van Peebles understands the magnetic attraction surrounding stereotypes of blacks in popular consciousness, and he often begins his narrative strategy from the comfortable vantage point of commonplace understandings. What is most significant in his narrative strategy is the way he then moves away from the stereotype, deconstructing and reformulating the familiar representation. Without a proper understanding of the nature of filmic signification, it is possible to commit the critical error many make in assessing *Sweetback* as exploitation cinema that wallows in depictions of horrid, animalistic sex.

In *Watermelon Man* (1968), Van Peebles crafts a plot in which the white protagonist is transformed into a black man. Godfrey Cambrigde plays the white main character in 'whiteface.' Obviously, attention to existing notions of reality and established conventions of the 'real' are of little interest to the filmmaker, who suspends the criteria of empiricism in the system of representation in order to elevate the fundamentally filmic element. This refusal of a simplistic notion of realism in order to create a filmic world that reflexively critiques the popular image or stereotype is found throughout Van Peebles' films, his theatrical work as well as his audio recordings.

Sweetback is a commentary on the fundamental structuring function that gender roles and sexual positioning imposes on society. There is the related focus on how social power is reproduced as the natural order of things in the classical narrative. Although the women seen at the beginning of the film are presented within the space of a whorehouse, they are not represented specifically as prostitutes. Prostitution is the commodification of a sexual act performed in exchange for some form of compensation, usually monetary. The system of relations developed in the act of prostitution is based on the dominant patriarchal paradigm that characterizes most other social relations and the distribution of power in society. It implies the terms of exchange that underline the organization of Western society, which are the positions establishing the distribution of power: master/slave; buyer/seller; active/passive; the one receiving pleasure/the one giving pleasure. In a sense, prostitution implies a certain defiance of established social positioning of the woman who refuses to play the accepted role of the female. Yet, inasmuch as prostitution as an act of exchange reaffirms the existing system of social relations, the rendering of the female body as a commodity functions in the service of the status quo.

The character of Sweetback is developed through the 'Nightclub' scene in the film's opening sequence. Sweetback is introduced as a performer in a nightclub sex act. The plot moves forward when the police seek a 'patsy' to satisfy their superiors, who want an arrest to satisfy top brass and local politicians that they are working to contain the explosive urban black revolt. But the narration is not so much concerned with this plot development item, for all this appears to be subsidiary to the activities of the nightclub show. The 'Nightclub' scene is presented using subdued lighting and rapid editing. It involves the presentation of several levels of reality. The nightclub act opens with a woman wearing an Afro-hair style with a long white streak down the center. This figure is dressed in a white knit dress with small-patterned holes that expose the skin. A bearded man who wears a hat, suit and carries a cane accompanies the woman on stage. The show features live sex entertainment. The style of acting is deliberately non-naturalistic. The dominant atmospherics exude an air of make-believe. The two figures are soon engaged in a semicomic sexual act simulating intercourse. The male figure is sexually positioned on top of the woman. The 'fairy godmother'—a man dressed in white impish skirt carrying a child's sparkler—enters. "I'm the good dyke's fairy godmother ... why, don't you know that all good dykes have fairy godmothers?" The question of exactly which reality is real continues to be a principal concern of the narration. At this point, a handheld camera technique is used. There is brisk movement, the use of close ups with rapid fades: Body wearing bra; hands take off bra; shot of male body; repeat of body wearing bra; shot of male body; repeat of body wearing bra; shot of male body; repeat of body wearing bra; Sweetback emerges from the female body wearing the bra; a shot of his penis; and the sex show continues. Spectators look on avidly, and the camera moves around the room to the music of Rhythm and Blues. There is a cutaway to the rear of the club where a couple of white detectives and the club owner, Beetle, are engaged in a conversation.

> **Beetle**
> We don't know nothing 'bout no dead man.
> **Detective**
> We know that, but the Commissioner doesn't.
> We just want to borrow one of your boys for a cou-
> ple of hours to make us look good . . . official-wise!
> **Beetle**
> Why me? I'm short a man already, George is sick.
> **Detective**
> You're our friend. We know you'd be willing to lend
> us a hand.
> **Beetle**
> Why you people all of a sudden so interested in
> black folks – dead or alive?
> **Detective**
> Progress!

On an empirical level, the 'Nightclub' scene involves risqué entertainment. However, there is a lot more going on involving different levels of reality, which reveals important information about the nature of film, sexual roles and the mechanisms that reproduce traditional ideologies in the cinema. The narration suggests that film is a fairy tale, a system of make-believe. The confusion of sexual positions resulting from the multiple signi-fiers of the 'dyke' plays havoc with the system of realist signifi-cation: At one moment, the figure appears to be a man, then a woman, and again a man. The narration focuses on the struc-ture of sexual pleasure in popular entertainment both in the live sex act and in the film as well. Momentarily, we see the large penis of Sweetback. This is followed immediately by the revela-tion of sexual confusion in the figure of the bearded man. Sweetback emerges the final agent of the series of visual trans-formations. This chain of filmic signification formulates the social options available to Sweetback: will Sweetback live the cas-trated existence of a sexual 'freak' performing in night club acts or will he realize the potential for revolt contained in the signi-fier of the castrated image, which exposes the fragility of his posi-tioning as an object of sexual desire and containment.

Whereas pornography is the graphic display of sexual acts for an onlooker's voyeuristic pleasure, the filmmaker uses the pornographic moment to the film's advantage. Were this a simple pornographic event, a different kind of cinematography would have been used. The camera would develop the eroticism of the body specifically for the specular pleasure of the viewer as voyeur. In this sequence, the images come and go in a rapid editing sequence. The viewer is unable to grasp them satisfactorily in order to savor their pleasure. The body is not represented in glamorous terms, although it is adorned to suggest sexual pleasure; ultimately it refuses to gratify the viewer and consummate his expectation. The sexual acts are simple, cold and mechanical. What is being contested in *Sweetback* and the controversy revolving around it is precisely our notion of reality – how we understand reality and how we represent it in our films.

The dominant way of seeing of any age operates to buttress the ideological interests of powerful social classes. The narration begins with the commonplace stereotype, but uses it in such a way as to force a new knowledge of the familiar. The tools the filmmaker uses include a formulation of film language that mitigates against the traditional experience of cinematic pleasure. The film language is experimental and explores the possibilities of filmic signification from the point of view of society's powerless. In the visual arts, the representation of blacks and women takes place within an ideological area that confirms their subordinate social status. *Sweetback* dares to use the stereotype, which the dominant society prefers to control and which the black middle class prefers to repress. Whereas the dominant society begins with the stereotype and ends with its reification, *Sweetback* places the popular image in crisis. But the problem facing filmmakers who seek to reformulate the familiar with new cinematic approaches is the need to re-educate the audience and to motivate new ways of seeing. Working-class viewers respond more favorably to *Sweetback* than middle-class audiences because it is valuable to them and deals frankly with the concrete conditions of their existence. Furthermore, it presents a character from the streets (a world they encounter frequently), who despite the seemingly impossible task of altering his life, strikes a small, but nonetheless important blow for his freedom.

THE DAWNING OF
A POLITICAL CONSCIOUSNESS

The opening sequence establishes the quandary of Sweetback's
social condition. He is a mere freak who exists in the underbel-
ly of urban America to provide sexual thrills for nightclub audiences. The narration makes no judgments about Sweetback's
profession or his lifestyle. These are presented as the product of
a certain historical reality that cannot be repressed whether we
seek to deny its existence or not. The narration also introduces
elements such as the Black Power revolt, the black revolutionary MooMoo, who, in contrast to Sweetback, is actively engaged
in a struggle to alter the course of history. Interestingly, the transition connecting the opening sequence of the film (which ends
with the police taking Sweetback away from the night club scene)
to the next scene (in which MooMoo is arrested) assumes an
importance as significant as the two sequences it connects. The
transition incorporates experimental use of filmic languages. We
see shots of Sweetback being taken away in the night and a neon-
lit sign "Jesus Saves" is interspersed with the night shots. But the
soundtrack immediately superimposes the raised voices of an
angry crowd over the visual image. The flow of sound and visual signifiers are chosen carefully for their filmic impact: the city
at night (nightlife); Jesus Saves (religion); urban rebellion; the
protagonist Sweetback in chains; and the young revolutionary
MooMoo captured. The images are varied. In and of themselves,
most are inconsequential; but when these images collide within
the filmic signification, powerful meanings are formulated. In
one filmic statement, the camera in a travelling shot depicts the
glitter of the nightscape as a policeman tells MooMoo, "You been
stirring up the natives, kid!" Then, the music rises in a bold unre-
strained statement, accompanied by the following dialogue:

> **Police Officer No. 1**
> Nice night for a drive!
> **Police Officer No. 2**
> Nice night for a walk too!

The dialogue is minimal. The narration then features abstract
images of machinery at work intermixed with extraordinary
color effects and superimposed images of the figure of Sweetback
on the run. Sweetback is motionless as the police beat MooMoo.
When he no longer can contain his anger at the severe beating

the young black man is receiving, Sweetback unleashes a torrent of spontaneous violence using the handcuffs that were used to chain the two men. Fanon observes that "violence is a cleansing force. It frees the native from his inferiority complex and from his despair and inaction; it makes him fearless and restores his self-respect" (1968, p. 94). However, Sweetback's violence to aid MooMoo cannot have the force of a revolutionary act for it is a spontaneous response, which is forceful but without direction. MooMoo is grateful, telling Sweetback, "Thanks man, . . . where we going?" Sweetback responds coldly, "Where you get that we Shit . . . ?" Whereas Sweetback responds to an act of inhuman suffering, he has not yet internalized the need for unity and struggle. As victim, he empathizes with other victims; but his political awakening and maturity is yet to come. The presentation of Sweetback as a character who undergoes a political awakening out of a deeply oppressive social condition is a critical moment in black cinema. Bourne describes Sweetback's transformation as the dawning of a political consciousness that evolves into a willingness to act on behalf of one's community: "It was one of the first African American films that, in effect, showed the growth and development of a political consciousness. It was an important moment in the evolution of black cinema which involved redefinition and initial struggle against one's fate in America" (1982, p. 56).

A major thematic strand of the film deals with Sweetback on the run. The visual statements focus on motion, movement and their continued repetition. The repeated shots and the repetitive actions do not function to integrate separate aspects of the narrative; they serve only to confound the viewer as to why there is so much emphasis upon Sweetback's running. In the opening sequences of the narrative, Sweetback's motion is without direction. What we know is that Sweetback had to act in order to save the young revolutionary; but the continued repetition of the visual signifier of the runner and the occasional emphatic shots of Sweetback's feet extend beyond the theme of escape. Sweetback has transgressed his established social position, and now exists in a disequilibrium signified through the figure of the runner. His running is not recreational, but more fundamental: Sweetback is running for his life. Fanon discussed this interest in movement among the oppressed: "The first thing the native learns is to stay in his place, and not to go beyond certain limits. This is why the dreams of the native are of action and aggres-

sion. I dream I am jumping, swimming, running, climbing"
(1968, p. 52). The narration proceeds with a series of events that
Sweetback experiences while on the run. Each succeeding event
poses a dilemma for him because as he makes good his escape,
he cannot ignore the fact that various people in his world act so
that his life can be saved. Sweetback's worldview begins to undergo a transformation, for he can no longer deny the acts of broth-
erhood he experiences while on the run. As a matter of fact, those
who help Sweetback elude the police do so at tremendous risk.
Despite torture and mutilation, Beetle still does not turn
Sweetback in to the police.

Sweetback is captured after leaving Beetle's apartment. He
refuses to co-operate and is beaten by them. A split-screen device
is used in which we see a half-dark, half-screen image of a police
car in an inner-city neighborhood. Some black teenagers
approach the police car offering to wash it. Soon the car is set
ablaze by those helpers who aid the hero's escape. The helper or
the agent that makes good the escape of the hero fulfils a significant ideological function in facilitating the success of the hero's
narrative quest. This moment allows a notable critique of the
system of the classical narrative because it confirms the cultural
basis of forms of social organization and the way narrative functions to help reproduce or transform them. Any narrative invokes
elements of magic. In traditional criticism, this is often referred
to as the willing suspension of belief. These narrative feats, which
the viewer decodes as legitimate events, provide support structures for the world-view of the narrative and seek to guarantee
its social and political system.

THE QUESTION OF
SEXUAL PLEASURE IN SWEETBACK

Still handcuffed, Sweetback seeks temporary haven in the room
of a woman friend. He wants her to remove the handcuffs. She
refuses and tells him to beg. Sweetback stands over her with his
chained hands, outstretched in a gesture of helplessness. He
refuses to beg. The woman demands sex before she will help him.
The ideology of the dominant society permeates deeply into the
consciousness of the oppressed: the woman demands a contrac-
tual agreement to aid *Sweetback*. Many view the woman's demand
for sex as implying a looseness and freakishness of the black
woman; but a careful analysis would demonstrate that the sexual positions in the sex contract (woman = buyer; Sweetback = sell-

er) are the reverse of the existing distribution of power in society. The woman takes off her panties and disposes of Sweetback's pants. Traditional sexual positions are disturbed because the woman functions as the sexual aggressor, but not in the sense that one encounters in the pornographic film. We might even juxtapose this sex contract scene with Sweetback's earlier delineation as a superstud. Certainly, the tables have been turned as Sweetback begins to undergo a transformation in the plot. Without any filmic embellishment of the sexual act, Sweetback settles between the woman's legs. She sighs. He is a very inert figure in the sexual encounter.

It is important to distinguish between images of eroticism produced principally for monetary gain and sexual images that defy the traditional signifieds of eroticism and pleasure made popular in the mass media. Once again, the narration presents the sexual act more in terms of shock than titillation. The sexual contract is fulfilled to the satisfaction of this woman in the narrative; but not for the audience – the silent but ever present partner. The filmic signification denies the sexual pleasure associated with a sex scene in the classical narrative. *Sweetback* would have to revert to traditional images of sexual pleasure to fulfil its contract with the audience. The viewer is not afforded the normal expectation of filmic pleasure he would find in a typical sex scene in the classical narrative. What the viewer sees is a motionless, stiff figure of Sweetback at a time when we expect ecstatic sexual rapture. This line of meanings is supported also when we consider the juxtaposition of this sex contract scene with the one that follows immediately:

> *Visual image of a motionless Sweetback positioned between the woman's legs. The soundtrack uses a voice over.*
>
> **Male Voice (Off-screen)**
> Where's Sweetback?
> *Cut to Beetle's apartment where he is being tortured by police. A pistol is shot next to his ear. Blood flows. Beetle refuses to talk. The police continue to torture him. There is a montage of nerve-shattering sound effects and abstract visual patterns. We then see Beetle's bloody face, a shot of a woman's face in church. The soundtrack resonates, "Oh Jesus . . ." Shots of Sweetback on the run are intercut with shots of faces from the church scene. At the*

front of the church, a preacher conducts a funeral. His
sermon eulogizes a man who died from an overdose of
black misery.

The narrative logic constructs axes of meaning at the level of the
chain of signification and not on the level of the individual visual or sound images. Most critics of the film make the error of
isolating individual images and fail to realize that statements in
the cinema begin with the individual visual or sound elements,
but are completed through the lexia – the chain of signification
– or the cinematic context that the narrative constructs.

The preacher, who wears African robes, is a figure of con-
trasts. He might be running a "farm" that feeds women into the
nightclub business or provides them haven from it. He admits
to Sweetback that he is preaching a social palliative, but explains
that he is only providing a little worldly comfort for downtrodden souls. Sweetback seeks a place to hide; and there is a quick
cut to a room where we see the image of a distraught black
woman screaming madly from a bed. She appears to be under-
going the pains of drug withdrawal. The preacher, too, is responsible for injecting this hope into the lives of the oppressed. At
this moment, there is an affinity with Sweetback, for the woman
expresses graphically what Sweetback has internalized.
Interestingly, this section of the film contains the most dialogue.
It is rare when Sweetback has dialogue in the narrative; and when
he does, he says very few words.

Preacher
(to Sweetback)
It is strange that when we die our souls like to
rejoice. But when it comes to the living, that's it . .
. them people inside . . . It ain't dangerous. I'm just
selling them a little bit of happiness, you know. . .
from the happy land. We're all gonna die, and all I
want them to have is some peace. It's my job to make
them believe that they're gonna get it better on the
other side. It's my job . . . MooMoo, the boy you
saved, and those other kids. They are laying down
the real religion. They got it. You're awful good
news to me, slapping on some white cops. Yes,
indeed. I'm gonna say a black Ave Maria for you.
Like the kids say, . . . later for whitey. You saved a

plant they were gonna pick in the bud. That's why
the man's down on you. That's why the man's down
on you. I'm still gonna say a black Ave Maria for you.

Sweetback, too, has died a certain death. It is possible within the
scope of the filmic signification that the preacher is presiding
over Sweetback's death. The preacher seems to be making a point
about Sweetback's death when he tells him, "when we die, our
souls like to rejoice." But the existence for the black underclass
continues to be one deprived of peace and happiness. The
preacher distinguishes between a false religion (which he uses to
bring some worldly peace to the restless souls of the oppressed)
and the political nature of his social position, for he subscribes
to the revolutionary cause, blesses Sweetback and helps drug
addicts. Within the system of the filmic signification, the preacher is selling religion as an opiate, but is using religion for its political and psychological advantages to the oppressed.

Sweetback continues his journey in search of help. At a gambling cellar, a group of men are playing cards seated around a
table. The manager, who is dressed in a two-piece suit, tells
Sweetback:

Manager
What does a dead man need bread for? So he can
whip him a brother? How many brothers have you
whupped? How many sisters have you zapped? Life
is tough baby, . . . a real struggle, from the womb to
the tomb. Every dollar we make, the guineas get 20;
the police get 40; and Goldberg gets 50. Anybody
can tell you that don't add up to a dollar and a dime.
That's why all us niggers are so far behind.
Man (Off-screen)
And Africa shall stretch forth her arms.
(The view is of the gambling table.)
Man
Yeah . . . , and bring forth a bloody stump.
(He takes a long drink of beer)
Man No. 2
Viva Puerto Rico libre!
The room breaks into applause and laughter.

The old Sweetback has died decisively in this sequence. He has undergone a series of encounters that have altered his social awareness. Now, he awakens to his social situation and there is the dawning of a political consciousness. In this sequence, the narration is preoccupied with imagery of death. The preacher presides over a funeral. The manager tells Sweetback that a dead man needs no money or worldly things. There are also the harsh realities facing blacks: life is tough; it is a game rigged against the oppressed. Off screen, we hear one man shout that, "Africa shall stretch forth her arms;" while another adds, "(to) bring forth a bloody stump." This cryptic allegory speaks also of a certain death in that the body of the tree has been felled; but there remains a bloody stump. Yet, there is also the implication of birth arising from death and unity among peoples seeking freedom.

The manager of the gambling cellar aids Sweetback by taking him away in a getaway car. As they drive along, Sweetback spots MooMoo roaming the streets and stops the car in order to pick him up. Once again, the nightscape includes repeated references to the neon sign "Jesus Saves," which is superimposed over MooMoo's face as he sits in the back seat of the car. The driver drops the two men at the edge of town, telling Sweetback that he's a dead man, so go buy a last supper. Actually, the old Sweetback dies in this "Political Awakening" sequence. A new Sweetback emerges when he stops the car to pick up MooMoo. This is a far cry from his earlier refusal to help the young revolutionary. The images of death are heavy. The images of a rising revolutionary consciousness are embryonic. The "Political Awakening" sequence is characterized by poetic dialogue. Whereas in the classical film narrative, dialogue serves usually as a slave to the visual image, the dialogue in Sweetback takes on a life of its own to parallel the searching and deconstructive tendencies of the visual image. At the end of this sequence, the narrative has given birth to a new Sweetback who makes a small sacrifice for his fellow brother of suffering.

RESISTANCE AND THE
STRUGGLE FOR LIBERATION

Chorus
They bled your Mama. They bled your Papa.
Sweetback
Yeah, but he won't bleed me.

Following the awakening of Sweetback's political consciousness, the narration presents a protagonist whose social awareness has been slowly aroused and whose actions now assume a purpose that was lacking earlier in the narrative. Sweetback is transformed from a character who passively lives in the world to one who now has a desire to actively impact upon it. This transformation is elaborated in the "Motorcycle Gang Scene" when MooMoo and Sweetback find themselves in the territory of a white motorcycle gang. Now, the cinematography differs from earlier sequences. In the "Motorcycle Gang" scene, multiple visual signifiers are superimposed over each other. The same shot and narrative action are repeated consecutively. The setting is lit using expressionistic lighting and the sequence features a montage editing style. As Sweetback and MooMoo are brought to the gang leader, they confront a powerful looking figure, whose back is turned against the camera and who is wearing riding pants, leather jacket and helmet. Prez, the leader, lifts a heavy motorcycle with bare hands. The gang demands that Sweetback and MooMoo pay because they have been caught trespassing on private property.

Prez throws a knife expertly, and the gang members call for a duel. Sweetback is given the right to choose the weapon. Prez removes the helmet to reveal a long flowing head of red hair. The gang leader is a female. Sweetback chooses a weapon or mode of duelling with which he is closely familiar. His weapon will be "fucking." Whereas at the start of the film, Sweetback made a living performing in live sex shows as nightclub entertainment, he now uses sex as a means of survival. The sexual scene with the female gang leader begins with Sweetback wearing only a derby hat. The white female gang leader walks nude to the arena of the sexual duel. This shot is repeated several times consecutively. The sex act is presented using multiple images, repetition of the same action, same shot and freeze frames. The use of these techniques makes it difficult for the viewer to fully experience the regular pleasures of viewing sexual activity in the cinema. More attention is given to cinematic elements, deconstruction of both the visual and aural signifiers, and the distanciation or estrangement of the sexual act. The mode of representing sexual activity in the Classical Hollywood cinema is conspicuously absent. Instead of using the camera as a slave to the narrative action to create a fuller illusion and develop a sense of reality that did not previously exist, the camera work in

Sweetback is more concerned with how film language and technique construct and deconstruct images. Contrary to popular opinion, Sweetback seems to have little regard for sexual titillation. There are no novel, exotic sexual positions that add spice to the narration. There is no exuberant sexual athleticism. There is little construction of the romanticization of the sexual act through careful shots of segmented body parts and bodily gyration or the use of editing patterns to construct images of eroticism in a scene filled with voyeuristic pleasure.

Several points of significance converge upon this scene. We have already discussed the narrative strategy of the film, which begins by presenting a traditional delineation or stereotyped concern, but then proceeds by altering the image through a process of deconstruction or a refusal to use the image within its expected 'normal' context of conventional meanings. This is developed through the script's minimalist approach to dialogue, which is a severe violation of the classical narrative tradition. The leader of the motorcycle gang is presented first within the codes of the male in society in terms of dress, appearance, actions, social status and physical prowess. Concealed beneath the recognizable male image is a woman. In traditional Hollywood delineations, the white woman signifies subordination and passivity. *Sweetback* works against these traditional conventions. When Sweetback chooses "fucking" as the weapon of the duel, he is irreverent in his assault on dominant social sensibilities and conventional morality. The signifieds associated with the white woman are Amazonian, Herculean, and yet feminine. Within her peer group of males, she has no match. Within the newly awakened consciousness of Sweetback, her rival in the duel is one engaged in a struggle for survival using weapons that he has mastered in making a living. Consequently, within the narrative system, Sweetback wins the duel. The stakes are high, for it is not a question of the survival of the lone individual; there is MooMoo, and by implication, the community.

Having won the duel, Sweetback and MooMoo are led by the motorcycle gang to a hideout. As the two men play pool in a room adorned with posters of naked pinup girls and a large wall mirror, two law enforcement agents arrive. Sweetback raises his hands submissively for the handcuffs. He feigns this action and strikes a blow to the face of the policeman, who blindly shoots off his weapon, wounding MooMoo in the shoulder. Sweetback strangles the policeman and uses a broken pool cue as a spear to pierce the heart of the other policeman. Like the earlier scenes, the narration uses the technique of consecutive repetition of the shot. The theme of death is codified in the narrative. Sweetback kills so as not to die at the hands of the police. The weapons of death are simple, but effective: the hands and a makeshift weapon in the form of a spear. Interestingly, the narration comments on the unpreparedness of the revolutionary who Sweetback (the survivor) saves on two occasions. The film seems to offer us the following: the black survivor without the black revolutionary is lost; and the black revolutionary without the black survivor will not survive. When the contact meets the pair, he tells Sweetback that only one passenger can go on the motorcycle:

> **Cyclist**
> I could only take one of yuh. I couldn't get ten feet with three people on this bike. And they told me to pick up Sweetback . . . , you, Sweetback, eh? (pause)
> **Sweetback**
> Take him!
> **Cyclist**
> You know what you're doing?
> **Sweetback**
> He's our future Brer, take him!
> *Sweetback shakes hand in solidarity with MooMoo. The young revolutionary is hurt and can hardly remain seated on the bike. At last, the cycle takes off leaving Sweetback.*

FREE AT LAST

At this point in the narration, the filmic signification introduces an innovative device incorporating elements of the black expressive tradition such as orature and signifying. The soundtrack features spoken word techniques as the visuals show Sweetback on the run.

> **Sweetback (Off-screen)**
> Come on feet, cruise with me, Trouble ain't no where to be. Come on feet, do your thing, You all know whitey's game. Come on legs, come on run. Come on knees, don't be mean, ain't the first you

ever seen. . . Feet, do your thing. Come on baby,
don't cop out on me, Come on, free at last . . .

The introduction of the oral tradition on the soundtrack complements Sweetback's liberation. Whereas the visual image had
already conceded Sweetback's transformation, the sound signifiers had refused to go along until the point where Sweetback's
consciousness is fully awakened and redirected. The narration
makes Sweetback's freedom contingent on leaving the ghetto.
He must escape the colony or reservation. When Sweetback stays
behind and allows the young revolutionary the opportunity to
take his place, his political awareness is heightened, and the narration intensifies its use of visual and oral signifiers. Now, there
is a harmony of the sound and visual images, not within the terms
of the classical narrative, but in the creation of new cinematic
forms. There is still little compromise in the film's use of the
realistic juxtaposition of sound and visual image. The sound
image signifies in the black oral tradition, while the visual image
constantly points to the plasticity of the medium. There is very
little lipsync dialogue. While the chorus and voice of the soundtrack often move the narration forward, the visual image often
becomes experimental seeking out new expressive forms. The
most naturalistic dialogue occurs in scenes involving the police.
When a brother talks to a brother, the dialogue takes on a poetic quality. Witness Sweetback's encounter with the preacher during the Funeral scene, the Gambling Cellar scene or the
call-and-response voice-over of the soundtrack featuring a chorus and Sweetback's responses. The use of naturalistic dialogue
brings with it the ideological baggage of the dominant society in
relation to its dominant meanings and its positioning of blacks:
in a briefing at the police station, the captain tells his men he
wants the cop killers. After indignantly informing them that he
wants those "niggers" caught, the captain calls two black police-
men aside.

Captain
I didn't mean anything by that word. Its' just a figure of speech, you know . . . You guys could be a real
credit to your race if you brought these guys in.

This kind of naturalistic dialogue is loaded and charged with ideological ramifications. Through this device, the film is able to

expose contradictions in society. The police captain makes an important speech at the City Morgue where the squad has gone to confirm Sweetback's death.

Captain

If things change, the majority of the people will decide where and how. This is a democracy. It's not communism. We are all going to respect the law or pay the consequences.

The camera moves out to include the heavily bandaged face of Beetle, who is seated in a wheel chair. Several faces including Beetle's look curiously and slowly in harmony at the body in the morgue. Beetle, who is surrounded by the police, is slow and quiet.

Captain

As a citizen, you are required to aid us in this investigation. Is this Sweetback's body?

Beetle

I ain't able to read lips yet.

Sweetback's use of naturalistic dialogue occurs strategically to penetrate the ideological facade so carefully constructed in popular cultural signification.

SWEETBACK'S BAADASSSS SONG

Following the City Morgue scene, the narration moves the plot to the streets. Increasingly, the narration introduces elements that complicate the narrative. It appears as though the narration is not concerned with the enigma so crucial to the police, who want to find out where Sweetback is. This is definitely Sweetback's "Baadassss Song" and not a traditional entertainment film, which would have had to play the game of the police and pursue their interest. This is a now the story of a community and not a lone hero. The camera now assumes the language of the documentary, interviewing community people, vox-pop style and interjecting random shots of street scenes. The people on the street do not know Sweetback and are not interested in his pursuit. A new kind of cinema has taken over. It offers no haven to the traditional concerns of the classical narrative film. Juxtaposed within the sequence of shots of images of the street is the visual image of an old woman who is caring for several young children in her apartment. Shots of street images are seen as the woman's voice (offscreen) repeats a series of words in quick succession. There is the image of a night club singer on stage making gestures to suggest that she is singing, but there is no sound to synchronize her movements and performance. Only the soundtrack theme provides background music. Offstage, the police interrogate the female singer, seeking knowledge of Sweetback's whereabouts. The woman is upset and angrily curses the police, telling them to get off her back. The next image shows her on stage, but this time she is actually singing.

At this point in the narration, a new kind of sound image emerges. It features poetry recited by a chorus and Sweetback's voice in a call-and-response pattern. This sound signification arises strategically at this juncture as Sweetback is clear of the imposed confinement of the ghetto reservation.

> **Chorus (Off-screen)**
> They bled your mama. They bled your papa.
> **Sweetback (Off-screen)**
> But he won't bleed me. Nigger scared. Pretend they don't see.
> **Chorus (Off-screen)**
> Just like you Sweetback.
> **Sweetback (Off-screen)**
> Just like I used to be. Work your black behind to the gumbs, and you supposed to 'Thomas' 'till he done.
> **Chorus (Off-screen)**
> You got to 'Thomas' Sweetback . . . They bled your brother. They bled your sister.
> **Sweetback (Off-screen)**
> Yeah, but they won't bleed me.

The spoken word soundtrack is interspersed throughout this section as the hero makes his escape. There is a curious and brief scene that occurs involving a black shoeshine man who polishes the shoes of a white patron. The man seems to be enjoying himself as he shines the white man's shoes with the seat of his pants. If we seek a literal understanding of this scene, certainly it raises signifieds of subservience and lowcomic stereotypes. However, the narrative pattern established and repeated throughout *Sweetback* cannot be read by paying attention to a single visual image. It must be considered within the context of a chain of signification. The fact is that in society, blacks are positioned to perform for the pleasure of whites no matter how comic and dehumanizing the nature of the performance. This was once the essence of Sweetback's existence and still continues to characterize the existence of many blacks. The insertion of the shoeshine man at this point helps to heighten the significance of Sweetback's decolonization. So long as some blacks take on and internalize the comic roles prescribed for them by the dominant society, Sweetback's heroism (given the point where he started), no matter how seemingly inconsequential, must be recognized and applauded.

HE WON'T BLEED ME

A helicopter joins in the search for Sweetback, flying over arid bush land somewhere in the Southwestern United States. A quick glimpse of a man is seen running through the bush. A police car gives pursuit and it appears that Sweetback is running away. As the man is apprehended, the police find that a white man is dressed in Sweetback's clothes. He tells that he "gave word that he would run" if anyone came after him.

> **Police Officer**
> Alright, now why did you run?
> **Man**
> Why did I run? I run cause I gave my word.
> **Policeman**
> You gave what word?
> **Man**
> I promised to run.
> **Policeman**
> You promised who . . . what?
> **Man**
> This guy gave me five dollars to change clothes with him. He told me if anybody came after me to keep on running.
> **Policeman**
> Was he a black guy?
> **Man**
> Yeah, he was colored.
> **Police**
> What did he look like?
> **Man**
> Like a buddy I used to pal around with in Denver.

Policeman
Now, would you say that he was this tall,
about this size.
Man
. . . about that.
Policeman
What was he doing?
Man
Poorly.
Policeman
You mean how he was doing?
Man
Yeah, . . . Poorly.

Once again, the first introduction of the image is misleading.
The man turns out to be someone else. The narration goes to
extreme lengths to warn us that things are not always what they
appear to be. The man refuses to collaborate with the police and
only gives vague, nondescript information. The narration presents this white man as Sweetback's brother inasmuch as they
occupy the same position in the system of power and they are
depicted wearing each other's clothes. In *Sweetback*, there is a
sense of community that reaches across racial categories.

"YOU TALKIN' REVOLUTION, SWEETBACK"

Sweetback crosses the desert wearing the borrowed clothes of
the white man. The soundtrack presents the religious song "Bye
and Bye," and the off-screen call-and-response pattern continues between the chorus and Sweetback. At this point in the narration, the dialogue is uncompromising and the soundtrack
explicitly foregrounds the political struggle for liberation.

Chorus
Progress, Sweetback.
Voice (Off screen)
Yeah, that's what he wants you to believe,
Chorus
No, progress Sweetback.
Voice (Off screen)
We ain't seen progress for 400 years, and he don't
intend to for a million.
Chorus

> He sure do us bad, Sweetback. We can make him do
> us better. Chicken ain't nothing but a bird. White
> man ain't nothing but a turd. Nigger ain't shit.

Although weary, Sweetback moves on in the scrappy environment of the Southwest. His journey has taken him from the city to the hinterland using a freight train, hiding on the roof of a truck and riding in the back of a farm truck with Hispanic workers. The chorus introduces the religious song "Wade in de Water," which was used by escaping slaves to signal secret messages to those using the Underground Railroad to freedom. This song, which functions as a helper in the narrative, encouraged runaway slaves to travel by streams and rivers' edges because water creates difficult conditions for trackers and dogs to follow. Sweetback suffers a hideous stomach wound that is very disturbing to look at. He uses water from a mud pool to wash his face. To heal his wound, he urinates in the sand and uses the mixture to form a mudpack that he places on the wound. In the desert, when Sweetback is hungry, he eats roots and catches lizard for protein. As Sweetback's transformation into a new person is achieved, the film introduces the signification of the guerrilla who lives off the land using available means for survival. Now, the soundtrack begins to call explicitly for revolt.

> **Voice (Off screen)**
> Get my hands on a trigger.
> **Chorus (Off screen)**
> You talking revolution, Sweetback
> **Voice (Off screen)**
> I wanna get off these knees
> **Chorus (Off screen)**
> You talking revolution, Sweetback.
> **Voice (Off screen)**
> Somebody listen to me . . . He won't waste me.
> **Chorus (Off screen)**
> **(Breaking into song)**
> Let it shine, let it shine, let it shine.

As the sound images become less prosaic, the narration progressively becomes explicitly political, especially in its use of spoken word technique. Whereas prose describes the world, poetry is a more fundamental discourse. At this point in the narration, the sound image appears to have become extremely desperate.

> **Chorus (Off screen)**
> The man know everything Sweetback. The man
> know everything.
> **Voice (Off screen)**
> Then he ought to know I'm tired of him fucking
> with me.
> **Chorus**
> Use your feet baby. Run motherfucka. Run
> Sweetback.
> **Voice (Off screen)**
> He won't bleed me.

An interesting feature of *Sweetback's* narration is its creation of a
space for the viewer who does not simply watch the film, but gets
involved in talking back to the film and giving Sweetback opinions. This mechanism is an important characteristic of black
expressive forms.

The dialectical relationship that has developed between the
visual image and the soundtrack supports the point of view that
Sweetback's narration is constructed on the premise of refusing
the traditional representation of reality in cinema. In the
Classical Hollywood cinema, filmic reality is generally a unify-
ing enterprise in which the system of continuity strives to create a harmonious filmic world. In its emphasis on filmic unity,
the traditional cinema features compatible uses of sound and
visual images so that there is an attempt at closure of meanings,
which functions ideologically to reinforce the dominant system
of values. *Sweetback's* critique of the real world and the filmic
reality denies this excessive structuring and the closure of social
possibility that is integral to the classical narrative. The narration concedes only the reality of the world we live in and its system of power relations. The system of power in society is real in
so far as it exists independently of individual subjects; but it is
not a transhistorical reality or truth of nature. The narration in
Sweetback suggests that cinematography is an art that is constructed on the deconstruction and re-presentation of various
elements. In this view, the significance of filmmaking is found in
its ability to shatter the illusion of the real so that a new series
of social and political relations may arise and not in its sophisticated narrative illusions of reality, which function to conceal or

repress aspects of the real world that are inconsistent with dominant ideologies.

As Sweetback plans to make good his escape across the desert
into Mexico, the film offers a theme of solidarity with the
Chicano people who work the farms in the Southwest and who
help his escape from the hands of the law. The narration fashions a landscape that is different from the city. Instead of
Sweetback attempting to find his freedom in the urban area, he
heads for the hinterland and away from the confines of the city.
African drums are introduced at this point on the soundtrack. At
a picnic, a female folk singer sings a ballad, but her performance
is interrupted by the police who fan through the area searching
for Sweetback. The last sexual scene in the narrative presents
Sweetback and a woman in each other's arms as a ruse to avoid
capture. The sheriff looks on voyeuristically, enjoying the sexual embrace of the couple. He dismisses the scene as one of mistaken identity. For Sweetback, sexual activity has progressed from
initiation into adulthood, sex as commodity relations and
voyeuristic entertainment for night club audiences, to the use of
sexual acts to effect escape, and now the pretense of sex to avoid
capture. In retrospect, each sexual act in the film is presented
within a context that functions against traditional sexual enjoyment or is developed with a use of filmic signification that develops an antivoyeuristic experience.

The entire enigmatic structure of the narration unravels in
the Dog Chase sequence as Sweetback approaches the Mexican
border. We want to know will Sweetback die and is that
Sweetback's blood in the water after the dogs have been released
to pursue him? But each bit of visual information the narration
gives after the first visual statement contradicts itself when subsequent shots are presented. The odds are against Sweetback.
All he has is a pocketknife and his will to survive. The three tracking dogs are ferocious in their eagerness to start the hunt. To
reach the hills in the distance, Sweetback must cross a body of
water. Echoing the crossing of the Middle Passage several centuries earlier when the enslaved Africans were transported across
the ocean, Sweetback must now negotiate a body of water to gain
his freedom. The dog trainer and the sheriff fight over the release
of the dogs; however, the dogs are freed and they begin the hunt.
Soon, the river is red with blood. Beneath the water, there is an
unidentified figure submerged in the water. Subsequently, the
narration reveals it to be that of a dog and we learn that the blood

we saw earlier was a dog's blood. Of the three tracking dogs, one survives – a solitary figure – lapping water from the river. The camera shows a view of a mountainous landscape that signifies Mexico and the words "A Baadassss Nigger is Coming Back to Collect Some Dues" are superimposed on the screen.

NARRATION AND FILMIC SIGNIFICATION IN SWEETBACK

The development of an alternative heroic tradition, the use of the black expressive tradition and a new formulation of narrative are fertile areas for exploration in black cinema. One area of *Sweetback's* success can be found in its different and creative use of limited resources and technical facilities. Film budgets escalate with the attempt to construct the narrative realism that we associate with Hollywood film. A talking picture full of wonderful dialogue and elaborate film sets only makes filmmaking more expensive. Part of the astuteness of the narration in *Sweetback* is its minimal use of lip-sync dialogue. This technique takes us back to the creative founding moments of cinematography before it became commonplace that the image must speak what is being seen. *Sweetback* develops the possibilities of cinematic expression: the visual image and the sound image do not have to do the some thing or even provide the same meaning. Most of all, the film does not have to talk all the time. The world of sound is wide and varied, and dialogue is but a small part of it. *Sweetback* refuses to reproduce the narrative realism of the Classical Hollywood cinema. Rather, it moves discussion of the cinematic image from the conventionalism of whether it is real or unreal, moral or immoral to the control of these images, their reproduction, and their place in the political and economic system.

Sweet Sweetback'sBaadasssss Song is an important film in the history of contemporary cinema and it is a seminal work in the exploration of an alternative cinematic expression in popular cinema. A viable black cinema cannot assert itself when it is constructed upon the very ideologies that have supported its historical oppression. Consequently, the narration in *Sweetback* refuses to reproduce Hollywood's cinematic grammars and syntax. Van Peebles uses his camera not to represent a comfortable realism, but as a tool to question conventional uses of the cinema. His sound images are not simple confirmations of the visual image, for they function dialectically, often engaging in a critique of the visual image. In undertaking this enterprise, the filmmaker disturbs the traditional positioning of the viewer as consumer.

The film's use of the human body provides another example of the rejection of the paradigms of institutionalized cinema. In the Hollywood cinema, there is an ideology of the body developed around a preferential use of particular body types. The star system functions as one such crystalization of body types in the cinema through which sexual and racial ideals are transformed into heroic proportions for widespread popular consumption. In general, the classical film narrative represents the female body as voyeured object signifying a perverse erotic pleasure around which the economic apparatus of the film industry is built. In *Sweetback*, there is a barrage of sex-related images, a seeming orgy of sexual acts; yet, the filmic signification within which the sexual image is presented does not foster a syndrome of erotic pleasure. Rather, it disturbs in that it refuses to gratify the voyeurism associated with the Hollywood cinema. In *Sweetback*, there are no perfectly formed, luscious, erotic sexual creatures. The women in the film are not developed voyeuristically for or by the camera. Only a stark, unwelcome reality is created, which operates to disturb and shock, rather than provide sexual gratification to the viewer. In simple terms, *Sweetback* does not allow the kind of sexual pleasure one usually encounters in pornographic film.

Contrary to a popular opinion, *Sweetback* is no simple pornographic film. Pornography in the cinema is constructed upon the economic and voyeuristic exploitation of the female body – that is, the submissive and dominated body – and its control by the male. Pornographic film is a celebration of unequal relations in society through its exploitation of the body strictly in sexual and economic terms within the system of patriarchy characteristic of society. However, the use of the body in *Sweetback* augurs more shock than titillation. The refusal of the illusion of realism in the cinema contributes to the development of an alternative cinematography, for the illusion of reality tends to reproduce only a limited view of society and its social relations. When black cinema affirms the illusory quality of the Hollywood-type narrative, it legitimizes the subordinate position of the powerless within the social structure and the dominant cinema. As a filmmaker, Van Peebles is concerned with attacking the illusion this vulgar realism creates in order to foster an alternative knowledge of social reality.

In the classical film narrative, the viewer focuses principally on the progression of the narrative and becomes engaged in a pursuit of the story line through the enrapturing moment-to-moment unraveling of the plot. However, the narration in *Sweetback* allows no such luxuries. It shifts our attention forcefully to the uses of cinematic languages and to other political and ideological questions. Students who are schooled in the consumerist aesthetics of pleasure associated with the Hollywood cinema often respond to the film by saying that all *Sweetback* does is run.

Because blacks have been positioned negatively and subordinately since the opening of the New World to the Europeans, a primary project of black social existence has been the struggle for liberation. There has been a historic attachment of political struggle to almost all areas of black life. The experimental narration in *Sweetback* locates itself within a tradition of signification opposed to the established cinematic conventions that represent a narrative world in which existing reality is reproduced with an almost sacred status. As a matter of fact, the social critique extended by this new breed of films contends that inasmuch as film assumes a position in the system of exchange as a prized commodity, it tends to support traditional social relations and ideologies. *Sweetback's* use of filmic signification refuses to conceive of film as principally consumer entertainment; rather film is viewed as an instrument for transforming social existence through its own expressive modes.

Chapter Seven

Narration as Cultural Memory in *Daughters of the Dust*

J ulie Dash's *Daughters of the Dust* is a landmark achievement in black cinema. It not only transforms traditional subject matter and imagery, but productively engages film form and narrative. *Daughters* offers us a fresh use of aesthetic sources. Foremost is its feminist appropriation of narrative through its specific use of the African American woman as producer of meaning. It repositions discourse about black women in film and initiates a discussion of film language as a site of resistance in African American cinema. In the classical cinema, the black woman has been vilified—desexed as 'mammy' and oversexed as 'mulatto vamp'. Although African American cinema has provided broader parameters and expanded the discourse about the black woman, Problems still remain in her representation. *Daughters* signals an important moment in black cinema because of its successful shift from a preoccupation with "positive images" and "inclusion" to foreground two important concerns—the textual production of the black woman and the black woman as producer of meaning. In that black women speak so eloquently and incisively in their own voices, *Daughters* is an important document in American cinema and in black film. It draws on the black experience, utilizing folklore, the oral tradition, the blues and cultural memory to shape its narrative and film style.

BLACK WOMEN'S CULTURAL EXPRESSION

Black women have had to contend with a history of neglect within a system of social relations marked by racial and patriarchal concerns. Their experiences and their culture "and the brutally complex systems of oppression which shape these are in the 'real world' of white and/or male consciousness beneath consideration, invisible, unknown" (Smith, 1982, p. 157). In spite of the fact that white society and black patriarchy attempted to render black women's existence invisible, a distinct tradition of African American cultural expression has existed since the 19th century, and black women have long fought to transform their social situations in order to reconstruct the ways in which they were represented. Slave narratives serve as an early expression of black women's identity in the face of popular historical stereotypes. These narratives challenge the male-defined genre and the established criteria of autobiography (Stetson, 1982, p. 71). Black women activists such as Harriet Tubman, Sojourner Truth, Frances Harper, Ida B. Wells and Mary Church Terrell have always played important roles in the resistance movement from slavery to the Civil Rights era. The Combahee River Collective finds that these women "had a shared awareness of how their sexual identity combined with their racial identity to make their whole life situation and the focus of their political struggles unique. Contemporary black feminism is the outgrowth of countless generations of personal sacrifice, militancy, and work by our mothers and sisters" (1982, p. 14).

Zora Neale Hurston's *Their Eyes Were Watching God* exemplifies the potential of a black woman's aesthetic for the resolution of critical aesthetic and political problems in black independent cinema. A distinct "black women-identified folk culture is manifested through symbols, language, and modes of expression that specifically reflect the realities of black women's lives in a dominant white/male culture (Bethel, 1982, p. 177). Barbara Smith argues that writers such as Zora Neale Hurston, Margaret Walker, Toni Morrison, and Alice Walker incorporate traditional black female activities of rootworking, herbal medicine, conjure, and midwifery into the fabric of their stories in a way that is not coincidental. Furthermore, their specific use of black female language to express their own and their characters' thoughts is not accidental (1982, p. 164). In this same vein, *Daughters of the Dust* resonates richly and profoundly with this tradition when intertextually referenced to the forms and narrative of black women artists. Because black women writers explore "form and language . . . nothing like what white patriarchal culture requires or expects," critics need to extend their evaluative criteria to seek intertextual sources, "precedents and insights in interpretation within the works of other black women" (Smith, 1982, p. 164).

The fabric of black women's cultural expression is part of the aesthetic framework that makes black filmmaking intelligible. Of specific importance is the way writers such as Margaret Walker, Audre Lorde, Alice Walker and Toni Morrison explore black female consciousness in their project of articulating the language of the black woman and investigating the mythic structures of black women's experiences. These writers consider art to be an "instrument of power, engaging its readers' minds and emotions" (McDowell, 1980, p. 20). In asserting that innovativeuses of form were often aesthetically superior to more structured modes, Margaret Walker was a generation ahead of others. This is directly relevant to the narrative structure one encounters in a film such as *Daughters of the Dust* because Walker's poetry and fiction early on incorporated "gospel, blues, and folk song as specific motifs and as structural patterns" (McDowell, 1980, p. 23).

A central strategy in black woman's cinema is the act of naming and validating. These are important and function to identify one's self and other black women as "inherently valuable" (Bethel, 1982, p. 184). It is a way of giving black women a place as subject, a way of positioning them to play a central role in the production of meaning (Christian, 1980). Black women filmmakers, such as Julie Dash and Zeinabu Irene Davis, are creating a new cinematic language and are forging new ontological relationships between the viewer and film. In Lorde's view, the black woman artist creates for "women for whom a voice has not yet existed, or whose voice has been silenced" (1983, p. 104). She is committed to the creation of a new world, using her own voice to articulate her own vision and to foster self-definition. Gloria Gibson-Hudson argues that within a black feminist aesthetic, film functions as a vehicle to address the effects of marginality or social invisibility. "In expressing their concern for, and connectedness to, other women and other people, the artists' philosophy is to capture and reconstruct reality through texts they hope will enlighten, empower and redress the 'invisibility' of African American women" (1991, p. 46).

Defining space and giving shape to it is a significant aspect of a black feminist aesthetic developed in the writings of bell hooks. She is proud to point out that her sense of an aesthetic was influenced by "black women who were fashioning an aes-

thetic of being, struggling to create an oppositional world-view
for their children, working with space to make it livable" (1990,
p. 112). This oppositional world-view is articulated in black
women's films through the particular use of iconography and
space. "Stemming from black feminism the philosophical core
of which is the desire for complete recognition and understanding of black woman's life experiences as valuable, complex, and
diverse, the films of black women function as a cultural micro-
cosm. They provide narratives that relate to historical occur-
rences and conditions, their cinematic frames challenge decades
of 'structural silence' levied against the black woman" (Gibson-
Hudson, 1994, p. 366).

NARRATIVE STRUCTURE IN
DAUGHTERS OF THE DUST

Toni Cade Bambara writes that "the thematics of colonized terrain, family as liberated zone, women as source of value, and history as interpreted by black people are central to the narrative
of *Daughters of the Dust* (1993, p. 121). Set in the Sea Islands off
the South Carolina coast, Daughters is the story of the Peazant
family, some of whose members are about to migrate North.
Members of the extended family gather for a last meal together
before setting out on their journey. The film's setting—Ibo
Landing—captures a formative moment in the cultural identity
of African Americans. The narrative structure of *Daughters of the
Dust* reveals the problem of who the Peazants are, where they
come from and their struggle, that is, where they are headed.
The plot consists of the specific presentation of individual personalities of the family members and the particular flow of events
as they debate the crossing. Some believe that going North is
progress; others are strongly attracted to their home and its connection with their ancestors. The environment of the islands (the
dark earth and the ocean) functions as a physical memory of the
African American experience and the family's stories preserve the
complementary fabric of their cultural memory. The narrative
emphasizes motifs such as the dust, hands, water, the womb, food
and African iconography in carvings, hairstyles and so on. Cade
Bambara observes that while *Daughters* uses "the unities of time,
place, and action" in that the family reunion takes place in one
day (beginning with the arrival of family members and ending
with the departure for the North), it is not a Hollywood classical narrative, but is classic in the African sense, using "digres

sions and meanderings" as one encounters in cinemas that employ features of the oral tradition (1993, p. 123). The narration in *Daughters of the Dust* rejects the sexual and racial politics of Hollywood film, emphasizing black women's subjectivity as opposed to an 'objective' rendering of historical time. History is not an account of the past, but it is the way the past co-exists with the present.

The narration is generated by multiple voices that weave a quilt-like texture. It is structured as memory around the narration of the great-grandmother, Nana (the ancestral link who is the family's matriarch); her great-granddaughter Eula, (who is impregnated after being raped); and Eula's Unborn Child (who comes from the future). Memory plays a key role in cultural identity, which is not a pre-existent phenomenon that transcends place, time, history and culture. "Cultural identities come from somewhere, have histories. But like everything which is historical, they undergo constant trans-formation" (Hall, 1992, p. 223). This process of 'being' as well as 'becoming' offers a framework to examine the particular formulation of cultural identity Dash articulates through her use of film form. The past speaks to us not as a simple factual account, but is "constructed through memory, fantasy, narrative and myth" (Hall, 1992, p. 224).

The control of space is a central concern of cinematic narration. In *Daughters*, Nana's view of space echoes Booker T. Washington's appeal to blacks to remain on the land in the South. Yet, Dash's multiple narration also allows her characters a sense of agency to choose how they will orient themselves. Some decide to go North. Although the film presents the South as a nurturing environment, it still remains a threatening place given the pivotal position Eula's rape plays in the narrative events and the references to the anti-lynching movement. Diawara explains the urgency to reformulate film space in independent black film. He notes that "Common sense reveals that characters that are more often on the screen, or occupy the center of the frame, command more narrative authority than those that are in the background, on the sides, or completely absent from the frame" (1992, p. 14).

In the classical cinema, space is very often delineated as an arena for confrontation and dramaturgical conflict, but *Daughters* celebrates African American conceptions of space, suggesting a complex quilt, a mosaic of black women's voices. There is richness in the different voices, but no attempt is made to develop difference within a system of dramatic conflict. Framing devices help to define space in the cinema. When they are used in this film, they don't function to break up the space of the frame, but offer protection. In *Daughters*, space is ludic. It is a paradise for children. As a matter of fact, the narrative contains several references to childhood. In St. Julian's Last Child's letter to Iona, he writes: "Our love is very precious, very fragile flowering of our most innocent childhood association," and the Unborn Child's narration tells us, "I remember how important the children were to the Peazant family."

Dahtaw Island, where the Peazants live, is a protected zone. The outside is a threatening space. Eula's rape and lynchings are part of the larger story. While the narration acknowledges these threats, its plot finds no need to present these pathologies normally favored in the Hollywood classical narrative. Yet, *Daughters* does not present an idyllic John-Boy Walton family existence for the Peazants. The narrative is set at Ibo Landing, a place where Africans took their own lives instead of submitting to slavery. Eula also tells Yellow Mary about the story of the slave girl who was drowned by her master at Ibo Landing. Yellow Mary cautions Eula not to tell Eli who was responsible for the rape because "There's enough uncertainty in life without having to sit at home wondering which tree your husband is hanging from." There is the metaphor of the North, a place physically removed from the ancestral memories alive in the South. Nana tells Eli, "When you leave this island, . . . you ain't going to no land of milk and honey." The South is a place that carries a direct connection with Africa. It is a land of magic, in which time seems to stand still. Haagar describes the Sea Islands as backward.

Although the narration in *Daughters* treats the family's traditions as the norm, in its making of myth it refuses to romanticize the ancestral memories of the Peazant family. In the Classical Hollywood cinema, when the narration transforms a character into heroic proportions, a corresponding maneuver takes place, which simultaneously functions to demonize the other. The Western film genre is a case in point. The other is an entity that exists on the margins of discourse. In Christian theology, the other is a demon who lives in hell. In that the discourse of black feminism informs *Daughters*, black women occupy the center of the narration. Whites are marginalized, but are not transformed into the other. Yet, the narration clearly is critical of an oppressive system that creates subordinate gender and racial positions.

In the use of film space in the classical film narrative, women are presented as objects to be looked at and controlled through mise-en-scene. *Daughters* reformulates these relationships and allows its characters to exist with respect in their own private spaces. Despite trying circumstances, the Peazants retain a sense of dignity. Yellow Mary is able to return home without shame. Eula is raped, but the community does not treat her as a victim who is to be pitied and shunned. The terms of reference presented by the narration are quite different. The diegetic space of the narrative is mediated by a black woman's point of view, and black women are fully enfranchised individuals. This gives the spectator options not available in the Hollywood cinema. Generally, the spectator identifies with the position of the camera-narrator. Thus, in *Daughters*, a new set of relations of identification emerges. Characters have multiple names—several names in addition to a given name. Interestingly, identity is fluid, less fixed than in the classical cinema. Furthermore, there is identification with the female protagonists, identification with multiple narrators, and identification with the landscape. When viewers initially have difficulty with the narration in *Daughters*, it is this shifting of identifications that they find difficult. Dash uses the film's diegetic space as a site of resistance to the structure of domination that is built into the classical film narrative. Her cinema is based on the principle that film is capable of functioning as part of a transformational discourse that can help restructure unequal relationships in respect to social space.

In many traditional narratives and in folklore, we know the story line and its ending. Yet, we still can find pleasure in such forms of narration. In contrast, the ending is a carefully guarded secret of the time-based narratives of Classical Hollywood cinema. As a result, it is necessary to seek alternative evaluative criteria for narratives such as *Daughters*, which unfold in space. The viewer is generally more familiar with narratives whose construction is based on the dramatic manipulation of time. In these films, time is phallic; it has a continuous forward thrust. Phallic time is based on a paradigm of dramatic conflict in which the heroic force wins in the end, thereby achieving specific narrative goals. It is related to the fetishized notion of progress in Western history. Progress is important even if it means despoiling the environment, oppression of native peoples and destruction of one's soul. In the Hollywood cinema, the viewer uses a goal-oriented narrative paradigm and a 'canonic story' format that demands justice (punishment) be meted out as the response to a specific action in the diegesis. For example, in a murder mystery, the detective initiates an investigation with the goal of bringing a killer to justice. Diawara argues that the construction of time is problematic in the classical cinema. "White men drive from East to the West, conquering wilderness and removing obstacles out of time's way. Thus the 'once upon a time' which begins every story in Hollywood also posits an initial obstacle in front of a white person who has to remove it in order for the story to continue, and for the conquest ideology of whiteness to prevail" (1992, p. 12). However, in the African American aesthetic tradition, we find that narratives foreground spatial exploration and can develop paying more attention to the existential performative requirements of the narration. I am not suggesting that the African American tradition does not include goal-oriented narratives, merely that in seeking to reach the goal, other experiential elements can come into play and temporarily assume narrative importance. Viewers need to bring this improvisational quality that has developed as an integral part of the African American tradition to the viewing situation of a film such as *Daughters of the Dust*. It is in this sense that narration as a cultural construct plays out differently across cultures.

The technology of the camera occupies a central role in the narrative. After all, Viola has brought the photographer Snead to record an historic moment in the family's life and Dash uses the camera—that very device used for objectification and subjugation of women in the Hollywood cinema—as a narrative device in her film. Whereas phallic time is not foregrounded, movement is. There is movement from Africa to America and from South to the North. Viola and Yellow Mary return to the family home for the reunion. The narrative empowers the Peazants through the way their freedom is spatially validated. The men even impact on history through their involvement with the antilynching movement. The filmmaker skillfully reflects on the camera technology as it is used to record historical event. Although we use the camera to record history, Dash questions our tendency to rely on it as a documentary tool when the Unborn Child appears in a group photograph in Snead's viewfinder. Snead is visibly shaken. The Unborn Child violates linear time and actually appears for fleeting moments in the space of the family picnic. This character wreaks havoc with the traditional use of temporal devices such as flashbacks and flashfor-wards. Consistent with the film's notion of history, not so much as occurring in time, but as unfolding in space, the device of the Unborn Child actually reaches into the future, enters the pre-sent as well as goes back into historical time. There is a sense that history is spatially organized with past and future having a contiguous relationship to the present. The progressive unfold-ing of events in time is less important to the narrative than a sense of time in which the past and future co-exist and impact on the present. It is at this moment that the narration engages in cultural restitution because it provides a canvas for a discourse on African American history, which has been repressed by the dominant society.

The absence of cultural devices to keep time, such as clocks, is not surprising. Yet, the marking of time is present through nat-ural events such as morning and sunsets. In the narration, time is conflated. We don't know for certain whether the events of the narrative take place over several hours, one day or two. The conception of time in Hollywood film as a race against the clock is just not that important to the filmmaker's aesthetic system. The narration is omniscient, using flashforwards and flashbacks in a circular notion of time. It hides very little and the viewer knows what it knows. Its ambiguity lies in the information indi-vidual characters have that no one else has. For example, only Eula knows her rapist. We want to know Yellow Mary's story and the nature of her relationship with Trula, but the narration never reveals it. A black feminist aesthetic necessarily reorients our relationship to foreground and background information.

The film uses the criteria of documentary realism in its mise-en-scene, especially as it relates to verisimilitude of behavior and verisimilitude of historical space. It presents the viewer with a structured account of events—a plot—which helps to establish the story of the Peazant family. However, the filmmaker's shot construction and shot sequencing are preoccupied by other con-cerns. The film uses a mix of narrative strategies, which produces an aesthetic driven more by visual and oral expression than lit-erary form. It is a cinema of resistance and transformation, which insightfully sets its narrative in the South, an area generally back-grounded in African American cinema. Reflecting a black woman's film practice, *Daughters* questions the dominant male-centered aesthetics of the black film movement and repositions our concept of the African American voice, conceiving of it in communal terms not as a single dominant voice, but a texture of multiple voices.

The narration develops using elements of characterization and dramatic conflict that we recognize from Aristotelian poetics. To some degree, the film's characters are goal-oriented and enter into conflict with each other. Some characters—for example, a daughter Viola, the Christian missionary and Haagar, a daughter-in-law—are presented in opposition to the 'backwardness' and old ways of the island as dramatized in Nana. We see the conflict of African-based tradition and white Christian religion. Although the narrative's sequence of events appears to use classical plot devices, the narration is different, never allowing these elements favored in classical cinema to determine its shot-by-shot unraveling. The filmmaker's style becomes an important player in the unfolding of the narrative. This is precisely the significance of the blues form as developed within the intertextual space of the Harlem Renaissance artists in what we now call, the blues aesthetic (Powell, 1989). In the narration, there are moments when the flow of events becomes secondary to cinematic elements such as editing. However, although the film privileges concerns with the expressiveness of style, it is not a self-conscious use of cinema like in European-based art cinema.

Because *Daughters* has a loose interest in plot, it does not present a heavily pregnant causality that drives forward the dramatic action. Neither does it present an open-ended causality that fosters a character's subjective realism. It invokes the figure of cultural memory, which functions as an external authority. Dash's narrative logic is built around cultural memory as elaborated in its paradigm of the intimate connection of past and future, in Nana, an ancestral figure who has a healing influence and the Unborn Child, who is the future. Although the filmmaker as author is relevant here, she exists within a tradition. She does not seek to exercise the kind of liberties one finds in the work of art cinema directors or in Jean-Luc Godard's eclectic style.

AESTHETIC SOURCES IN
DAUGHTERS OF THE DUST

The filmmaker creates a space for an active viewer who must make assumptions and inferences about a polyvalent narrative that transgresses linear time and de-emphasizes an Aristotelian narrative structure. In this way, the film unfolds like the performance of a group of rappers or the improvisational strategies of an ensemble in African American classical music. Initially, some viewers have problems with the narrative. This must be expected because the viewer usually constructs story information based on an identifiable scheme of things, using a sense of causality, space and time gleaned from the classical narrative. However, in this aesthetic, extra-textual elements help the viewer to understand the film. This does not mean that as artistic expression, *Daughters* is inferior. All it suggests is that the traditions that give meaning to the film are not yet as readily understood by viewers as the ubiquitous devices of the classical film narrative.

This film derives its power and force precisely because of its grounding in the black woman's experience. It sets out not to represent a black Hollywood, but importantly locates its struggle at the level of how we structure values and the forms we use to articulate them. What we witness in the unfolding of the film is the cinematic transformation of elements—for example, improvisational techniques—that are deeply embedded in the African American tradition. In the context of African American cinema, *Daughters of the Dust* elevates style to a dominant role in its narrative. Style is used to shape the way historical events are narrated. It functions as more than mere decoration. It is a determinant, a player in the organization of cinematic space and time. Dash attempts a tricky enterprise. Her subject is history, but her film is not driven by a bourgeois realist preoccupation with linear time. The filmmaker allows cinematic possibility to mediate her film's narrative. What we find is that style plays a primary role in this aesthetic. This also resonates with the central importance of improvisation in the African American tradition and the use of folkloric devices and myth as integral elements of narrative construction in black women's writings. Essentially, the structuring needs of the historical events of the narrative are subordinated to issues of form and style. Although *Daughters* may utilize narrative elements from the Classical Hollywood cinema and art cinema, intertextual references from the African American tradition in general and black women's expression offer a richer reservoir for approaching the film's aesthetic system.

MIGRATION AS A GRAND SIGNIFIER
IN BLACK CULTURAL EXPRESSION

In the relation between the conscious and unconscious of a culture, we find certain key metaphors, which function as grand signifiers that articulate the deep structures of a culture. Migration functions as a grand signifier that informs African American expression. In the black cultural tradition, it is a richly symbolic metaphor. Migration is a central element of diasporic consciousness. It speaks to origins, linking the discourse of history with the discourse of utopia, representing the language of power and the language of desire. In *Daughters of the Dust*, it is the signifier of creation, the myth of death and rebirth, a narrative of the descent into hell and the ascent to heaven.

A powerful iconography of migration is developed in the film and in the black cultural tradition: Africans shackled in slaveships; survivors of the crossing, or a people rising from the bowels of the ocean to labor on the plantations of the Americas; the exodus of blacks from the post-slavery South; and the physical or psychic return to Africa. This iconography revolves around empowerment and is articulated in black expression, for example, through signifiers of transportation such as the Underground Railroad or spirituals that offered solace to African while encoding messages of escape and redemption. *Daughters of the Dust* skilfully invokes the metaphor of migration in that its story is set during the period of the Great Migration of blacks from South to North, from rural areas to urban centers, and from the islands to the metropoles. The lure of reverse migration also had a powerful psychic appeal as masses of blacks throughout the Americas hailed Marcus Garvey's "Back to Africa" message. As a grand signifier of the African diasporic experience, migration has deep structural power that informs narrative activity in the black cultural tradition. African American folklore and musical forms such as the blues and jazz improvisation also reveal these influences. Any meaningful understanding of the African American tradition must take into account these key signifiers that articulate fundamental information about the black experience. The degree to which African American expressive culture mines this rich source of knowledge is directly related to its artistic success within the African American cultural tradition.

Chapter Eight

The Historical Narrative in Black Film

The historical narrative serves as a repository for a society's official memory and a vehicle for legitimizing the values of dominant social groups. Narrative is a mode of writing, a form of representation that structures a society's experience of the past and transmits information from generation to generation. It seeks to construct a meaningful reality out of past events, giving them a structure that, in themselves, they do not possess. The narrativization of historical events often functions to establish moral authority reflecting the interest of powerful social groups. Narration may also work as a cognitive mechanism to provide structures through which we make sense of historical events and things around us. This helps explain why the lived experience of African Americans has been at odds with the historical narratives of the dominant culture and why black filmmakers are motivated to contest traditional modes of representation. In the official history books and films, blacks have been represented as marginal beings existing on the fringes of history. In the dominant system of representation, the same mechanism has operated to repress knowledge of women's history and women's role in culture formation and institution building.

THE PROBLEM OF THE HISTORICAL FILM

In the cinema, the writing of history is subject to the structural constraints or shaping influences of narrative. The historical epic lends itself readily to cinematic manipulation because it appears to be based deceptively on empirical events and "real" people. Whereas there is no denying that some particular person actually lived or that a specific event did occur, it is possible to contest the representation of that said person or event as history. The core difficulty is that history is a privileged and foundational enterprise in human understanding, and the traditional approach to historical discourse attempts to efface the very nature of its undertaking by laying claim to a monolithic view of the past and discounting other accounts. This is also the problem of the historical film, which appears to be more "real" and "true" than other film genres because at some point in time, there was an actual reference in the real world to the series of events actualized in the film. To more clearly understand the historical film as a genre, we must remember that knowledge emanates from specific cultural reservoirs; that history itself is determined within a particular cultural environment encompassing its own ideologies, laws, politics and social relations; and that cinematic languages and technologies arise within these determinations.

It has already been established that this paradigm of cinema based upon the conventions of the Hollywood classical narrative is endowed with a series of structuring mechanisms that work to retard progressive social development in the favor of society's dominant classes through the recuperation and maintenance of the status quo. The traditions and forms of institutionalized narrative fulfil an ideological function through the perceptual and intuitive blinders imposed upon the experiences and knowledge it offers us by way of its restricted views and conceptions of reality. Certain items subject to narration will be represented or repressed according to dominant ideologies, which subsequently impacts on the openness of the narrative form.

FRANCISCO'S STORY

The Cuban film *The Other Francisco* (1977) examines the process of narrative construction and the way narrative closure works in the cinema. It undertakes the project of reformulating historical discourse through its emphasis on the development of alternative forms of narrative. *Francisco* demonstrates the structuring influences film form brings to bear on storytelling, the construction of meaning and the reproduction of dominant ideologies. It challenges the commonplace approaches to historical understanding. Its significance lies precisely in this reformulation of narrative expression. The film examines historical events and the realism of the classical narrative cinema through its interrogation of the conditions that produce filmic signification.

The *Other Francisco* focuses on the story of a slave as narrated in Cuba's first anti-slavery novel, *Francisco: The Sugar Plantation of the Delights of the Country* (1839). The anti-slavery novel which represents the system of narration associated with classical narratives, itself, is based on a narrative written by Juan Francisco Manzano (1797-1854), a slave who was freed and then achieved prominence in 19th century Cuban literary circles. Manzano's original narrative chronicles the first three decades of his life.

> From birth (which probably occurred in 1797) until approximately the age of twelve, he lived with his parents who were servants to the Marquesa de Santa Ana. Upon the death of the latter, the family passed into the service of the Marquesa de Prado Ameno, a cruel and capricious mistress from whom Manzano eventually fled to Havana. Manzano was largely self-taught . . . After his escape from the Marquesa de Prado Ameno, he obtained permission to work independently in Havana. He married a mulatto pianist, Delia, in 1835. (Mullen, 1981, p. 14)

Manzano's *Autobiography*, which was completed in 1839, graphically exposes the cruelties of slavery. Coulthard states that this "account of the sufferings of an intelligent and fairly well educated slave is one of the most valuable documents of the period. . . The deepest impressions left by this autobiographical sketch are of the arbitrariness and meanness of the masters, and the total denial of any kind of rights to the slave" (1962, p. 20). Historians have pointed out striking similarities between Manzano's *Autobiography* and *The Life and Times of Frederick Douglass* (Mullen, 1981, p. 24).

Dr. Richard Madden was an Irish physician employed by the British Colonial Office from 1833 to 1839 in Jamaica and Cuba. In Havana, he was the British Crown Agent charged with observing violations of the Anglo-Spanish treaty forbidding the slave trade. Madden published an English translation of Manzano's narrative in 1840 called *Poems by a Slave in the Island of Cuba*. Manzano's *Autobiography* is considered part of the African American literary tradition and similarities can be found in techniques, themes and modes of narration. "If one considers the fact that the English version was extant for some hundred years before the publication of the Spanish text . . . in 1937, it is legit-

imate to consider Madden's translation as a work of Afro-
American literature in the broadest and most universal sense of
the term" (Mullen, 1981, p. 4). Madden had a reputation as an
abolitionist, who the Spanish Captain-General of Havana
described as "a dangerous man from whatever point of view he
is considered, and living in this island he will have far too many
opportunities to disseminate seditious ideas directly or indirectly . . ." (Murray, 1972, p. 49). Madden's views on slavery influenced Cuban abolitionist writers of the period. In addition to his
official diplomatic role, he became involved with a group of
Cuban writers who met at the home of Domingo del Monte, a
prominent Creole intellectual. The group included Anselmo
Suarez-Romero—a white author from a slave-owning family—
who wrote the important abolitionist novel, *Francisco: The Sugar
Plantation of the Delights of the Country* (1839).

THE TWO SYSTEMS OF NARRATION
IN THE OTHER FRANCISCO

The Other Francisco revolves around the story of a slave rebellion. It utilizes Suarez-Romero's narrative as source material and
constructs a meta-narrative that provides a critical commentary
and intervenes strategically in the flow of Suarez-Romero's narrative. Suarez-Romero's *Francisco* presents a traditional paradigm—a romantic triangle—to dramatize the narrative problem
of the main character. The conventions of the classical narrative
shape a particular kind of hero and a certain kind of conflict. It
uses narrative closure to avoid questions the narration seeks to
marginalize or repress. Filmmaker Sergio Giral's meta-narrative
opens up the space of an alternative narrative, which interrogates
Suarez-Romero's narration and presents background information about slavery. This meta-narrative functions as a subversive
narrative, refusing closure and pointing the viewer to another
history that is carefully elided in the traditional modes of historical representation.

　　The Other Francisco can be classified within the genre of the
historical film; however, the filmmaker separates his work from
the romanticized narratives that usually characterize the genre
of historical film. Suarez-Romero's narration of Francisco tells
of a slave captured from the West Coast of Africa at the age of
ten, who is brought to the Americas and becomes the property
of a slaveowning family. The mistress, Senora Mendizabal, raises the boy as a houseslave, who grows up playing with her son,

Ricardo. As an adult, Francisco falls in love with the mixed-race slave woman, Dorotea, who bears him a child. The mistress forbids their love affair and she disapproves of their subsequent disobedience. The couple's happiness is thwarted when the young slavemaster Ricardo falls in love with Dorotea and completes the love triangle. Francisco suffers severe punishment. When Dorotea can no longer bear the pain of her lover's unfortunate circumstance, she gives in to Ricardo to lessen Francisco's punishment. Upon learning of Dorotea's submission to the advances of the slavemaster, Francisco is distraught. Suarez-Romero's narration ends with Francisco's suicide, apparently from heartbreak on learning of Dorotea's relationship with Ricardo.

Francisco's story bristles with powerful dramatic agents, deeply rooted conflict and emotionally stirring ingredients favored by the classical film narrative. For example, one finds the noble slave who suffers the inhumanity of his fellow man; the beautiful mulatto woman who loves him; the "evil" slavemaster who also loves the mulatto woman and rivals the downtrodden hero for her love; the brokenhearted woman who submits to the advances of the slavemaster to put a halt to the cruel punishment her lover suffers; the two lovers torn apart from each other because of the "sin" of the woman; and finally the eventual suicide of the hero who prefers death to living a life in which he cannot have the woman he loves. Suarez-Romero's narration develops precisely along these stereotyped lines of character and plot development. However, Giral is interested in calling attention to the way ideological considerations influence decision making and choice in narration. Suarez-Romero's plot emphasizes a peculiar interpretation of historical event that foregrounds dramatic values based on romantic love, brutal conflict, sensational plot elements and viewer empathy.

In contrast to the established conventions of the genre of the historical film, *The Other Francisco* refuses the teleology of the classical narrative and opens up the diegesis to observe the mechanisms that impose closure and operate to structure a specific kind of narration. *The Other Francisco* refuses the closure so closely identified with the system of Hollywood classical film. In the presentation of Francisco's story, Giral's narration adopts the cinematic techniques and patterns of narrative development characteristic of narrative realism. When Giral's narration presents its own version of Francisco's story, it foregrounds the analysis of a slave's life using Francisco as its example. The narration of

Suarez-Romero's *Francisco* uses a softfocus camera technique, which serves to intensify the sexual presence of the mixed-race woman. The close-up is also a prevalent feature of the classical system of narration as it functions to draw the viewer emotionally into the story through intimate identification with the characters of the diegesis and the systemic flow of the narrative. However, later as Giral's narration seeks to penetrate the system of the classical narrative, it becomes necessary to do so through the use of different technical-craft codes more related to the development of an alternative cinematic tradition.

DRAMATIC CHOICES IN THE CLASSICAL FILM NARRATIVE

The following is a summary outline of the climax of the original narrative presented at the beginning of the film:

> *The camera moves in slowly to show a thoughtful Francisco, seated at the water's edge. The water surges and a bell tolls. Close-up view of Francisco looking intensely into the camera, which then reframes to give Extreme Close-up shot of his eyes. Cut to Extreme Close-up shot of Dorotea's eyes in soft focus while quiet, soothing orchestral music underscores the visual images. Francisco rises from his seated position, moves aside and walks into the camera view. Close-up shot of Dorotea's face as she starts to move away. Long shot of Dorotea as she runs into the woods. Francisco runs into the frame from the bottom of the screen. The two lovers meet. They hug and caress. The camera moves in much closer to picture their emotions and their embrace. Teardrops flow from Dorotea's eyes as her face is pictured in extreme close-up. The camera view opens to provide a two-shot of the couple: Extreme close-up shot of Dorotea's face with teardrops in her eyes. The camera view opens up to provide a twoshot of the couple.*

Dorotea
Wait Francisco, . . . the truth is that we cannot get married.

Francisco
Why not? They've pardoned me, my darling.
Francisco takes Dorotea in his arms, gently and lovingly, swirling her around.

We'll go back to Havana with our baby, to serve the mistress and be together.

Medium Close-up of the two lovers in each other's embrace. Extreme Close-up shot of Dorotea.

Dorotea

They forgave you, but not to stay together. I'll go back to Havana with the mistress; but you have to stay here.

Francisco

What's happened now?

Dorotea

I can't stand it anymore, Francisco. All I did was for you. . . to save you. I went to bed with the master. Now, I don't deserve your love. I'm not yours. I'm not yours anymore Francisco. Otherwise he would have killed you, and I want you to live even if I never see you again. Forgive me, . . . forgive me, . . . Goodbye . . . forgive me.

Close-up shot of Francisco

We won't see each other again . . . Forgive me.

Long shot of Dorotea running away. Francisco follows, running into the camera's view and going after her. Medium close-up view of Francisco who is distraught and angry. He runs madly through the forest throwing himself blindly around. He falls to the ground beating the earth with his fists. Francisco looks up slowly. We see his face and eyes in Extreme close-up. Long shot of the master Ricardo and the overseer Don Antonio. They are in a clearing in the woods. Ricardo is perched on his horse and Don Antonio stands next to the horse. They both look up and beyond the camera.

Suarez-Romero (Off screen)

Later, the master and his overseer saw that buzzards were flying around a tree.

Camera tilts up to show Francisco's body hanging listlessly.

And from the top branch, they saw a black man hanging, the body swollen, half-rotten and eaten by buzzards. It was Francisco.

Medium shot of the Author Anselmo Suarez-Romero in a parlor reading from his manuscript at a party of intellectuals and bourgeois *socialities who share antislavery sentiments.*

Suarez-Romero
Neither Senora Mendizabal nor Dorotea found out
until later when Master Ricardo wrote them about
it. The brown girl, overcome by pain, wasted away.
The camera zooms in slowly.
After a few years, she died.

The opening sequence of *The Other Francisco* establishes the main
characters and outlines the plot development of Francisco's story.
Giral's narration interweaves plot details that lead to the climax
throughout the first section of the film, which presents exposi-
tory material and develops character. But the narration introduces the voice of a commentator, who is empowered to stop the
flow of the narrative, dissect it and furnish additional information that the original narrative does not give. In contrast to using
the narrator's commentary to confirm the flow of visual and
sound images and to impose a unified structure on the narration,
The Other Francisco creates the device of a subversive narration,
which presents its own concerns about the framed narrative and
adds much more information than usually is the case in classical
film narrative.

The narrator in the classical film narrative system is usually
concealed behind the voices of characters in the plot. When these
films use the device of a commentator, this figure anchors or confirms those meanings in the narrative that are difficult to pin
down or to establish solely through the actions and characters
presented in the development of the plot. The system of classical narration seeks to guarantee a social order consistent with
dominant ideologies. Characters and events of the narrative are
developed to have a purposeful existence. The actions of the hero
are presented as legitimate. They are represented as moving one-
dimensionally toward the resolution of the narrative conflict. In
this system of narration, there is little room for representing a
complex character or complex events outside the regime of
meanings presented in the plot. For example, Suarez-Romero's
narrative of Francisco portrays the hero to be a character full of
human emotions who has the capacity to fall in love. Its entire
system of narration hinges around the love story of Francisco
and Dorotea. The wickedness and violence of the slavemaster is
only represented because somehow it relates to Francisco's love
story. Thereby, it provides a powerful emotional system antagonistic and pessimistic in nature, but it functions dramatically to

establish the hero Francisco as a noble character worthy of the
viewer's empathic concern. It is possible to encounter a character endowed with complexity in classical narrative cinema; however, this complexity is of a limited and limiting variety because
it works to repress another knowledge regarding the richness
and diversity of the real world.

Suarez-Romero's narrative positions Francisco as a slave in
love, The abolitionist sentiment of the original narrative pays
inordinate attention to the capability of the slave to love, to serve
the Christian religion and to possess a bourgeois nobility. The
question then arises as to how can the slaveowning society
enslave such a noble human being? It is certainly an important
question; however, it is more appropriate at the historical
moment of the beginnings of the slave trade and in its heyday
than at a time when it has become economically inefficient and
financially difficult to maintain. Undoubtedly, this type of sentiment is important to the Western society, for, at least, it concedes the slave's humanity. In the regime of 18th and 19th
century literature, grave doubts still lingered concerning the
humanity of the slave. Whereas Suarez-Romero's narration presents the hopes and desires of a slave who is full of passion, it
also conceals the truth of its intentions, which uses the camou-
flage of the slave's humanity to attack the slave system. In contrast, its ideological concerns have to do with a crisis in the
socio-economic system of plantation slavery and the emergence
of industrial capitalism as a superior system of social and economic organization.

Suarez-Romero's narration ends with Francisco's death at
his own hands. Within the dramatic conventions of this
Aristotelian schema, what other recourse is there for a character who possesses the nobility of Francisco in this Godforsaken
circumstance. The system of classical film and its narrative realism reflect elements of philosophical idealism, which find an
eternal essence in human nature. In these terms, men fall in love
and die for love; a slave can be a good man, while the master can
be a wretch. Certain common values are assumed to traverse
social classes and historical periods. In the Aristotelian system of
classical narrative, we develop an empathic relationship with the
slave Francisco. We pain with him in his punishment and hate
the cruel master for his vicious inhumanity. Anger seethes within us, but the narrative invokes the device of catharsis to provide
a vehicle for containing our dissatisfactions. Classical narration

resolves the crisis of the plot within the terms of the complication, which the narrative develops. This system of narrative
throws the world into some sort of crisis and then resolves it
within its own careful terms of reference. Hence, we can point
out the conservative function of the classical narrative: it is fundamentally concerned with rehabilitating the narrative in the
service of the status quo as well as rehabilitating the individual
viewer to maintain the social order of the dominant society.
Consequently, there is the negation of the possibility of social
change, which the narration occasionally brings to the surface
through its guise as an anti-slavery novel. Ultimately, there is a
creative resolution of this problem by foregrounding the major
plot action as that of a slave in love as opposed to the evils of
slavery, which lurk in the background of the story. The narration is incapable of resolving the romantic triangle and the inhuman brutality it produces. However, while raising the question
of slavery as a system of exploitation, the social and economic
inequality around which the social order is organized is never
fully represented as the scourge it really is.

THE SUBVERSIVE NARRATIVE

Because the system of pleasure characteristic of the classical film
narrative over-determines forms of consumerist narrative at the
expense of social change and narrative innovation, narrative closure is imposed as a means of intensifying the entertainment
value of a film. *The Other Francisco* begins with similar historical
actors and events as any typical film on slavery; however, its system of narration opens up its story to subvert the ideological
operation of the classical narrative. In Suarez-Romero's novel,
the author's point of view is the supreme guide in the narration.
It assigns points of view and social positions to the characters of
the narrative all the time concealing the origin or point of view
of the narration. In contrast, the narration in *The Other Francisco*
identifies its narrative interests and the diversity of ideological
positions in the story. Initially, Giral's narration wants to find out
whether Suarez-Romero's narrative provides a real view of the
slave, and it questions the ideological intentions of the young
bourgeois intellectuals who support the anti-slavery movement.
The subversive narrative presents its commentary as a mode of
clarifying and elucidating the contradictions of the narration
without attempting to repress their utterance. It also features the
commentator as an interlocutor who undertakes a process of

interrogation and contextualizes plot events.

In contrast to the cinematic techniques of the classical narrative, which emphasize a stylized realism through which Suarez-Romero's narrative is presented, the reformulated narrative uses a documentary ambience that de-emphasizes elements of dramatic unity and entertainment values. *The Other Francisco* is photographed in black and white. This technique de-emphasizes "the illusion of cinema," which strives to create an imaginary fullness and an apparent logical completeness to narrative events that reaffirm the legitimacy of the dominant social order. Because advances in color photographic technique seem to bring us closer to commonplace conceptions of reality, we tend to believe that this is a necessary and modern way of filmmaking. The use of black-and-white photography in *The Other Francisco* can be seen as an aesthetic choice, which allows the viewer to understand that film is a cultural product fabricated within a particular social system, and that it can have other important values beside entertainment. In these terms, the black-and-white photography becomes a conscious choice informing the viewer that what is being seen is plastic and not reality itself. Color photography also involves additional finances.

Let us now take a look at the nature of Francisco's crime. Ricardo provides helpful information when he tells the overseer that the slave impregnated the mistress' favorite seamstress. This act was most unthinkable because Francisco is expected to have known better in that he was raised in the "big house" and learned to read and write. Francisco is described as an "ingrate" who "ruined" Dorotea. Despite the anti-slavery tone of Suarez-Romero's narration, there still remains fundamental questions concerning the slave's humanity. We may relate this to the system of sexual repressions underlining the narrative and the actions of characters. The narrative imbibes the predominant ideologies of the day, which espouse the humanity of the slave, but finds it impossible to endow blacks with human characteristics. Dorotea has been 'soiled,' or in other words she has sinned. Francisco, the house slave, is not to be conceived as a sexual creature. He is to be desexed because of his upbringing in the big house. As punishment, Francisco is sent to the fields. Suarez-Romero builds a certain anti-slavery sentiment into his narration and presents a graphic depiction of the violence surrounding the life of the slave.

However, the subversive narrative penetrates this superficial sympathetic sentiment of the slave to suggest that the appearance of the novel occurred at a time when the slave economy had become inefficient, and that it was in the interests of the bourgeoisie to provide a rationale for the emerging system of capitalism, which would yield more profits for their investment. Thus, while seeking to arouse sympathetic public sentiment for the anti-slavery movement, Suarez-Romero's narration acts in its own ideological disposition to further its class interests as well as display the limitations of its class consciousness regarding the degree of humanity granted to the slave. For example, the Padre blesses the slaves telling them, "Your body may be enslaved; but your soul is free to fly one day to the happy manse of the chosen." But he also condones the actions and philosophies of the slaveowning class.

In Suarez-Romero's narration, audience identification with the suffering of the slave is powerfully effected. We are moved by the sheer brutality of the slave system and tend to look with pity upon those who are caught up within it and have been entrusted with its enforcement. The subversive narrative seeks to bring the characters and events back to the realm of history. Whereas Suarez-Romero's narrative is overly concerned with the sexual passions of the young master Ricardo, the commentary points out that other circumstances may explain the reason why Ricardo set out to cause pain to Francisco and Dorotea because, at the time, millowners had other motivations.

> **Commentator (Off screen)**
> The sugar slavelords entered capitalism with a deep
> class-consciousness, The advent of the steam engine
> speeds up production and worsens slave exploita-
> tion. The Cuban millowners seek ways to get more
> out of their slaves. Slavemaster relations were based
> on production.

Our identification with Francisco and our suffering for the tragic love between him and Dorotea keep our attention focused on the peculiar vagaries of romantic love and away from a fuller consideration of the life of the slave. Francisco's undying love for Dorotea is over-determined by the Suarez-Romero's narration, which does not allow the articulation of other questions concerning sexual relations of the slave and sexuality in 19th century society. We learn that Dorotea was a "brown Creole girl"

whose mother nursed Ricardo. Although the mistress refused
Francisco's wishes to marry Dorotea, the two lovers courted
secretly for two years until Dorotea became pregnant, and their
love affair was uncovered.

In order to reveal the repressed aspects of the narrative, the
moving image is stopped on occasion and replaced by a still photograph. The narrator then presents information that has been
overlooked by the original narrative.

> *Medium shot showing a freeze frame image of Dorotea*
> *taking her seat in carriage next to the mistress, Francisco*
> *clasps her hands assisting as she enters.*
> **Commentator (Off screen)**
> But the real facts of life and love were that the slave's
> love and sex relations were limited
> *Medium long shot of Slave woman crouched over her*
> *work.*
> by the numerical imbalance of the sexes.
> *A white plantation worker sneaks up from behind.*
> *He assaults the woman carrying her off to rape her.*
> The few slave women were used for the pleasure of
> white plantation workers who mated with slaves to
> reproduce.

The narration of the subversive narrative commandeers Suarez-
Romero's narrative to direct its flow by injecting a critique of the
sexual relations of plantation society. For example, we learn that
pregnant women worked the fields until the ninth month; that
plantation mortality was extremely high, and this ruled out
increasing the slave labor force through natural reproduction
given the fact of the AngloSpanish pact on ending the slave trade;
and that the slave women aborted themselves avoiding preg-
nancy.

When the subversive narrative takes control of the flow of
narrative events, a different type of filmic signification is utilized.
The music assumes a different texture, tonality and expressive
form. Whereas the music of the classical narrative is European,
the music of the subversive narrative is African. In the scene
where a slave woman gathers leaves and herbs to prepare a mixture to induce abortion, flute music is used. The music builds as
the woman grinds the mixture in a small mortar. She drinks the
bitter concoction and then struggles through the woods where

she keels over in pain clutching her stomach. As Suarez-Romero's narrative reverts to its romanticized style, symphonic music returns. Toward the conclusion of Giral's narrative as the slave revolt begins, the sound image features African drums and other distinctly non-European percussion instruments.

Suarez-Romero's narrative literally overflows with acts of violence. There is the constant punishment of black male slaves who are shackled with hobbles and neck chains. They are tortured. The women are raped and brutalized. In the classical narrative, violence functions as a condition that seeks to guarantee the continuation of the existing social formation through the representation of power in terms of superior force. The terms of power in plantation society are delineated in Suarez-Romero's narrative, but only in relation to a social system it renders decadent. However, the capacity to own or possess is usually reserved for the powerful in society. There is also the power over sexual activity, which positions the black male and the female in terms of a deficiency in relation to the dominant Euro-patriarchal paradigm of power. Francisco's sexual threat is contained by the violence of the white overseer and the master, Ricardo. He ends up hanging from a tree in a dumb stoic submission and the woman is made to be the exclusive property of the white male. The black slave women are assaulted and raped. The mixed-race woman who is filled with sensuality is proscribed in her relationship with the black man. She is made to succumb to the terror of the slave-master, who beats her as well as has sexual intercourse with her.

In principle, the signification of sexuality in the classical narrative implies possession. The phenomenon of possessing human beings was manifested in the system of chattel slavery and in the silence imposed on the condition of women. Whereas the classical narrative attempts to link these with the decadent slave system, it represents the emerging capitalist system as an improvement in the conditions of slavery and in terms of its efficient machines. But the subversive narrative is capable of challenging the representation of power and sexuality in the classical narrative. There is the myth of the omniscient power of the dominant society. Francisco seems to have no way out. His narrative actions take place within the limitations established by the system of the classical narrative. However, the subversive narrative introduces the efforts of the slaves in their revolts and their acts of resistance.

We are told now that the dominant system of power is not

as ubiquitous as its ideology would have us believe; that the slaves constantly sabotaged the workings of the sugar mills; that the slavewomen committed abortions and refused to give birth to slave children; that whenever the opportunity arose, the slaves struck a blow for their freedom. The commentary then observes that long before the writing of the Suarez-Romero novel, there was a wave of uprisings that occurred and continued through the 1840s. There is the additional information of the slave revolt in Santo Domingo, which led to the setting up of the first black republic in the New World and the existence of maroon communities in the hills where free blacks live.

The final sequence of *The Other Francisco* deconstructs the smooth veneer of the classical narrative. Once again, the narration presents the summary ending of Suarez-Romero's narrative. However, this time, it is represented by the use of still shots depicting the beginning of the sequence; and later as it concludes, there is the repetition of still shots. On these occasions, the sequence of visual images is juxtaposed with a commentary that refuses the closure of meanings Suarez-Romero wishes to impose. With the final repetition of the original visual sequence, the slave revolt is in progress and the commentary advises: "This is the real situation of the slaves: Would Francisco kill himself? Despite the novel's idealized view of the slave, it was censored. Publication in Cuba was out at the time. But would Francisco have hanged himself? And precisely for love? Suicide was one form of slave rebelliousness, but there were others." The visual images return at this point to the events of the slave revolt in which slaves burn the fields.

Another intervention occurs when Madden interviews the author Suarez-Romero about the influences and presuppositions he used in writing the novel. The commentary brings us back to the novel, but with contrary intentions. The commentator wants to reconsider the novel taking a look at the "real situation of slavery and a true picture of a mill-slave of the times." The filmic signification is shorn of the illusory romanticism of the classical narrative. The documentary image that replaces it is harsh and uncompromising. Much of the time, the overseers are taken up with runaway slaves, who the narration presents as involved in organizing themselves to escape or commit acts of resistance. The violence against the slaves is brutal and swift. The recaptured slave Crispin tells Francisco of freedom in a land found on the other side of the mountain where the blacks live as free as they did in Africa, and where there is no master. Yoruba ritual is fused heavily with political agitation by the high priest, who tells of the hardships of a slave's life, emphasizing that " . . . de slaves tired of dying and getting a white heaven." The slaves beg for strength to kill the white master and for leadership to find their way to freedom. The spirit of this Revolt Sequence intensifies when the slave Crispin calls out for his freedom and proclaims "but we got to purify de massa's land."

As the slave revolt begins, the slaves set fire to the cane fields and plantation property. The sound image is percussive using distinctively African rhythm instruments. The overseers are in hot pursuit of the rebellious slaves. Even their dogs give chase. The editing patterns of the sequence are built according to dialectical juxtapositions of disparate visual images and the intensity of the percussion sounds. In a progression of images from this sequence, a slave fights off a vicious hunting dog using a stone; slaves run to the hills; percussion instruments are heard; cut to a close-up of a chess game piece being moved and the commentary informs us, "Slaves striving for their freedom didn't interest the ideologists who relied on the mass of free blacks and even some poor whites." In a subsequent interview with Richard Madden and the Creole intellectual Domingo del Monte, we learn that further importation of slaves would harm economic progress because of the industrialization of the sugar production process. Interestingly, the slavemaster Ricardo expresses a frightening fear when he remarks "what can we do? Wait until the devils gobble us up?" This is followed by the castration of a dead runaway slave in front of a group of slaves who are forced to witness the event. When Ricardo rapes Dorotea, the scene is intercut with slaves sabotaging the mill. Francisco is chosen to be punished as an example for the mill sabotage. This information helps develop the notion of the slave Francisco not simply as a slave in love, but one who refuses his oppression. Furthermore, we see the response of the slaver to the slave's acts of rebellion.

The slaves are savage in their revenge. The black slave-driver is attacked and killed by a group of men and women. The killing is a communal act. The overseer is strangled with his own whip. But, significantly, the subversive narrative does not succumb to an idealistic fairy tale ending in which the slaves triumph. The revolt is contained, in keeping with historical fact; however, the slaves put up a good fight and many escape to join the maroons in the hills. They cause serious damage to the sugar mills and their rebellion pushes the slave system closer to oblivion. At the end of the reformulated narrative, the superior weaponry of the slavemasters, which comprises firearms and gunpowder, defeats the spears and bows-and-arrows of the slaves. In their brief victory, the whites chop off the hands of blacks. A leader of the slave revolt is decapitated and his head paraded around the plantation. Captured runaways are hung from meat hooks. The final scene of the film offers the sound image of African drums and visual images of blacks climbing the hills to freedom. From on high, the escapees look down on the enslaved land below.

THE IMPACT OF FILM FORM
ON HISTORICAL CONTENT

In its reformulation of the narrative, *The Other Francisco* moves away from the problematic of the classical film narrative to explore an alternative mode of narration that fosters fresh approaches to the dialectic involving film form and historical content. The basic criticism offered by *The Other Francisco* is that the writing of history in the classical narrative structures historical material within narrow ideological guidelines that operate to restrict the richness of history and the divergent forces extant within a particular era. Whereas Suarez-Romero's novel is based on an amorous triangle, which becomes the source of Francisco's suffering, *The Other Francisco* remolds the question to ask whether a typical slave of the time would be likely to react in the manner of Francisco who acts simply out of romantic considerations? The fallacy inherent in the classical narrative is its tendency to reduce the complexity of society to the point of view of the dominant social class in a particular historical period. While the classical narrative accepts the universality of concepts such as romance and romantic love, the reformulated narrative seeks more information to make it possible to place Francisco's story within a proper historical context. Historical cross currents and competing ideological assumptions are explicitly foregrounded. In a scene featuring an interview between Madden and Suarez-Romero, the latter's ideological interests in the narrative are revealed. We learn that the Suarez-Romero's family members are plantation owners experiencing financial instability because of the economic inefficiency of the slave system. He writes the story of *Francisco* for financial reasons and tells Madden that creditors are running the mill. Furthermore, we also learn that

Francisco was written so that the author could gain income as a novelist. In essence, the slave Francisco is a representation that exists principally for a narrative value that is based on economic returns. Speaking of Francisco, Suarez-Romero observes, "Can a person groaning under the slave yoke be as tame and peaceful as Francisco? He's a freak, an exception who helps me to denounce the horrors of slavery." As a result, the classical narrative endows the slave with a Christian resignation and stoicism that is not a permanent condition of a slave, but a strategic survival mechanism.

Any alternative cinema must address the core problem of the constitution of power in society and the sexual and racial positions it prescribes. Regarding the representation of women, the reformulated narrative breaks from the historical stereotype. The slave women are represented as active makers of history. They are involved in the resistance struggle and are central to the ensuing slave revolt. The characterization of Dorotea and the mistress, Senora Mendizabal, is derived from their delineation in the classical narrative. Dorotea is the sensual mixed-race woman who is craved by the white master. The mistress is a solitary figure of a woman. She is the white matriarch who has given the responsibility for running the sugar mill business to her son; but there are some questions that we might ask about Dorotea and Senora Mendizabal. The matron typifies the bourgeois woman of the time. She prefers the Havana life to the harder conditions of the country. According to the original narrative, no mention is made of her husband and there is no male companion for her. The matron was responsible for shaping Francisco to her likes. He was a privileged slave, who worked in the big house. When Francisco's affair with Dorotea is discovered, the matron decides to take revenge by ordering Francisco to be physically punished, while sending Dorotea away to serve as a seamstress to a French woman. The mistress does have an unusual interest in Francisco, who is her male slave. It would appear that the physical punishment meted out to Francisco and his banishment to the sugar mill to do the work of field slaves was excessive for his sexual affairs, which contravened the wishes of the mistress. The question then arises why is Francisco so severely punished and why is the mistress unable to forgive him? The narrative of Suarez-Romero represses any knowledge of interracial sexual relations between the white bourgeois woman and the slave. But the deep-seated anger of the mistress may, according to Barthes' symbolic code, imply a repressed sexual interest in Francisco. This theme of sexual relations between the slaveowning aristocracy and their slaves was limited in Suarez-Romero's novel to Ricardo's interest in Dorotea and the white plantation workers' sexual raids on the black slave women. However, we may formulate an additional enigma concerning the identity of the mixed-race slave, Dorotea, who is described as a brown Creole girl whose mother nursed Ricardo. Interestingly, Suarez-Romero's narrative provides specific information on Francisco. We learn that he was taken from Africa at the age of ten; but it is silent on Dorotea's origins. We can point out that Dorotea was born on the plantation because her mother was the nurse to Ricardo. The narrator states during the course of the film that the few male slaves were used for the sexual satisfactions of the white female workers, Even Ricardo's sexual obsession with Dorotea provides a case in point. Regarding Dorotea's identity, it is possible that she is a relation of the Mendizabal family?

In the film, the white male signifies the established social order. The white plantation workers seem to enjoy the harsh, brutal nature of their work as well as the unceasing violence they administer. The fragility of the Euro-patriarchal social order is uncovered through the narrator's additional information of a long history of slave revolts as well as Suarez-Romero's mention of slaves who sabotage the mill, which then causes Francisco to be subjected to further punishment. Although the original narrative does present the violence of the overseer against the slaves as harsh, we can still point out how the act of official violence is a pillar for the maintenance of the status quo. In the reformulated narrative, the violence of the slavemaster is met by acts of resistance and revolt by the slaves. In the narrative, as in society, violence emanates from a symbolic framework, which has as its objective the control, domination and possession of aspects of the world perceived to be threatening to the imaginary fullness that society represents. The violence of the slavemaster seems to intensify as a means of system maintenance. This violence betrays the myth of slave docility and subservience.

An important element of the critique extended by *The Other Francisco* is that the political uses of cinema proceed beyond a concern with content to analyses and reformulations on the level of the formal structures of the film. By actually breaking up the flow of the narrative as a means of highlighting the nature of its repressive system, the reformulated narrative opens up an avenue for the development of films that seek to rewrite history. But this approach to narrative requires a new orientation of the viewer to the film, who must engage the reformulated narrative as an adventure in exploration and knowledge generation. The viewer is liberated from the colonial submissiveness, the missionary position in which one comes to the cinema as a voyeur to experience and witness the parade of life as it passes by from a vantage point of imagined safety.

Bibliography

Abrahams, Roger D. (1976). *Talking Black.* Rowley, Massachusetts: Newbury.

Agee, James. (1948). "David Wark Griffith." In R. A. Maynard, ed., (1974). *The Black Man on Film: Racial Stereotyping.* Rochelle Park, New Jersey: Hayden Book Company.

Anderson, Victor. (1995). Beyond Ontological Blackness: *An Essay on African American Religious and Cultural Criticism.* New York: Continuum Publishing Company.

Aristotle. (1987). Richard Janek, trans., *Poetics.* Indianapolis: Hackett Publishing Company.

Asante, Molefe K. (1990). *Kemet, Afrocentricity and Knowledge.* Trenton, New Jersey: Africa World Press.

_____. (1987). *The Afrocentric* Idea. Philadelphia: Temple University Press.

Baber, Ceola Ross. (1987). "The Artistry and Artifice of Black Communication." In G. Gay and W. L. Baber, eds., *Expressively Black: The Cultural Basis of Ethnic Identity.* New York: Praeger, 75 - 108.

Baker, Houston. A., Jr. (1984). *Blues, Ideology, and Afro-American Literature.* Chicago: University of Chicago Press.

_____. (1981). Generational Shifts and the Recent Criticism of Afro-American Literature. In A. Mitchell, ed., (1994). *Within the Circle: An Anthology of African American Literary Criticism from the Harlem Renaissance to the Present.* Durham: Duke University Press.

Barrett, Michele et al. (1979). *Ideology and Cultural Production.* New York: St. Martin's Press.

Barthes, Roland. (1977). *Mythologies.* New York: Hill and Wang.

_____. (1974). S/Z: An Essay. New York: Hill and Wang.

Beardsley, Monroe C. (1972). "Problems in Aesthetics." In Paul Edwards, ed., *The Encyclopedia of Philosophy.* New York: MacMillan and the Free Press.

Belton, John. (1994). *American Cinema, American Culture.* New York: McGraw-Hill.

Bennett, Lerone, Jr. (September 1971). "The Emancipation Orgasm: Sweetback in Wonderland." Ebony, 106-108.

Bethel, Lorraine. (1982). "This Infinity of Conscious Pain: Zora Neale Hurston and the Black Female Literary Tradition." In Gloria T. Hull, Patricia Bell Scott, and Barbara Smith, eds., *But Some of Us Are Brave.* Old Westbury, NY: The Feminist Press.

Boal, Augusto. (1979). *Theatre of the Oppressed.* New York: Urizen Books.

Bobo, Jacqueline. (1995). *Black Women as Cultural Readers.* New York: Columbia University Press.

Bogle, Donald. (1994). *Toms, Coons, Mammies, Mulattoes and Bucks: An Interpretive History of Blacks in American Films.* New York: The Continuum Publishing Company.

_____. (1974). "Uptown Saturday Night: A Look at its Place in Black Film History." *Freedomways: Quarterly Review of the Freedom*

Movement 14: 4.

Bontemps, Arna. (1966). "Introduction." In Langston Hughes and Arna Bontemps, eds., *Book of Negro Folklore*. New York: Dodd, Mead and Company.

Bordwell, David and Thompson, Kristin. (1997). *Film Art: An Introduction*. New York: McGraw-Hill.

Bordwell, David (1985). *Narration in the Fiction Film*. Madison: University of Wisconsin Press.

_____, Janet Staiger, and Kristin Thompson. (1985). *The Hollywood Classical Cinema: Film Style and Mode of Production to 1960*. New York: Columbia University Press.

Bourne, St. Clair. (May 1988). "Bright Moments." *The Independent*, 10-13.

_____. (1994). "The Continuing Drama of African American Images in American Cinema." *Black Stage and Screen* 7: 2, 20-22.

_____. (1982). "The Development of the Contemporary Black Film Movement." In G. L. Yearwood, ed., *Black Cinema Aesthetics: Issues in Independent Black Filmmaking*. Athens, OH: Ohio University Center for Afro-American Studies, 93-105.

Bowser, Pearl. (Winter 1973). "History Lesson: The Boom is Really an Echo." Black Creation: *A Quarterly Review of Black Arts and Letters* 4 (2), 32-34.

_____, and Spence, Louise. (1996). "Identity and Betrayal: The Symbol of the Unconquered and Oscar Micheaux's Biographical Legend." In D. Bernardi, ed., *The Birth of Whiteness: Race and the Emergence of U.S. Cinema*. New Brunswick, NJ: Rutgers University Press, 57-80.

_____. (1981). "Introduction." *Independent Black American Cinema*. New York: Third World Newsreel.

_____. (1982). "Sexual Imagery and the Black Woman in Cinema." In G. L. Yearwood, ed., *Black Cinema Aesthetics: Issues in Independent Black Filmmaking*. Athens, OH: Ohio University Center for Afro-American Studies, 42-51.

Heath, Shirley Brice. (1983). *Ways With Words: Language, Life and Work in Communities and Classrooms*. New York: Cambridge University Press.

Browne, Roscoe C. Jr., (1973). "Film as a Tool for Liberation." *Black Creation: A Quarterly Review of Black Arts and Letters* 4 (2), 36-37.

Cade Bambara, Toni. (1993). "Reading the Signs, Empowering the Eye: *Daughters of the Dust* and the Black Independent Cinema Movement." In M. Diawara, ed., *Black American Cinema*. New York & London: Routledge, 118-144.

Campbell, Joseph. (1968). *The Hero with a Thousand Faces*. Princeton, NJ: Princeton University Press.

Carmichael, Stokely and Hamilton, Charles V. (1967). *Black Power: The Politics of Liberation in America*. New York: Vintage Books.

Cham, Mbye. ed., (1992). *Ex-Iles: Essays on Caribbean Cinema*. Trenton, NJ: Africa World Press.

_____ and Andrade-Watkins, Claire, eds., (1988). *Blackframes: Critical Perspectives on Black Independent Cinema*. Cambridge, MA: The MIT Press.

Christian, Barbara. (1980). *Black Women Novelists: The Development of a*

Tradition, 1892-1976. Westport, Conn.: Greenwood.

Collingwood, R. G. (1938). *The Principles of Art.* Oxford: Oxford University Press.

The Combahee River Collective. (1982) "A Black Feminist Statement." In G. T. Hull, P. Bell Scott, and B. Smith, eds., *All the Woman Are White, All the Men Are Black, But Some of Us Are Brave.* Old Westbury, NY: The Feminist Press.

Cortissoz, Royal. (1924). "The Post-Impressionist Illusion." *Three Papers on Modernist Art.* New York: American Academy of Arts and Letters.

Coulthard, G. R. (1962). *Race and Colour in Caribbean Literature.* London: Oxford University Press.

Coward, Rosalind and Ellis, John. (1977). Language and Materialism: *Developments in Semiology and the Theory of the Subject.* London: Routledge and Kegan Paul.

Cox, Kenyon. (1913). "The 'Modern' Spirit in Art." *Harper's Weekly*, March 15, 1913.

Cripps, Thomas. (1978) *Black Film as Genre.* Bloomington: Indiana University Press.

_____. (1996). "The Making of *The Birth of a Race*: The Emerging Politics of Identity in Silent Movies." In D. Bernardi, ed., *The Birth of Whiteness: Race and the Emergence of U.S. Cinema.* New Brunswick, NJ: Rutgers University Press.

_____. (1982). "New Black Cinema and Uses of the Past." In G. L. Yearwood, ed., *Black Cinema Aesthetics.* Athens, OH: Center for Afro-American Studies, 19-26.

_____. (1977). *Slow Fade To Black: The Negro in American Film*, 1900-1942. New York: Oxford University Press.

_____. (1990). *"Sweet Sweetback's Baadasss Song* and the Changing Politics of Genre Film." In Peter Lehman, ed., *Close Viewings: An Anthology of New Film Criticism.* Tallahassee: Florida State University Press.

_____. (1993). "Oscar Micheaux: The Story Continues." In M. Diawara, ed., *Black American Cinema.* New York: Routledge.

Cruse, Harold. (1967). The Crisis of the Negro Intellectual. New York: William Morrow and Co.

Crusz, Robert. (1986). "Black Cinemas, Film Theory, and Dependent Knowledge." In H. A. Baker, Jr., M. Diawara and R. H. Lindeborg, eds., *Black British Studies*: A Reader. Chicago: University of Chicago Press.

Davis, Zeinabu Irene. (1989). "The Future of Black Film: The Debate Continues." In M. T. Martin, ed., (1995)., *Cinemas of the Black Diaspora: Diversity, Dependence, and Oppositionality.* Detroit: Wayne State University Press.

Diakite, Madubuko. (1980). *Film, Culture and the Black Filmmaker.* New York: Arno Press.

Diawara, Manthia. (1993) "Black American Cinema: The New Realism." In M. Diawara, ed., *Black American Cinema.* New York: Routledge, 3-25.

_____. (1993) "Black Spectatorship: Problems of Identification and Resistance." In M. Diawara, ed., *Black American Cinema.* New

York: Routledge, 211-220.

DuBois, W. E. B. (1903). *The Souls of Black Folk*. Chicago: A. C. McClurg & Co.

Dufrenne, Mikel. (1987). *In the Presence of the Sensuous: Essays in Aesthetics*. Atlantic Highlands, NJ: Humanities International Press, Inc.

Eco, Umberto. (1976). *A Theory of Semiotics*. Bloomington: Indiana University Press

Fanon, Frantz. (1967). *Black Skins, White Masks*. New York: Grove Press, Inc.

_____. (1968). *The Wretched of the Earth*. New York: Grove Press.

Fine, Elsa Honig. (1973). *The Afro-American Artist: A Search for Identity*. New York: Holt, Rinehart & Winston.

Floyd, Samuel. (1995). *The Power of Black Music*. New York: Oxford University Press.

Folb, Edith. (1994). "Who's Got the Room at the Top? Issues of Dominance and Nondominance in Intracultural Communication." In L. Samover and R. E. Porter, eds., *Intercultural Communication: A Reader Seventh Edition*. Belmont, CA: Wadsworth, Inc.

Foucault, Michel. (1973). *The Order of Things: An Archaeology of the Human Sciences*. New York: Vintage Books.

Fowler, Carolyn. (1981). *Black Arts and Black Aesthetics*. Atlanta: Carolyn Fowler.

Franklin, John Hope and Moss, Alfred A., Jr. (1994). *From Slavery to Freedom: A History of African Americans*. New York: McGraw-Hill.

Gabriel, Teshombe. (1982). *Third Cinema in the Third World: The Aesthetics of Liberation*. Ann Arbor: UMI Research Press.

_____. (1988). "Thoughts on Nomadic Aesthetics and the Black Independent Cinema: Traces of a Journey." In M. B. Cham and C. Andrade-Watkins, eds., *Blackframes: Critical Perspectives on Black Independent Cinema*. Cambridge, MA: The MIT Press.

Gates, Henry Louis, Jr. (1987). *Figures in Black: Words, Signs and the Racial Self*. Oxford/New York: Oxford University Press.

_____. (1993). "Looking for Modernism." In M. Diawara, ed., *Black American Cinema*. New York: Routledge.

Gay, Geneva. (1987). "Expressive Ethos of Afro-American Culture." In G. Gay and W. L. Baber, eds., *Expressively Black: The Cultural Basis of Ethnic Identity*. New York: Praeger.

Gayle, Addison, Jr. (1971). "Introduction." In A. Gayle, Jr., ed., *The Black Aesthetic*. Garden City, NY: Doubleday, xx-xxiv.

Gerima, Haile. (1982). "On Independent Black Cinema." In. G. L. Yearwood, ed., *Black Cinema Aesthetics: Issues in Independent Black Filmmaking*. Athens, OH: Center for Afro-American Studies, 106-113.

George, Nelson. (1992). *Buppies, B-boys, Baps & Bohos: Notes on Post-Soul Black Culture*. New York: HarperCollins Publishers.

Gianetti, Louis. (1996). *Understanding Movies, Sixth Edition*. Englewood Cliffs, N.J.: Prentice-Hall.

Gibson-Hudson, Gloria. (July-Oct. 1991) "African American Literary Criticism as a Model for the Analysis of Films by African American Women," *Wide Angle* 13 (3 & 4).

_____. (1994). "Aspects of Black Feminist Cultural Ideology in

Films by Black Women Independent Artists." In D. Carson, L. Dittmar, and J. R. Welsch, eds., *Multiple Voices in Film Criticism.* Minneapolis, MN: University of Minnesota Press.

Green, J. Ronald (1993). "Twoness in the Style of Oscar Micheaux." In M. Diawara, ed., *Black American Cinema.* New York: Routledge.

Guerrero, Ed. (1993). *Framing Blackness: The African American Image in Film.* Philadelphia: Temple University Press.

Hall, Stuart. (1992). "Cultural Identity and Cinematic Representation." In M. Cham, ed., *Ex-Iles: Essays on Caribbean Cinema.* Trenton, NJ: Africa World Press, Inc.

Harding, Sandra (1987). "Introduction: Is there a Feminist Method." In S. Harding, ed., *Feminism and Methodology.* Bloomington and Indianapolis: Indiana University Press.

Harrison, Paul C. (1972). *The Drama of Nommo.* New York: Grove Press.

Heath, Stephen. (1981). *Questions of Cinema.* Bloomington: Indiana University Press.

Hogue, Lawrence. (1986). "Literary Production: A Silence in Afro-American Critical Practice." In J. Weixlmann and C. J. Fontenot, eds., *Studies in Black American Literature Volume II: Belief vs. Theory in Black American Literary Criticism.* Greenwood, FL: The Penkevill Publishing Company.

hooks, bell. (1993). "The Oppositional Gaze: Black Female Spectators" In M. Diawara, ed., *Black American Cinema.* New York: Routledge.

_____. (1990). *Yearning: Race, Gender, and Cultural Politics.* Toronto: Between the Lines.

Hughes, Langston. (1926). "The Negro Artist and the Racial Mountain." In A. Gayle, Jr., ed., (1971). *The Black Aesthetic.* Garden City, NY: Doubleday.

_____, and Meltzer, Milton. (1968). *Black magic: A Pictorial History of the Negro in American Entertainment.* Englewood Cliffs, NJ: Prentice-Hall, Inc.

Hurston, Zora Neale. (1995). "Spirituals and Neo-Spirituals," *Folklore, Memoirs, and Other Writings.* Library of America, 873.

Jerome, V. J. (1950). *The Negro in Hollywood Films.* New York: Masses and Mainstream.

Johnson, Albert. (Fall 1959). "Beige, Brown or Black." *Film Quarterly XIII,* 38-43.

Jordan, June. (1989). "Black Studies: Bringing Back the Person." *Moving Towards Home: Political Essays.* United Kingdom: Virago.

Kant, Immanuel. (1960). J. T. Goldthwait, trans., *Observations on the Feeling of the Beautiful and the Sublime.* Berkeley: University of California Press.

Karenga, Maulana. (1971). "Black Cultural Nationalism." In A. Gayle, Jr., ed., *The Black Aesthetic.* Garden City, NY: Doubleday, 32-38.

Kochman, Thomas. (1981). *Black and White: Styles in Conflict.* Chicago: The University of Chicago Press.

Kovel, Joel. (1971). *White Racism: A Psychohistory.* New York: Random House.

Kuumba Workshop. (1978). *From a Black Perspective: A Searching and Critical Analysis of the Hit Film—Sweet Sweetback's Baadasssss Song.* Chicago: Kuumba Workshop.

Lanier-Seward, Adrienne (1987). " A Film Portrait of Black Ritual Expression: The Blood of Jesus." In G. Gay and W. Baber, eds., *Expressively Black: The Cultural Basis of Ethnic Identity*. New York: Praeger.

Lardner, Joyce (1972). "Introduction to Tomorrow's Tomorrow: The Black Woman." In S. Harding, ed., *Feminism and Methodology*. Bloomington and Indianapolis: Indiana University Press.

Lawson, Bill E. (1994). "Jazz and the African American Experience: The Expressiveness of African American Music." In D. Jamieson, ed., *Language, Mind and Art*. Netherlands: Kluwer Academic Publishers, 131-142.

Leab, Daniel, J. (1975). "A Pale Black Imitation: All-Colored Film, 1930-1950." *Journal of Popular Film* IV, 345-56.

Lewis, Samella S. (1978). *Art: African American*. New York: Harcourt Brace Jovanovich.

Locke, Alain. (1936). *The Negro and His Music*. Washington: Associates in Negro Education.

Lorde, Audre. (1983). "The Master's Tools Will Never Dismantle the Master's House." In C. Moraga and G. Anzaldua, eds., *Radical Women of Color*. New York: Kitchen Table: Women of Color Press.

Lott, Tommy, L. (1991). "A No-Theory Theory of Contemporary Black Cinema." *Black American Literature Forum* 25.

Lubiano, Wahneema. (1991). "But Compared to What? Reading Realism, Representation, Essentialism in School Daze, Do the Right Thing, and the Spike Lee Discourse." *Black American Literature Forum* 25 (2), 253-281.

Luhr, William and Lehman, Peter. (1977). *Authorship and Narrative in the Cinema: Issues in Contemporary Aesthetics and Criticism*. New York: G. P. Putnam and Sons.

Malraux, Andre. (1974). S. Gilbert, trans., *The Voices of Silence*. London: Paladin.

Mapp, Edward. (1972). *Blacks in American Films: Today and Yesterday*. Metuchen, NJ: Scarecrow.

Martin, Tony. (1983). *Literary Garveyism: Garvey, Black Arts and the Harlem Renaissance*. Dover, MA: The Majority Press.

Masilela, Ntongela. (1993). "The Los Angeles School of Black Filmmakers." In M. Diawara, ed., *Black American Cinema*. New York & London: Routledge.

McDowell, D. E. (1980). "New Directions for Black Feminist Criticism." *Black American Literature Forum* 14.

McDowell, M. B. (1987). "The Black Woman as Artist and Critic: Four Versions." *The Kentucky Review* 7 (1), 1941.

Mercer, Kobena. (1988). "Diasporic Culture and the Dialogic Imagination: The Aesthetics of Black Independent Film in Britain." In M. B. Cham and C. Andrade-Watkins, eds., *Blackframes: Critical Perspectives on Black Independent Cinema*. Cambridge, MA: The MIT Press.

Mitchell, Angelyn. (1994). "Introduction." In A. Mitchell, ed., *Within the Circle: An Anthology of African American Literary Criticism from the Harlem Renaissance to the Present*. Durham, NC: Duke University Press.

Morrison, Keith. (1995). "The Global Village of African American Art."

In David C. Driskell, ed., *African American Visual Aesthetics*. Washington: Smithsonian Institution Press.

Mullen, Edward J. (1981). *The Life and Poems of a Cuban Slave: Juan Francisco Manzano, 1979-1854*. Hamden, CT: The Shoe String Press, Inc.

Murray, David R. (Spring 1972). "Richard Robert Madden: His Career as a Slave Abolitionist." *Studies 61*.

Murray, James P. (1973). *To Find an Image: Black Films from Uncle Tom to Superfly*. New York: The Bobbs-Merrill Company.

_____. (1973). "The Subject is Money." *Black Creation: A Quarterly Review of Black Arts and Letters* 4 (2), 32-34.

Neal, Larry. (1972). "The Black Arts Movement." In A. Gayle, ed., *The Black Aesthetic*. Garden City, NY: Doubleday & Co., Inc., 257-74.

Newton, Huey P. (1972). *To Die for the People*. New York: Random House.

Noble, Peter. (1948). *The Negro In Films*. London: Skelton-Robinson.

Nicholson, David. (1989). "Which Way the Black Film Movement?" In M. T. Martin, ed., (1995)., *Cinemas of the Black Diaspora: Diversity, Dependence, and Oppositionality*. Detroit: Wayne State University Press.

Patterson, Lindsay, ed. (1975). *Black Films and Film-makers: A Comprehensive Anthology from Stereotype to Superhero*. New York: Dodd, Mead and Company.

Pines, Jim. (1988). "The Cultural Context of Black British Cinema." In M. B. Cham and C. Andrade-Watkins, eds., *Blackframes: Critical Perspectives on Black Independent Cinema*. Cambridge, MA: The MIT Press.

Powell, Richard J. (1997). *Black Art and Culture in the 20th Century*. London: Thames and Hudson.

_____. (1989). *The Blues Aesthetic: Black Culture and Modernism*. Washington, D.C: The Washington Project for the Arts.

Reddick, Lawrence. (Summer 1944). "Educational Programs for the Improvement of Race Relations: Motion Pictures, Radio, The Press and Libraries." *The Journal of Negro Education* XIII.

Reid, Mark. (1993). *Redefining Black Film*. Berkeley: University of California Press.

Rombauer, Irma S. and Rombauer Becker, Marion. (1973). *Joy of Cooking*. New York: A Plume Book/New American Library.

Rose, Vattel. T. (1982). "Afro-American Literature as a Cultural Resource for a Black Cinema Aesthetic." In G. L. Yearwood, ed., *Black Cinema Aesthetics: Issues in Independent Black Filmmaking*. Athens, OH: Ohio University Center for Afro-American Studies, 27-40.

Sampson, Henry T. (1977). *Blacks in Black and White: A source Book on Black Films*. Metuchen, NJ: The Scarecrow Press.

Sanders, Leslie. (1986). "Dialect Determinism: Ed Bullins' Critique of the Rhetoric of the Black Power Movement." In J. Weixlman and C. Fontenot, eds., *Studies in Black American Literature Volume II: Belief vs. Theory in Black American Literary Criticism*. Greenwood, FL: The Penkevill Publishing Company. , 161-175.

Schiller, Frederich Von. (1795). E. M. Wilkinson, trans. and ed., (1966). *On the Aesthetic Education of Man*. Oxford: Clarendon Press.

Simpson, Donald. (March-April-May 1990). "Black Images in Film: The 1940s to the Early 1960s." *The Black Scholar: Journal of Black Studies and Research* 21 (3), 20-29.

Smith, Barbara. (1982). "Toward a Black Feminist Criticism." In G. T. Hull, P. Bell Scott, and B. Smith, eds., *But Some of Us Are Brave*. Old Westbury, NY: The Feminist Press.

Smitherman, Geneva. (1977). *Talkin and Testifyin: The Language of Black America*. Boston: Houghton Mifflin.

Snead, James. (1994). *White Screen, Black Images: Hollywood from the Dark Side*. New York & London: Routledge.

Solanas, Ferdinand and Getino, Octavio. (1979). "Towards a Third Cinema." In B. Nicholls, ed., *Movies and Methods: An Anthology*. Berkeley: University of California Press.

Stetson, Erlene. (1982). "Studying Slavery: Some Literary and Pedagogical Considerations on the Black Female Slave." In G. T. Hull, P. Bell Scott, and B. Smith, eds., *But Some of Us Are Brave*. Old Westbury, NY: The Feminist Press.

Taylor, Clyde. (1988). "St. Clair Bourne." *The New American Filmmakers* Series. New York: Whitney Museum of American Art.

_____. (1989). "The Paradox of Black Independent Cinema." In M. T. Martin, ed., (1995), *Cinemas of the Black Diaspora: Diversity, Dependence, and Oppositionality*. Detroit: Wayne State University Press, 431-441.

_____. (1993). "The Ironies of Palace-Subaltern Discourse. In M. Diawara, ed., *Black American Cinema*. New York: Routledge.

_____. (1988). "We Don't Need Another Hero: Anti-Theses on Aesthetics." In M Cham and C. Andrade-Watkins, eds., *Blackframes*. Cambridge: The MIT Press.

Turkle, Sherry. (1978). *Psychoanalytic Politics: Freud's French Revolution*. New York: Basic Books.

Vlach, John Michael. (1989). "Quilting the Blues." In R. J. Powell, ed., The *Blues Aesthetic: Black Culture and Modernism*. Washington, D.C: The Washington Project for the Arts, 67-69.

Wallace, Michelle. (1993). "Race, Gender, and Psychoanalysis in Forties Film: Lost Boundaries, Home of the Brave, and The Quiet One." In M. Diawara, ed., *Black American Cinema*. New York: Routledge, 257-271.

Weitz, Morris. (1967). "The Role of Theory in Aesthetics." In M. C. Beardsley and H. Schueller, eds., *Aesthetic Inquiry: Essays on Art Criticism and the Philosophy of Art*. Belmont, CA: Dickenson Publishing Co., Inc.

Wittgenstein, Ludwig. (1953). *Philosophical Investigations*. Oxford: Basil Blackwell.

West, Cornel. (1993). *Keeping Faith*. New York and London: Routledge.

_____. (1993). *Race Matters*. Boston: Beacon Press.

Woodyard, Jeffrey Lynn. (1995). Locating Asante: Making Use of the Afrocentric Idea. In Dhyana Ziegler, ed., *Molefi Kete Asante and Afrocentricity: In Praise and Criticism*. Nashville, TN: James C. Winston Publishing Co., Inc.

Wright, Richard. (1959). "Foreword." In Paul Oliver (1963). *The Meaning of the Blues*. New York: Collier Books, 7-12.

Wynter, Sylvia. (1992). "Rethinking Aesthetics: Notes Toward A

Deciphering Practice." In M. B. Cham, ed., *Ex-Iles: Essays on Caribbean Cinema*. Trenton: Africa World Press.

Yearwood, Gladstone L. (1982). "The Hero in Black Film." *Wide Angle* 5: 2, 42-50.

_____. (1982a). "Introduction: Issues in Independent Black Filmmaking." in G. L. Yearwood, ed., *Black Cinema Aesthetics: Issues in Independent Black Filmmaking*. Athens, OH: Center for Afro-American Studies.

_____. (1987). "Expressive Traditions in Afro-American Visual Arts." In G. Gay and W. Baber, eds., *Expressively Black: The Cultural Basis of Ethnic Identity*. New York: Praeger.

INDEX

PRINTED IN CANADA